DENNIS POTTER: BETWEEN TWO WORLDS

KING ALFRED'S COLLE

WITHDRAWN FROM
THE LIBRARY

UNIVERSITY OF
WINCHESTER

D0234774

Dennis Potter
Between Two Worlds

A Critical Reassessment

Glen Creeber

First published in Great Britain 1998 by
MACMILLAN PRESS LTD
Houndmills, Basingstoke, Hampshire RG21 6XS and London
Companies and representatives throughout the world

A catalogue record for this book is available from the British Library.

ISBN 0–333–71389–3 hardcover
ISBN 0–333–71390–7 paperback

 First published in the United States of America 1998 by
ST. MARTIN'S PRESS, INC.,
Scholarly and Reference Division,
175 Fifth Avenue, New York, N.Y. 10010

ISBN 0–312–17774–7

Library of Congress Cataloging-in-Publication Data
Creeber, Glen, 1962–
Dennis Potter : between two worlds : a critical reassessment /
Glen Creeber.
p.   cm.
Includes bibliographical references (p.) and index.
ISBN 0–312–17774–7 (cloth)
1. Potter, Dennis—Criticism and interpretation.   2. Television
plays—History and criticism.   I. Title.
PR6066.O77Z62 1998
822'.914—dc21   97–26514
                                                    CIP

© Glen Creeber 1998

All rights reserved. No reproduction, copy or transmission of this publication may be made
without written permission.

No paragraph of this publication may be reproduced, copied or transmitted save with
written permission or in accordance with the provisions of the Copyright, Designs and
Patents Act 1988, or under the terms of any licence permitting limited copying issued by
the Copyright Licensing Agency, 90 Tottenham Court Road, London W1P 9HE.

Any person who does any unauthorised act in relation to this publication may be liable to
criminal prosecution and civil claims for damages.

The author has asserted his right to be identified as the author of this work in accordance
with the Copyright, Designs and Patents Act 1988.

This book is printed on paper suitable for recycling and made from fully managed and
sustained forest sources.

10   9   8   7   6   5   4   3   2
07 06 05 04 03 02 01 00 99

Printed in Hong Kong

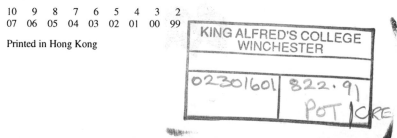
KING ALFRED'S COLLEGE
WINCHESTER

0230|60| 822.9|
POT |CRE

For Mum and Dad

Contents

List of Plates

1 *Blue Remembered Hills* (1979): Audrey (Janine Duvitski) and Angela (Helen Mirren) are literally caught between two worlds.
2 *Son of Man* (1969): Potter's Christ (Colin Blakely) is crucified.
3 *Where the Buffalo Roam* (1966): Willie (Hywel Bennett) and his mother (Megs Jenkins) grapple with the printed word.
4 *The Singing Detective* (1986): Philip Marlow's (Michael Gambon) loathing of women is physically turned in on himself.

All photographs are reproduced by kind permission of the BBC Photograph Library and Archive.

Acknowledgements

This book originally began as research for a PhD thesis at the University of East Anglia. Very special thanks therefore goes to my supervisor Professor Roger Sales for his invaluable help, support and continued encouragement. My thanks also goes to the British Academy who funded my research and made it possible for me to visit the Museum of Television and Radio in New York (where Potter's work was the subject of a comprehensive retrospective in 1992). To the staff at the BBC Written Archives Centre at Caversham and at the BBC Television Script Unit (sadly no longer in existence). To Stephen Lesley at the BBC who helped me to obtain copies of video material and to John Wyver and Philip Purser for their help in acquiring archive material. Thanks should also go to the members of various conferences who kindly commented on papers which were incorporated into the final book – in particular the 1994 and 1995 *Screen* Studies conferences at Glasgow University and the 1994 conference of 'The Romantic Child' held at the University of Keele. Finally I would like to thank my commissioning editor Charmian Hearne for her help and support, and all those who kindly gave their permission to reproduce copyright material. Particular thanks to Faber and Faber, *Media, Culture and Society* and the Judy Daish Associates Ltd.

A book of this kind is always built upon a deeper foundation than those who helped specifically with its construction. Thanks must therefore go to all my friends and colleagues at the University of North London, Lancaster University, the University of East London and the University of East Anglia. Very special thanks to Rita and Melonie Broughton, Claire and James Buckland, Warren Buckland, Dani Cavallaro, Jack Creeber, Kevin Donnelly, Tony Gillings, Laurel Goss, Clifford Harris, Pat Jackson, Jason Jacobs, Cormack Kirby, David Lewis, Alan McMurtrie, Jane Scott Moss, Dermot Power, Derek and Pam Newland, Georgia Poulopoulou, David Shaddick, Eileen Spowart, Karl Swainston, Delia Toberty, Jane Woolf, Eckart Voigts Virchow, 'Z Block 94', and to all my students past and present. Finally, very special thanks to Karen Broughton, without whom none of this would have been possible.

The author and publishers gratefully acknowledge the following for permission to reproduce copyright material:

THE GLITTERING COFFIN © Dennis Potter Published 1966 Victor Gollancz

SON OF MAN © Dennis Potter Published 1970 Andre Deutsch

PENNIES FROM HEAVEN © PFH (O) Ltd Published 1980 Quartet Books

THE NIGEL BARTON PLAYS © Dennis Potter Published 1967 Penguin Books

THE CHANGING FOREST © Dennis Potter Published 1966, 1996 Secker & Warburg

BRIMSTONE & TREACLE © PFH (Overseas) Ltd Published 1978 Eyre Methuen

SEEING THE BLOSSOM © PFH (Overseas) Ltd Published 1994 Faber & Faber Ltd

Between two worlds life hovers like a star,
 'Twixt night and morn, upon the horizon's
 verge:
How little do we know that which we are!
 How less what we may be!
Byron, Don Juan (Canto XV, 99)

Introduction: 'Switch on, tune in and grow.'

I first saw television in my late teens. It made my heart *pound*. Here was a medium of great power, of potentially wondrous delights, that could slice through all the tedious hierarchies of the printed word and help to emancipate us from many of the stifling tyrannies of class and status and gutter-press ignorance. We are privileged if we can work in this, the most entrancing of all the many palaces of varieties. Switch on, tune in and *grow*.

Dennis Potter, The James MacTaggart Memorial Lecture, 1993. (Potter, 1994, p.55).

Dennis Potter devoted his life to television in a prolific and celebrated career which spanned over three decades. While many of his contemporaries left to make a name for themselves in the theatre and the cinema, Potter doggedly persevered to make a mark on what he liked to think of as the most 'democratic medium'. As Melvyn Bragg has put it, '[h]is is one of the few talents which made television the true national theatre and the place where this country talked to itself' (Potter, 1994, p.x). From *Stand Up, Nigel Barton* and *Vote, Vote, Vote for Nigel Barton* (1965) through to *Pennies from Heaven* (1978), *Blue Remembered Hills* (1979), *The Singing Detective* (1986) and *Cold Lazarus* (1996), his work provided some of the most acclaimed and talked about drama ever to be produced for the small screen anywhere in the world. With plays and serials such as *Son of Man* (1969), *Brimstone and Treacle* (1976) and *Blackeyes* (1989) he acquired a reputation for being both challenging and controversial; a writer determined to take risks and experiment with a medium which had nurtured his unique talent. Gradually and consistently he revolutionised the standards by which we have come to judge television, turning 'the box of varieties' in the corner of the room into a multi-layered, self-referential and 'non-naturalistic' medium – blurring the lines between 'high art' and 'low culture' and forcing audiences

1

to confront their individual notions of 'reality' in the very privacy of their own homes.

At the time of his death from cancer in 1994, Potter had written 30 single television plays, six original television serials, five television adaptations, one television documentary, four novels, two works of non-fiction, one stage play and seven screenplays for the cinema; as well as pursuing a notable career in journalism.[1] This prolific intensity was matched only by his work's constant need to experiment and expand his own personal vision of the world. 'His boldness and his willingness to take risks with himself in subject matter and technique made it possible for *us* to take risks', Andrew Davies (best known for his television adaptations of *Middlemarch* and *House of Cards*) explained in his 1994 Huw Wheldon Lecture. 'The sheer volume of his work, the intensity at which he operated, and his technical innovations put him in a class of his own.'[2] For Davies, Potter was a television 'prima donna', one of those few writers who dared to use the medium for his own original vision. His drama always tackling intensely difficult, painful and personal subjects, refusing to be controlled or contained by the so-called guardians of 'the public interest'. Potter's work uncompromisingly confronted the Grand themes of Sex, God and Death, frequently exposing his characters to the extremities of physical, mental and emotional breakdown.

Love of place and of the past, the ambiguous fascination for popular culture and popular music, the dark and dangerous forces of male sexuality, the guilty and anguished arena of social class and politics, the despair and disgust at modern life, the longing to go back and reclaim the tortured but homely landscape of childhood, the spiritual thirst for a redeeming and redeemable 'God', and the painful introspection brought about by illness, betrayal and abuse are themes which make Potter one of the most characteristic and important of all contemporary British writers. Added to this is his work's continual desire to portray the *interior* world of his characters' lives, rejecting the surface and 'naturalistic' reflection of 'reality', to dramatise and project their memories, fantasies and repressed desires. Past, present and future merging and colliding together, blurring the frontiers between 'fact' and 'fiction', 'fantasy' and 'reality', 'imagination' and 'memory'. Yet central to this heady and complex mixture is an unmistakable humanity and humour in the work. At its finest, the writing produces a unique form of 'tragicomedy' which attempts to convey the absurd and surreal dreams of so-called 'ordinary people'. Whilst almost beaten down by the mundane predictability of their lives, his characters never quite stop yearning to live, like Arthur Parker, in a world 'where the songs come true'.[3]

As a writer, Potter's career uniquely reflects post-war British history. Born in 1935 his work charts the enormous changes which have taken place in the social, cultural and political landscape of Britain during the second half of the twentieth century. It has spanned and reflected a changing political climate which saw the post-war reconstruction of the 1945 Labour government and the establishment of the Welfare State, through to the consumerist and privatised landscape of Thatcherism and beyond. Culturally the shift has been just as great, from the very British socialism of writers and critics like George Orwell, Richard Hoggart and Raymond Williams, through to the slippery surfaces of an apparently 'postmodern' and 'post-feminist' world. Yet, Potter's other influences plunge us back even deeper into the Romanticism of William Hazlitt, William Wordsworth and Samuel Taylor Coleridge, through to the modernist texture and dynamics of novelists like Virginia Wolff and Marcel Proust, film-makers like Alain Resnais and Ingmar Bergman, and playwrights like Samuel Beckett, Harold Pinter and John Osborne. Potter's drama lies somewhere between them all, struggling furiously to work and re-work ideas and techniques which have fuelled and driven his entire oeuvre.

As the forms of television in Britain evolved from live studio-based dramas of the 1960s to the feature-length film productions of the 1990s so Potter's work continually adapted and exploited these changing possibilities. From the single drama of '*The Wednesday Play*' he came gradually to realise the full potential of the television serial to provide all the complexity and subtlety of the novel. Potter's achievement was to push that complexity to its limits, without ever losing a mass appeal. His drama always attracted an audience of millions, making him one of the most widely-known and watched dramatists Britain has ever produced.[4] Both as a playwright and a journalist he continued to take television seriously, pushing it beyond its dubious status as an ephemeral 'window on the world', and gradually forcing both critics and audiences to re-examine the power and potential of the small screen. Yet Potter's work, at least in his life time, was notoriously undervalued by 'serious' criticism. According to the dramatist

Trevor Griffiths, 'if he had worked in the theatre he would have
been the [Bernard] Shaw of our day . . . It remains a scandal that
because he worked in television he was somehow "downgraded",
you don't belong in that high category of "High Art." Well Dennis
does, if anybody does.'[4]

In recent years, however, Potter's work *has* finally attracted
'serious' critical attention. Books such as Peter Stead's *Dennis
Potter* (1993), Graham Fuller's *Potter on Potter* (1993), W. Stephen
Gilbert's *Fight & Kick & Bite: The Life and Work of Dennis Potter*
(1995) and John R. Cook's *Dennis Potter: A Life on Screen* (1995)
have all attempted to offer a critical account of the writer's dramatic legacy. Surprisingly perhaps, they all approach the subject
in a remarkably similar manner, offering a general critique of
the work in a strict chronological, historical and frequently biographical analysis. While the historian Peter Stead gives little
more than a general and chronological impression of the plays,
Graham Fuller's interviews with the writer provides Potter with
the opportunity to discuss the work almost entirely on his own
terms. Although W. Stephen Gilbert offers a more detailed critique, his examination of the life and the work ultimately fails
to produce either a successful piece of biography *or* criticism –
offering a lively but ultimately confusing selection of facts and
critical evaluations.

Despite John Cook's claim that his book is the first extensive
academic account of Potter's work, it offers little variation of
form and content. After a lengthy biographical introduction he
begins his analysis with a chapter on 'the *Wednesday Play*', followed by the '*Play for Today*' era and so on. Like Gilbert and
Stead, Cook describes every play, serial, novel and screenplay
in strict chronological sequence. Consequently each new 'text' is
regarded as a continuation and development (both thematically
and stylistically) of the last. 'The aim of this book', he tells us in
its conclusion, 'has been to . . . "follow the yellow brick road" of
Potter's artistic life on screen, with a view to showing a consistency and progression of "authorial" themes.'[6] Such an approach
clearly presents Potter's career as a neat and containable 'journey';
one which, with careful analysis, can be analysed in a simply
chronological, historical and even biographical sequence.[7]

In my own research into Potter's drama, however, I have been
increasingly forced to question exactly how much 'consistency'
and 'progression' there actually is in the work. Undoubtedly he

is one of the most 'repetitious' of all contemporary British drama-tists, 'ploughing the same stretch of land' (Potter, 1994, p.59) with obsessional devotion to both content and style. The 'lip-synch' technique, for example, was first glimpsed briefly in *Moonlight on the Highway* (1969), it reached the foreground of the action in *Pennies from Heaven*, performed a complex and ambiguous role in *The Singing Detective* and was later re-employed in *Lipstick on your Collar* (1993). Similarly, themes, references sometimes even dialogue reoccur with surprising regularity, presenting a series of cryptic allusions (or 'clues' as Cook puts it) tailor-made to delight the discerning critic and the observant viewer alike. Yet beneath this apparent veneer of repetition and consistency, Potter's work is actually driven and determined by a series of obsessions which are, in themselves, surprisingly contradictory. The love of the past is matched by a fear and loathing of the narrow, restrictive and abusive world it comes to symbolise. An almost evangelical zest for a 'religious' sense of the universe is equalled by a passionate hatred of organised religion and traditional Chris-tian morality. The dreams and visions evoked by the shiny and sentimental nuances of popular culture is matched by a bitter contempt and disdain for its corrupt and corrupting commercialisation of modern life. And the passionate need for transcendence through sex is overshadowed by a fear and a disturbing aggression towards women, who inevitably bring temptation to his tortured male protagonists.

It is these hidden paradoxes and contradictions which actu-ally make Potter one of the most interesting and exciting dramatists to have appeared in Britain since the Second World War. Yet, in their desperate desire for consistency and progression, critics have unanimously failed to appreciate the profoundly dialectical nature of the work as a whole. For a writer as prolific, as complex and as multi-layered as Potter the approach followed by critics like Cook and others can only grant us with an 'over-view' portrait of the man and his career. As useful as that has been, what is now needed is an original critique which is willing to investi-gate – selectively and discriminately – some of the less 'consist-ent' issues which lie at the heart of the work; to analyse individual dramas out of their strict chronological sequence so that many of the hidden contradictions and ambiguities as a whole can at last be revealed and investigated.

No longer tied to a strict chronological or biographical

framework, I can now call into question the whole notion of authorship and biography. While this book is still dealing primarily with a single 'author', it will produce the first ever detailed critique of Potter's drama to call into question the critical assumptions so frequently made between the 'life' and the 'work', the 'author' and the 'text.' My focus on 'cultural history' will enable me to connect the drama with crucially important cultural and theoretical traditions frequently ignored by critics who have tended to treat Potter's drama as purely 'literary' or 'televisual' artefacts. Links with Romanticism and British Culturalism will offer an original and revealing interpretation of the work, while my use of feminist, psychoanalytic, film and television theory will help me to analyse the underlying thematic and stylistic structures in the work as a whole. Such an approach will offer an extensive and original interpretation of Potter's drama, applying a broadly 'cultural studies' agenda to its themes and stylistic conventions. For only the *interdisciplinary* nature of cultural studies can accommodate and explain the contradictions, ambiguities and sheer variety of the work which previous critics have tended either to ignore or neutralise in order to preserve their *own* critical teleology.

Firstly, Potter's own status as an 'author' needs to be 'deconstructed' as much as any of the plays. As will be discussed in Chapter One, he built a mythology around his work and his name which itself was highly complex and often paradoxical. While claiming to be intensely private and reclusive by nature, he was probably one of the most *public* of all contemporary British authors. He openly talked about his life in interviews, journalism, lectures and pieces of non-fiction. A consummate self-publicist, intoxicating and charismatic both on page and on screen, he often allowed the media's own obsession for the television *writer* to deflect from the collaborative nature of the medium in which he worked. From his controversial appearance on the BBC's *Does Class Matter?* in 1958, through to his celebrated interview with Melvyn Bragg in 1994, he used the circumstances of his own life to promote and discuss himself and his work. Surprisingly perhaps, he also appeared to 'use' the details of his own life in his drama, yet consistently refused to accept that it was in any way 'autobiographical'. This book will be the first extensive critique to distinguish between the 'life' and the 'work', – to criticise the very way the drama has been conceived and discussed in the past. It will ask questions about 'authorship' and 'biography' which have been ignored in the critics' desire to construct Potter as the 'single author'. Finally, it will present an alternative means by which he as 'the author' can be re-evaluated and re-assessed.

Such contradictions and ambiguities are reflected in the drama as a whole, not least its portrayal of the past. Indeed, for many, Potter was the *dramatist of nostalgia*. Much of the work revolves around an apparently warm portrayal of British life in the 1930s, 1940s and 1950s; not only appropriating the popular songs of the period but frequently presenting an 'organic' and working-class childhood during the Second World War. Potter, however, disliked the term nostalgia intensely, arguing that it was a 'second-order emotion', one which offers a 'Technicolour version' of an imaginary world (Fuller, 1993, p.22). While he is right to point out the complexity of his work's portrayal of the past, there is nonetheless a discernible ache and a longing in his characters to return to a world which seems far simpler and less cynical than the present. Narrowness of horizons and of expectations is there and shown to be there in a community which frequently stands for intolerance, and yet, and yet . . . the past – its music, its culture, its costume, its look – is lovingly evoked. As discussed in Chapter Two, it is an ambivalence which lies at the heart of the archetypal 'scholarship boy' and reflected in the work of writers like Richard Hoggart and Raymond Williams. Torn from the warm embrace of his working-class roots, the 'scholarship boy' learns to condemn and despise his background, yet yearns secretly to go back and be accepted once again by the family, friends and community he has seemingly lost forever. Added to this is an ambiguous form of patriotism for an English past which is itself clouded in memory and regret.

In Chapter Three the apparent contradictions and ambiguities in the work's 'religious' view of the world will be examined and explored. As the quotation marks around the word suggests, the drama does not offer any orthodox or traditional interpretation of the 'religious' experience. Indeed, Potter was frequently accused of blasphemy and indecency by members of the Christian establishment who were often morally offended by the work. On the surface, the majority of his protagonists appear to be atheists, ranting and raging at a world in which God is significant only by His absence. Their secular lives become morally vacuous, a breeding ground for all sorts of evil and corruption. When the pious and religious do occur in the work, it is usually to be mocked or to have their beliefs undermined in some way. Yet the work, as a whole, is awash with religious imagery, its very language is saturated in the hymns, psalms and the King James's version of the Bible. Even the structure of the work itself reflects an intensely 'Christian' view of the world, the Genesis notion of the 'Fall' repeatedly used as a recurring and pivotal motif; his protagonists desperately and secretly yearning for spiritual redemption. Added to this, there is an unmistakably 'Romantic' influence in the work which clearly celebrates the power of the human spirit to transcend the purely physical limitations of the material world. Such a paradox suggests the complexity of the work which refuses to accept the cosy and traditional view of religion, yet is driven and fuelled by a passionately *spiritual* sense of the universe.

A similar paradox appears to arise in Potter's treatment and appropriation of popular culture. As will be discussed in Chapter Four, his work is filled with references and allusions to pulp fiction, tabloid journalism, grade-B Hollywood cinema, radio, television and of course, popular music. The very titles of his plays are frequently borrowed from popular songs, while the melodies themselves are sometimes brought to the foreground of the action by having his characters mime or 'lip-synch' to them in a bizarre subversion of the Hollywood musical. Subsequently, Potter has often been regarded as a triumphant *promoter* of 'pop culture', a television writer whose own career is seen to celebrate the apparent breakdown between 'high' and 'low' art. Yet, with a little investigation it becomes clear that much of his work actually takes a less than positive view of so-called 'mass culture'. Indeed, it implicitly condemns its increasingly dominant influence on British society, especially upon the lives of the working-class. Many of his plays reflect the influence of writers and critics like F. R. Leavis, George Orwell and Richard Hoggart who believed that an 'organic' English culture had become soiled and corrupted by the newer mass arts; especially those imported from America. Yet, while seemingly denouncing popular culture, there is a fascination and deeply held affection for its form and content that suggests an ambiguity which is as rich and as complex as it is apparently contradictory.

Finally in the last chapter, the most disturbing of all of Potter's 'inconsistencies' will come under scrutiny. While he argued that his drama was an attempt to 'get inside people's heads', those 'people' are almost invariably *men*. The women in his plays are, in comparison, 'shadowy' or 'one-dimensional' creatures, simply fulfilling some impulse or reflection of the main (male) protagonist's deepest desires. Frequently they fit into the stereo-type of either 'angel' or 'whore', a form of wish-fulfilment uncon-sciously manufactured by the imagination of its sick and central protagonist. In Freudian terms many of his male characters appear to display profound anxieties around the memory of the mother, unable to come to terms with a form of infantile sexual neuro-sis. The intense sexual problems which these men inevitable dis-play are often acted out in violent and fatal assaults on women, the rapturous pursuit of sex instantly followed by a neurotic and uncontrollable disgust for the physical act. Yet in some of Potter's later work this portrayal of women comes under greater scru-tiny in the writing itself. Successfully *and* unsuccessfully the drama came to be increasingly self-conscious and self-critical about its predominately male perspective, constantly trying to re-write and re-construct the inherent structures by which it was itself prone to view the dangerous arena of sex, gender and sexuality.

Such paradoxes, ambiguities and inconsistencies have rarely been addressed satisfactorily by critics who have tended to play down the dialectical nature of Potter's work in their desire to present a progressive and often uncritical trajectory. In contrast, this book will bring these very issues to the fore, exploring and examining the means by which they actually *drive* and *determine* the entire shape and nature of the work. Potter's characters are consistently torn between 'two worlds'; caught on a dangerous collision course between one culture and another, between the past and the present, childhood and adulthood, memory and repression, the organic and the commercial, fantasy and reality, good and evil, the innocent and the corrupt. This book is an attempt to tie all these dialectical threads together, to go beyond previous critiques by comparing and contrasting dramas from various points in his career, bringing themes and techniques together so that the intricate and complex nature of the work can be assessed in a way never before undertaken.

Within a broadly 'cultural studies' agenda it will take an original perspective on familiar and less familiar work, enabling lesser-known productions to help illuminate more well-known and celebrated plays and serials. By *selectively* discussing the familiar and unfamiliar outside of their chronological sequence I will be able to show how Potter's drama constantly worked and re-worked themes and techniques throughout his entire oeuvre *as a whole*. My intention is to produce a radical and original re-appraisal of Potter's drama, attempting to offer a new and revealing perspective on one of the most important and original writers television has ever produced.

NOTES

1. While a dramatist, Potter worked as a journalist and television critic from the early 1960s until 1978; first working for the *Daily Herald*, *The Sun* (as the *Herald* became), the *New Statesman* and later for *The Times* and *Sunday Times*.
2. Andrew Davies, 'The Huw Wheldon Memorial Lecture: Prima Donnas and Job Lots,' BBC TV, 1994. As well as his television adaptations Andrew Davies is known for original television drama such as *A Few Short Journeys into the Heart* (1994).
3. Dennis Potter, *Pennies From Heaven*, Faber & Faber, 1996, p.163. See also John Wyver, 'A World Where the Songs Come True', part of the brochure which accompanied a complete retrospective of Potter's work at the Museum of Television and Radio, New York, 23 January – 31 May 1992.
4. During its first run on British television *The Singing Detective* built up an audience of around 10 million – an enormous achievement for a drama which was both stylistically and conceptually radical.
5. Trevor Griffiths interviewed in *Dennis Potter: A Life in Television* (*A Late Show Tribute*), BBC 2, 7 June 1994.
6. John Cook, *Dennis Potter: A Life on Screen*, Manchester University Press, 1995, p.282.
7. To my knowledge only Eckart Voigts-Virchow's *Mannerphantasien: Introspektion und gebrochene Wirklichkeitsillusion im Drama von Dennis Potter* (1995) – a German PhD thesis not published in English – seems to vary this structure.

1

In Search of an Author: Biography, Authorship and Methodology

The way in which authors are produced, or constructed, must be explicated. And the complexity of their works, which escapes any unifying formula, must be capable of recognition.

Janet Wolff, *The Social Production of Art* (1981)[1]

'The Author', he said eventually, spitting out the word. 'He is the one. He – arranges things, plots, writes them down, pins me on the – the p . . . page.'

Dennis Potter, *Hide and Seek* (1973), p.7.

Mrs Mary Whitehouse (President of the National Viewers' and Listeners' Association) talked in 1989 about the reasons she had been offended by Potter's highly acclaimed six-part serial, *The Singing Detective* (1986). Expressing her concern to Dr Anthony Clare in an interview on BBC radio 4 *In the Psychiatrist Chair*, she complained about a scene in which a young boy secretly watches his mother make love with a stranger. From this piece of dramatic action she concluded that like his character the reason Potter had *himself* become ill was because, as a child, he had caught his mother in a similar compromising position. 'The heart of the problem', she said, 'was the fact that Dennis Potter, the reason for all his skin trouble . . . was shock. You see, as a child he had seen his mother having sex with a strange man in the grass'.[2] The playwright's own mother, Mrs Margaret Potter, was understandably upset by Whitehouse's comments. As a result, she sued the BBC for libel and won. In an apology, *The Listener* (which had published the interview) reported that 'Mrs Potter remained faithful to her husband throughout their married life,

11

and the scene in question was written entirely from Mr Potter's imagination'.[3] Whitehouse responded by explaining that she had temporarily 'blacked out' halfway through the interview and made her analysis after coming round. 'I am quite certain', she said, 'in more normal circumstances I would never have made such a remark'.[4]

Extreme as this example may seem, this is precisely the sort of critical analysis which has all too frequently been applied to Potter's drama. Journalists, critics and academics have continued to look at his biography as a means of understanding and interpreting the work. Interviews, articles, television programmes and books have all focused on the events of his life, constructing around his work a collection of biographical 'facts' and personal details which are almost as well known as the drama itself. His working-class childhood in the Forest of Dean, the difficulties surrounding his transition to Oxford, and the well-documented circumstances of his ill health (the playwright suffered from psoriatic arthropathy, a debilitating combination of psoriasis and arthritis) have become the stock and trade of journalistic profiles, as well as attracting serious critical attention. So why has Potter's life been allowed to play such a large role in the interpretation of his work and what are the consequences of discussing his fiction in such explicitly biographical terms? This opening chapter will explore the construction of Potter both as a *'personality'* and an *'author'* so that the reasons for my own critical methodology can be clearly outlined before attempting to offer a detailed analysis of the work itself. It is essential that these concerns are immediately addressed, as the critic's approach towards the issue of biography and authorship will ultimately determine the way the work itself will be conceived and interpreted as a whole.

ONLY MAKE BELIEVE?: THE QUESTION OF BIOGRAPHY

Potter himself cannot be regarded as entirely blameless for the media's obsession with the details of his personal life. His television drama, journalism, novels, screenplays, interviews and even the occasional lecture all drew heavily on seemingly biographical material. 'Base Ingratitude?', his first published article in 1958 talked openly about his family, his background and his life as a working-class 'scholarship boy'.[5] As did his first book *The Glittering Coffin* (1960) and his earliest television programme *Between Two Rivers* (1960), a documentary in which he took the BBC cameras back to his place of birth in the Forest of Dean (see Chapter Two). In his debut year as a television dramatist both *Stand Up, Nigel Barton* (1965) and its companion piece *Vote, Vote, Vote for Nigel Barton* (1965) seemed to reflect his own experiences at Oxford and his unsuccessful attempt to run for parliament as a Labour candidate in 1964.[6] Later plays such as *Only Make Believe* (1973) and *Double Dare* (1976) centred around writers who showed signs of illness and had a background surprisingly similar to Potter's own.[7] His first novel, *Hide and Seek*, concerned a writer who was brought up in the Forest of Dean, had been educated at Oxford and was suffering from psoriatic arthropathy. *The Singing Detective* centred around a writer suffering from the same illness and tormented by childhood memories which had striking similarities with Potter's own, while the posthumous *Karaoke* (1996) portrayed a television playwright from the Forest of Nead (Dean spelt backwards) suffering from a similar form of incurable cancer from which Potter died.

Potter even seemed eager to discuss certain details of his own life in public. His journalistic writings were frequently autobiographical. Take for instance 'Dennis Potter Exposed' (from the pre-Murdoch *Sun*) in which he spent his time furiously attacking his critics and celebrating a brief remission in his illness. 'The alien world leapt up in a blaze of euphoria when I discovered that I had been given back my health and strength', he wrote. 'Yes. It's true. I can open jars again. And hold a pen in a proper grip. . . . On Friday I ran again, Friday was also my thirty-third birthday – and I hadn't run since I was 27.'[8] It is also surprising that a man who consistently referred to himself as 'reclusive by nature' would feel the need to give so many interviews, often going over profoundly personal details and facing the same biographical questioning. In fact, Potter became something of a media celebrity in his later life, giving interviews not only to British 'art programmes' like *Omnibus*, *Arena* and *The Southbank Show*, but chat shows like *Whicker!* and *Wogan*.[9] He would frequently recall the same memories about learning to read at the age of three, the Biblical imagery in which he first saw the Forest of Dean, and the terrifying impact of his illness when it first descended on him as a young man.[10]

Potter even revealed that he had been sexually abused as a young child in a preface to a collection of published plays in 1984.[11] However, while prepared to make known this most intimate of facts he consistently refused to give any further details. His 1993 'MacTaggart Memorial Lecture' included, by his own admission, a great deal of 'autobiographical' and 'recycled material' (Potter, 1994, p.33) – even choosing the occasion to again refer to his childhood abuse.[12] Indeed, the lecture itself seemed more like a personalised 'sermon' than a public address to the British television industry. He even consented to one last televised appearance in 1994 when diagnosed as suffering from a form of terminal cancer. In a BAFTA award-winning interview with Melvyn Bragg for Channel 4 *Without Walls*, he talked openly about his life, his work and his imminent death, producing what one critic later described as one of television's 'most extraordinary events'.[13]

This interview with Bragg provided a curiously fitting platform for Potter's caustic personality. Complete with a flask of liquid morphine to ease the pain of cancer, he seemed to embody all the essential elements of the 'Romantic artist' (see Chapter Three). Struggling to complete his last work of art before his untimely death, he spoke movingly of 'seeing the blossom' outside his window with a renewed clarity and vision; and how the very nearness of death meant that he could finally experience life in 'the present tense' (Potter, 1994, p.5). Let us not forget, however, that Potter must have been only too aware that he was ultimately engineering the way his death (and life) would later be perceived. As Jenny Diski has since put it, '[t]he death of Dennis Potter may have been authored by God, but it was adapted for television by Dennis Potter'.[14] Part of its purpose, after all, was an attempt to convince Channel 4 and the BBC to collaborate on his final two pieces of work.[15]

Yet how reliable were the playwright's accounts of his own life? W. Stephen Gilbert has already cast doubt on some aspects of the Potter mythology. He questions the early poverty which the playwright frequently described in some detail. 'Potter', he tells us, 'perhaps selected the facts a little, building myths around himself.'[16] Later he even reconsiders the reality of Potter's childhood abuse.[17] While reserving my own judgement on such private details, I suggest that the critic needs to be more than a little careful when taking any biographical material purely at face value. As Potter himself put it, 'I do not believe what writers say about themselves, except when they think they are not saying it about themselves. This is ... because the masking of the Self is an essential part of the trade. Even, or especially, when "using" the circumstances, pleasures and dilemmas of one's own life.' (Potter, 1984, p.13)

Despite his apparent willingness to talk about his own life, Potter held an almost neurotic dislike of any work purporting to tell a person's life-story. 'Autobiography is the cheapest, nastiest, literary form', he told Graham Fuller, 'I think only biography beats it.' (Fuller, 1993, p.10) In his last play *Cold Lazarus* (1996), he typically has the central male protagonist's last request to be simply 'no biography' (Potter, 1996, p.213). Furthermore, he consistently denied that his own work was in any way autobiographical. 'I've always deliberately, as a device, used the equivalent of a novelist's first-person narrative', he told Bragg in his last interview. 'You know when the novelist says I, he doesn't mean I, and yet you want him to mean I, and I've used, for example, in *The Singing Detective*, I used the physical circumstances of psoriatic arthropathy ... and geographical realities, and it seemed so personal then, but I often do that. It isn't. I make it up, the story.' (Potter, 1994, p.12) In particular, he argued that he deliberately and consciously experimented with the notion of 'autobiography' in his work, rather than attempting to produce a straightforward autobiographical account of his life. 'I like in television playing around with the conventions of autobiography, as opposed to the reality of it', he told Paul Madden, 'because it's got much more charge to it, a much more personal feel about it, but it is artifice as much as any other form – a convention which one wishes to use, and which is very usable on television.'[18]

Predictably, then, the playwright himself consistently argued against any critical analysis which attempted to connect the *life* with the *work*. 'I don't think that biographical criticism is such an easy way of assuming you get the key to a body of work', he told John Cook. 'Nor am I interested in the sort of criticism that tries to make links between the work and the life. As a function of criticism I think it's invalid and impertinent. Biographical criticism doesn't really discover anything.'[19] This part of the interview with Potter is, however, omitted from Cook's subsequent book which surprisingly gives prominent attention to biography. '[T]he importance of Potter's early life to the subsequent work cannot be overstated', he declares in his introduction, before going on to discuss the playwright's childhood and his early life in considerable detail.[20]

Cook's critique, however, is no different from the great majority of the criticism which Potter's drama has attracted. It is believed that John Wyver's planned book on Potter was never published because he clashed with the playwright on the personal details which he had attempted to link with the work – especially in regard to sex.[21] 'Every writer is the product of his upbringing', Purser tells us, 'but here time and place and community conspired together with unusual attention to detail' (p.169).[22] At least W. Stephen Gilbert's (1995) was honest enough to proclaim his approach in his title – mixing, as he does, a combination of both biography and critical analysis of the plays. 'I am concerned with his biography only insofar as the circumstances of his life inform the work', Gilbert assures us. But, as he warns, '[t]his may prove uncomfortably far'.[23] Only Rosalind Coward's article attempts to investigate the validity of a biographical analysis. As Coward puts it, critics 'attempt to impose one meaning on Dennis Potter's work, either a meaning which can be explained by his life (themes) or by his character and distinctiveness (style)'.[24]

Unfortunately Coward proves to be the exception rather than the rule. What the majority of critiques (including countless articles, profiles, television programmes and interviews) all have in common is the unstated assumption that one can uncover the 'truth' about a work of art by discovering 'facts' about its author's life. The obsession with the playwright's illness, for example, makes an implicit connection between the writer's biography and the themes in his work. All too frequently, however, the physical effects of the illness are graphically described only in an attempt to construct Potter as a 'tortured genius' – suffering for his art and driven by 'inner demons'. Even the physical problems of holding a pen (Potter's hands were crippled by arthritis) becomes a metaphor for a much greater struggle. According to Cook, the 'fact of disease was literally the making of both him and his career'.[25] In this way, Potter's illness becomes implicitly linked with the *passion* of his vocation and the 'quality' of his writing. 'Great pain' equals 'Great Art'; biographical interpretation is disguised as critical analysis, and the connection between the life and the work simply taken for granted.

This approach to Potter's drama is all the more surprising when one considers that contemporary critical theory has tended to question the validity of analysing a 'text' through the life and 'personality' of its author. Roland Barthes's seminal essay 'The Death of the Author' argued that the 'text' (taken from the Latin *texere*, to weave) is a complex and intricate pattern of 'signs' which can never be satisfactorily reduced to a single authorial intention. The invention of 'the Author' as a *personality* only provides the critic with a mission to discover the 'man' or 'woman' beneath the work; 'when the Author has been found, the text is "explained" – victory to the critic'.[26] However, 'to give a text an Author', Barthes argues, 'is to impose a limit on that text, to furnish it with a final signified, to close the writing'.[27]

Barthes suggests that such an approach does little to help the critic to explain or understand the highly complex and frequently ambiguous workings of a 'text'. It should no longer be regarded as possessing a single 'theological' meaning, but should, instead, be seen for what it is, 'a tissue of quotations drawn from the innumerable centres of culture'.[28] Clearly Potter's biographical details provides a convenient, chronological and historical way of assembling and classifying, what is, ultimately, an unusually prolific, highly ambiguous, and frequently contradictory collection of 'texts'. As Michel Foucault explains in his essay 'What is an Author?', the 'Author-Function' simply allows the critic to include references to an author's life and personal motives as a convenient way of collating and ultimately containing the sometimes disparate elements within his or her work:

> The author explains the presence of certain events within a text, as well as their transformations, distortions, and their various modifications (and this through an author's biography or by reference to his particular point of view, in the analysis of his social preferences and his position within a class or by delineating his fundamental objectives). The author also constitutes a principle of unity in writing where any unevenness of production is ascribed to changes caused by evolution, maturation, or outside influence. In addition, the author serves to neutralize the contradictions that are found in a series of texts.[29]

Critics of Potter who have taken a biographical approach to the work are also in danger of neglecting one of its central themes. Indeed, his drama seemed to be unusually aware of the ambiguous connection between a writer's life and their work. Rather than simply offering a straightforward (if dramatised) reflection of his life, his work deliberately calls into question the whole notion of 'authorship'. Single plays, novels and serials such as *Only Make Believe, Double Dare, The Singing Detective, Blackeyes* (1989), *Karaoke* (1996) and *Hide and Seek* are self-consciously about the way personal identity is a mixture of both 'real' and *'imagined'* experience. They focus, in particular, on a writer's relationship with a piece of work, and the narrow, blurred and often dangerous line which frequently divides 'fact' from 'fiction' and 'fantasy' from 'reality'. Personal 'authorship' (or 'sovereignty' as Potter preferred to call it) is consistently portrayed as a 'fluid' combination of real, fantasised, repressed and memorised experience. Seen in this light, his own, well-known biographical similarities with many of his male protagonists simply adds a further and deliberately confusing dimension to the work, forcing the audience (and critic) to re-examine the means by which the interior landscape of his characters are constructed.

What my own approach to Potter's work will offer, then, is a long overdue attempt to study his television drama without allowing the almost mythological status of his life to dominate the critical agenda. Rather than simply accepting that the details of his biography are entitled to determine and organise the interpretation of the work, I shall examine the drama without explicitly referring to his personal life at all. While Potter's career in television is an important aspect of my analysis I shall *not* attempt to connect his life outside of television with themes in the work. Issues surrounding his illness or his own childhood abuse will be set to one side so that a *critical* examination of the plays can be conducted within a social and cultural context without reducing all analysis to a covert form of 'biography'. Interviews with Potter will, of course, be referred to, but only when they shed light on some aspect of the work or production, rather than adding to another unofficial 'biography'. Consequently, this critical appraisal will be the first extensive account to be consciously critical of the connections made between Potter's 'life' and his 'work'. It will allow his *work* to set the agenda, rather than insisting that the personal circumstances of his own life dictate how the work should be contextualised and examined. Not only is this what Potter himself would have wanted, it makes, as I will show, an enormous difference to the way the work is finally interpreted and understood.

SECRET FRIENDS?: THE PROBLEM OF AUTHORSHIP

If the question of biography was not problematic enough, television and film studies have both been troubled by the recurrent concern over authorship in general. Whereas in literary studies a text such as a novel or poem can be seen to be the product of one, identifiable writer, television and film are such highly collaborative media that it is not always clear which figure in the production team should be prioritised (if at all) as 'the author'. In both television and film a script will be interpreted and transformed by directors, producers, editors, actors, production designers, costume designers, choreographers, cameramen, composers and so on. As Edward Buscombe puts it '[t]aking all those before, during and after the work in the (television) studio the number of people working on a single drama series must run well into three figures if one includes those employed in the company infra-structure: accountants, telephonists, secretaries and so forth'.[30]

The collaborative nature of film and television has not been reflected, however, in the various discourses which surrounds these two media. On the contrary, both film and television have tended to prioritise one significant individual as the 'author' of an entire production. David Self has argued that in our natural desire to see film and television as an art form 'we try to make it fit in with our preconceptions that a work of art must be "pure", the unsullied product of genius, an individualist, working alone to express his or her vision'.[31] According to Self, this critical assumption, however, has its roots grounded more in 'Romanticism' than in 'logic'.

Yet why is it that film and television have taken two separately creative individuals as the focus of their attention? As John Wyver explains in his article 'The Great Authorship Mystery', 'cinema is assumed to be a director's medium. From the time of D. W. Griffith on, certain commercial directors, such as Hitchcock, have been recognised as the "author" of each of their films. . . . Television drama, in contrast, has always been identified as a writer's medium'.[32] As Wyver points out, the difference is deeply ingrained in both industries and is reflected in screen titles and the layout of magazines and journals like the *Radio Times*. For example, many television viewers will easily identify *The Singing Detective* with its writer Dennis Potter, but most will be unaware that it was directed by Jon Amiel. In the cinema, of course, the reverse is true. The majority of cinema goers will know that *ET: the Extraterrestrial* (1982) was directed by Steven Spielberg but will have little idea that the screenplay was actually written by Melissa Mathison. Such a significant difference in the approach to film and television authorship is also reflected in contemporary criticism.

So why has such a split been allowed to occur in the critical interpretation of the moving image? John Caughie's edited collection of articles entitled *Theories of Authorship: A Reader* (1981) certainly suggests the complexity of the debate within film studies. Put at its simplest, the '*auteur* theory' (which first gained significance within the pages of the French film journal *Cahiers du Cinéma* in the 1950s) has tended to prioritise the director as 'the artist' who 'created' the film. Despite its problematic history, the 'theory' has proved a remarkably resilient one, influencing film studies to the present day. As the American film critic Andrew Sarris has put it, the 'premise of the *auteur* theory is the distinguishable personality of the director as a criterion of value. Over a group of films a director must exhibit certain recurring characteristics of style which serve as his signature'.[33]

Television drama, in contrast, has continually preferred to focus its attention on the role of the *writer*. The reasons for this are partly historical and can be traced back to its early links with radio and its cultural identification with the theatre. The 'live' nature of television during the 1950s promoted the view that it was a 'window on the world' whose primary concern was with *relaying* live pictures directly into the home. Subsequently early television drama saw its role as simply transmitting live pictures from the West End theatres or else theatrical sets were reconstructed under stylised studio conditions, complete with intervals, prosceniums and curtains.[34] Furthermore, the BBC's notion of 'public service broadcasting' (under the directorship of John Reith) meant that television looked towards the classical theatre for its material and its artistic heritage. Indeed, what other name should proceed a transmission of *Hamlet* or *Macbeth* than that of its playwright William Shakespeare? It must have seemed a logical enough decision, especially to those who had been trained in radio and repertory theatre as so many of them had. As a result, early television drama developed few aesthetic properties of its own and the electronic studio became an extension of the theatrical stage as television gradually built its reputation as 'the largest theatre in the world'.[35]

This bias towards the writer continued when television began making its own specially written drama for the small screen in the late 1950s and early 1960s. The television producer Sydney Newman sent his team to scour the provincial repertory theatres in search of new writers. Directors like Ken Loach and producers like Tony Garnett also became significant individuals on the scene of British television drama during the 1960s, but the majority of the critical attention was still focused almost exclusively on the writer. Unlike the cinema, where a director's apparent use of film could be repeatedly analysed, the ephemerality of early television (recording techniques were primitive and expensive) meant that the task of the director was seen more in terms of providing *technical* rather than *creative* authority to a production. The early studio restrictions also meant that the television director was seen as 'directing' the flow of events around him or her (in the tradition of a theatre director) rather than actively constructing the *mise en scéne*. Furthermore, the relatively small dimensions of the television screen ensured that the spoken word was usually prioritised over the visual spectacle. While the writer of a television script is revered for his 'creative imagination', the 'technical' skills' of the production team are generally regarded as a means of simply *relaying* that original creative act to the screen.

The move away from studio drama in the early 1980s and the widespread use of film has meant, however, that there has been a shift in the way both television drama is made and conceived. The BBC's Drama Department is now called the Film Department, while the success of Britain's Channel Four Films (productions made with both cinematic release and a television broadcast in mind) has meant that the line which had previously divided television drama from film has become increasingly blurred. Yet the writer is still generally prioritised as the single creative will in television drama today. The answer for this may rest, however, with economic considerations rather than artistic ones. Identifying a drama series with a single, celebrated 'author' is often crucial for its economic survival. As Bob Millington puts it, authorship 'affords a neat mechanism around which programmes can be marketed'.[36] In Britain well-known writers such as Alan Bleasdale, Alan Bennett and Lynda La Plante can guarantee a relatively large audience to a new drama series on the strength of their past reputations alone; thus securing their authorial dominance.

A named 'author' also produces connotations of 'quality' onto a particular programme. Whereas the apparently formulaic conventions of the police or hospital series will not usually be associated with a particular writer or director, a named 'author' suggests a programme is the product of a single creative will, the result of an 'artist's' individual talent and sensibility. By foregrounding a single 'author' television is able to signal to the viewer that this is *quality* drama; the work of a *creative individual* rather than simply a formulaic television series. Thus the 'author' becomes the central figure by which 'quality drama' is both marketed and discussed. As Jon Cook (no connection with the former) has put it:

> a new series or play by Dennis Potter is both anticipated and received as a significant cultural event. It is discussed in terms of the evolution of the writer's vision and style, seen as the result of a single creative will, assessed in terms of an oeuvre, decoded in terms of its author's recurrent obsessions. When a television narrative is in this way identified with a named or known writer, it confers quality on the programme. The contrasting fate of the writers of soap operas makes the point.[37]

Many individuals working in television drama, however, have been less than happy with the amount of attention heaped upon a television playwright like Dennis Potter. Some have pointed out that the script is only *one* creative act, important as it is, in the overall production. Piers Haggard, the director of *Pennies from Heaven* (1978) argued that in 'a good director's hands other things develop – silences, moments. . . . Drama does not live by words alone.'[38] Indeed, Potter was perhaps unusual in the fact that his illness meant that for the majority of his career he actually had very little involvement in the production of his own scripts.[39] Often the director was given a surprising amount of artistic freedom. No doubt Potter himself discovered just how important the director's role *was* when he finally turned to directing his own screenplays in the late 1980s with disastrous results. Indeed, the disappointing reception of *Blackeyes* and *Secret Friends* (1992) left the writer feeling personally demoralised.

Just how influential a director could be in the production of a

Potter script recently came to light with Jon Amiel's discussion of *The Singing Detective*. As Amiel later explained in various interviews, his influence on the production came even before the first day's shooting. He persuaded Potter, in a series of early meetings, to alter crucial aspects of the script which included changes to the detective story, the role of Marlow's wife and even its ending.[40] His significance became even more pronounced during the actual shooting. In an article by Joost Hunningher, Amiel and members of his production team have even explained how the famous 'Dry-Bones' sequence was originally conceived without its playwright's involvement. Perhaps one of Potter's most memorable scenes (broadcast as an example of 'vintage Potter' by BBC's *One O'clock News* on the announcement of his death[41]) it was, in fact, a product of intense collaboration. While Potter's script had originally set the scene in a black void with skeleton costumes, it was Amiel, the designer Jim Clay and the choreographer Quinny Sacks who eventually came up with the idea of turning the hospital into a 'night-club' – complete with high-kicking nurses and the now famous Busby Berkeley dance routine.[42]

Yet such influences, however, were hardly acknowledged at the time of its first broadcast in the midst of the critics' obsession with the serial's *writer*. 'Very few of the reviews even mentioned me', Amiel later told Derek Malcolm, 'they called it Dennis Potter's *The Singing Detective*'.[43] This was in stark contrast to the critical acclaim Amiel later received for his direction of the Hollywood movie *Sommersby* (1992). 'That's the difference between television and film,' he argued, I did the same job on both. I made a significant contribution to the script and to the way it looked. But I got no credit for one and a lot for the other. It doesn't make sense.'[44]

To adopt Potter, then, as the single 'author' or '*auteur*' of a particular television production is, in itself, assuming a critical perspective. Those critics who choose to ignore this fact are simply in danger of refusing to acknowledge the detailed production processes through which a television script is eventually brought to the screen. I bring this to the reader's attention, however, not in an attempt to minimise or down-grade in anyway the enormous contribution which Potter's original script will have undoubtedly made to a production like *The Singing Detective* (indeed, Amiel has complimented Potter's 'visual' skills as a writer[45]) but to draw attention to the *complexity* of the moving image.

Potter was privileged to see his work produced for television by some of the most talented personnel of his age. Directors such as Gareth Davies, who directed nine of Potter's earliest dramas, including *The Nigel Barton Plays* and *Son of Man* (1969), and helped establish him as a writer of 'quality' and 'distinction' from the early 1960s. The same acknowledgement also applies to the hugely influential role of directors like Barry Gibson, James MacTaggart, Barry Davis, Alan Bridges, Piers Haggard, Jon Amiel and Renny Rye. The influence of Potter's long-term producer Kenith Trodd (who worked on 17 separate Potter productions) also needs to be emphasised, as well as acknowledging the influence of producers like Lionel Harris, Graeme McDonald and Rick McCullen. And, of course, the creative input of actors, editors, choreographers, and so on.

However, while I have no wish to see television studies adopt an unproblematic approach to authorship, it would surely be unwise to insist that a collection of television programmes *cannot* ever be interpreted around a significant individual; whether it be the writer, director, producer or any other member of the cast or production team. Authorship will always be a problem in television studies, but we must not allow it to become the reason why television drama ceases to receive the academic appraisal which other television genres (like the soap opera or police series) have enjoyed. As Graham Murdock has put it in his article 'Authorship and Organisation', '[t]he problem . . . is not whether to jettison the idea of authorship altogether, but how to explain its specific location, role and limits in the current situation'.[46] Because a collection of television plays or serials happen to share the same writer or director does not necessarily mean that they will be connected by strong thematic and stylistic similarities. Where similarities *are* shown to occur, however, the critic would be foolish to completely disregard them. By placing Potter's name on the cover of this critique I am, of course, centring my own approach around the role and significance of the *writer*. While I would certainly not want to portray Potter as the *only* creative force in a production, such a decision brings with it a certain critical perspective. What I ask the critic and reader to always keep in mind is the limits by which such an approach is ultimately contained.

COUNTING THE PENNIES?: A MATTER OF METHODOLOGY

The most obvious difference in approach between my critique of Potter's work and others already published is its refusal to analyse every single Potter production in strict chronological sequence. I would argue, however, that trying to acknowledge and describe every single Potter play, serial, adaptation, screenplay, novel and stage play means that wider issues and concerns cannot be given the scope and attention they undoubtedly deserve. Instead, the prolific intensity of his output has forced me to be *selective* and *discriminating* in what should and should not be discussed. While there is hardly a production I do not mention in my critique, only certain ones will be discussed in detail, choosing from what is undoubtedly a large and, in terms of quality, a variable body of work. My particular choice may not satisfy every reader, but I believe it gives a broad enough cross-section of his television drama, allowing both celebrated and well known productions to be discussed in detail along side lesser known but important single plays and serials.

Similarly, I have also chosen to break free from the critics' fanatical adherence to chronology. Complex and frequently contradictory themes such as class, nostalgia, religion, popular culture and sexuality do not conveniently arrange themselves in sequential order for the discerning critic, but need to be brought together under common and separate thematic headings. As a result, each chapter will deal with a separate and distinctive thematic issue which will be explored and analysed in detail with reference to three or four particular productions. This is not to say that an historical and chronological approach to the work has been dispensed with altogether. Indeed, the chapters progressively follow Potter's early days at the BBC and his first full-length television programme, through to his prolific involvement with the single play, his celebrated work for the television serial, his later attempt at directing his own scripts, and finally his two posthumous works. Such a structure will allow me to assess and evaluate Potter's 'epic' career in television and his growing development as a writer, while also enabling me to discuss plays and serials from different points in his career within the same thematic chapter. What this approach will provide is an original interpretation of Potter's drama which gives equal attention to the historical development of his career as it does to the thematic issues which lie at the heart of the work as a whole.

Some critics and students in television studies may feel that such a 'thematic' approach to Potter's work is somewhat 'reductive' and perhaps even 'old-fashioned', especially in the light of the recent concern for studying and locating the television *audience*. I would certainly agree that the reception of the work plays a crucial part in any contemporary critique of television. It would be impossible, for example, to discuss *Brimstone and Treacle* or *Blackeyes* without including such an analysis. Indeed, much of my critique will include extensive use of newspaper reviews and related archive material. Rather than playing down its critical significance I will attempt to promote the historical reception of Potter's work as a crucial and fundamental part of any contemporary analysis. While I am clearly not interested in carrying out empirical audience research I will still give a detailed, wide-ranging account of the work's reception and Potter's frequently controversial status within British culture. However, television drama like Potter's brings with it complex generic and televisual forms which are often difficult to discuss when analysed through the reception of its audience alone. Clearly there must still be room in television studies where the texts under scrutiny are the *programmes* themselves rather than their *audiences*.

It will become clear that I am not using 'text' here in any narrow or fetishised way. I shall explicitly relate these 'texts' to their *historical* and *cultural* contexts, to the history of television as an institution, to the archival material which surrounds their production and consumption, and to their transformation from script to screen. What I *am* attempting, in a spirit of co-operation with others working in television studies, is a combination of academic disciplines. Such an approach will provide readers with an historical, cultural and theoretical approach to Potter's drama. In other words, I have sought to provide an *original* interpretation of the work by drawing on a range of subjects; television and film studies, cultural history and literary criticism. In this sense, I shall not be pursuing either a conventionally 'literary' or 'sociological' view of Potter's work, but will instead lean towards the interdisciplinary nature of cultural studies – a discipline which, as I shall demonstrate, has an uniquely appropriate relevance to Potter's work as a whole.

NOTES

1. Janet Wolff, *The Social Production of Art*, Macmillan, 1981, p.123.
2. See 'Divine Purpose', an interview with Mary Whitehouse by Anthony Clare, the *Listener*, 10 August 1989, pp.10–11. See also 'Explicit sex scene vetted by Grade', *The Times*, 1 December 1986
3. 'Apology', the *Listener*, 11 October 1990, p.22.
4. Ibid. For a brief description of the history behind the Potter/Whitehouse conflict see 'Feuds Corner: Mary Whitehouse v Dennis Potter and his mum', *The Guardian*, 30 April 1992.
5. Dennis Potter, 'Base Ingratitude?', *New Statesman*, 3 May 1958, pp.561–2.
6. Potter stood as a Labour candidate in the 1964 General Election. The seat, however, (East Herts) had a rock-solid Conservative majority. He would later tell Graham Fuller that the experience was so demoralising that he didn't even bother to vote for himself (Fuller, 1993, p.14).
7. Like Potter, Christopher Hudson in *Only Make Believe* has 'crippled' hands. While Potter's hands were permanently damaged by arthritis, Christopher intentionally places one on the burning ring of an electric cooker. As a result he employs a typist to type out one of his television plays. The play he is writing just happens to be Potter's own *Angels are so Few* written three years earlier. Furthermore, Christopher is played by Keith Barron who had already played the central male protagonist in the two seemingly 'autobiographical' *Nigel Barton* plays. In *Double Dare* the television playwright Martin also admits to having trouble with his hands. He also appears to suffer from a mysterious illness which has forced him into virtual seclusion.
8. Dennis Potter, 'Dennis Potter Exposed', the *Sun*, 20 May 1968, p.12. Potter's journalism has unfortunately never be assembled into the one volume. For further references see bibliography.
9. See bibliography for full details.
10. All these autobiographical ingredients supplied the basis of his last interview with Melvyn Bragg; see Dennis Potter, *Seeing the Blossom: Two interviews and a lecture*, Faber & Faber, 1994.
11. '. . . something foul and terrible happened to me when I was ten years old, caught by an adult's appetite and abused out of innocence' (Potter, 1984, p.33).
12. '. . . at the age of ten, between VE day and VJ day, I had been trapped by an adult's sexual appetite and abused out of innocence' (Potter, 1994, p.50).
13. Peter Pearson, *Daily Mail*, 6 April 1994, p.47.
14. Jenny Diski, 'Made for TV', *London Review of Books*, pp.16–17.
15. Potter asked that *Karaoke* (1996) and *Cold Lazarus* (1996) be televised both by the BBC and Channel 4. See the conclusion for further details.
16. W. Stephen Gilbert, *Fight & Kick & Bite: The Life and Work of Dennis Potter*, Hodder & Stoughton, 1995, p.37.
17. Discussing a fictional piece of sexual abuse Potter employs in *Where Adam Stood* (1976) Gilbert suggests that it 'incurs a doubt as to whether

the incident of abuse in Potter's own childhood was itself fictionally introduced' (Gilbert, 1995, p.227).

18. Interview with Paul Madden, unpaginated programme notes for a National Film Theatre screening of the *Nigel Barton Plays*, November 1976.

19. This extract from Cook's interview with Potter appeared in Richard Brooks, 'A matter of life and death', *The Observer Review*, 4 June 1995, pp.2–3.

20. John Cook, 1995, p.8.

21. See Richard Brooks, 'Writers clash over Potter's life story', *The Observer*, 5 February 1995. John Wyver would later shorten much of the material from the proposed book to form his piece ('A World Where the Songs Come True') for the brochure which accompanied the 'Dennis Potter retrospective', the Museum of Television and Radio, New York, 23 January – 31 May 1992.

22. Philip Purser, 'Dennis Potter', in George W. Brandt (ed.), *British Television Drama*, Cambridge University Press, 1981, p.169.

23. W. Stephen Gilbert, 1995, p.33.

24. Rosalind Coward, 'Dennis Potter and the Question of the Television Author', *Critical Quarterly*, 29:4, 1987, p.84.

25. John Cook, 1995, p.20.

26. Roland Barthes, 'The Death of the Author', included in Roland Barthes, *Image, Music, Text*, Fontana Press, 1977, p.147.

27. Ibid.

28. Ibid.

29. Michel Foucault, 'What is an Author?', from *Language – Memory, Practice*, Basil Blackwell, Oxford, 1977, p.128.

30. Edward Buscombe, 'Creativity in Television', *Screen Education*, No. 35, Summer 1980, p.21.

31. David Self, *Television Drama: An Introduction*, Macmillan, 1984, p.70.

32. John Wyver, 'The great authorship mystery', *The Listener*, 14 April 1983, p.36.

33. Ibid., p.27.

34. For an account of the history of British television drama see Carl Gardener and John Wyver, 'The Single Play: From Reithian Reverence to Cost-Accounting and Censorship', *Screen*, Vol. 24, nos. 4–5. 1983, p.123.

35. More recently, however, Jason Jacobs has tended to modify this interpretation of television history, suggesting that although early television drama was inherently 'theatrical' it did still have some aesthetic properties of its own. See Jason Jacobs, *Early British Television Drama: Aesthetics, Style and Technology*, unpublished PhD, University of East Anglia, 1996.

36. Bob Millington, 'Boys from the Blackstuff', in George W. Brandt (ed.), *British Television Drama in the 1980s*, Cambridge University Press, 1993, p.20

37. Jon Cook, 'Film and Literature', in Thomas Elsaesser (ed.), *Writing for the Medium: Television in Transition*, the University of Amsterdam, 1993, p.131.

38. Quoted in David Self, 1984, p.81.
39. See interview with Potter in Graham Fuller, 1993, pp.32–33.
40. See Joost Hunningher, 'Who Done It?: The Singing Detective', in George W. Brandt (ed.), *British Television Drama of the 1980s*, Cambridge University Press, 1993, pp.234–57. Also see W. Stephen Gilbert, 1995, pp.267–70 and John Cook, 1995, 219–22.
41. The *BBC One O'clock News*, 7 June 1994.
42. George W. Brandt (ed.), 1993, p. 244.
43. Jon Amiel in interview with Derek Malcolm, 'Home defeat, away win', the *Guardian*, 22 April 1993.
44. Ibid.
45. As Amiel told Joost Hunninger, '. . . what Dennis's writing does, rather than insist on or direct you to do something, is to inspire you to do something with the same passion and same specificity. That's what's so remarkable about his scripts', George W. Brandt (ed.), 1993, p.241.
46. Graham Murdock, 'Authorship and Organisation', *Screen Education*, No. 35, Summer 1980, p.21.

2

Between Two Worlds: Class, Nostalgia and the 'Democratic Medium'

He cannot go back; with one part of himself he does not want to go back to a homeliness which was often narrow; with another part he longs for the membership he has lost, 'he pines for some nameless Eden where he never was'. The nostalgia is the stronger and the more ambiguous because he is really 'in quest of his own absconded self yet scared to find it'. He has gone beyond his class, feels himself weighted with knowledge of his own and their situation, which hereafter forbids him the simpler pleasures of his father and mother. And this is only one of his temptations to self-dramatisation.

Richard Hoggart, *The Uses of Literacy* (1957)[1]

In my rage and misery at being identified as 'different' in the sense that no working-class schoolboy *wants* to be different, I stayed behind after the final bell and wrote 'shit' on the blackboard so that I could be a hero again at the subsequent inquest.

Dennis Potter, *The Glittering Coffin* (Potter, 1960, p.77)

INTRODUCTION

Potter was, like thousands of other post-war British working-class children, a beneficiary of R. A. Butler's 1944 Education Act. Passed by a coalition Government, it introduced the 'tri-partite' system of schooling which attempted to divide children at the age of 11 into grammar, technical or modern schools depending on their measured ability. This meant that a small minority of working class-children were given the previously unimaginable

30

opportunity of winning a scholarship to grammar school and eventually to university. This sudden access to education was seen by many as one of the distinguishing influences of the post-war cultural scene. As the television director Don Taylor has put it, describing university life at Oxford in the late 1950s, '[a]ll the running in the social and intellectual life of my generation of students was made by people like myself, working-class grammar schoolboys. Dennis Potter and Brian Walden were the great political rivals in the Union and the Labour Club, and the theatre crowd was dominated by people like Ken Loach, Michael Simpson, Dudley Moore, Herbert Chappell and John McGrath'.[2] These changes in the British education system clearly helped produce some of Britain's most distinguished post-war writers, critics and intellectuals with names such as David Storey, Alan Bennett, Trevor Griffiths, David Mercer, Malcolm Bradbury, Richard Hoggart and Tony Harrison all from the same route provided by the post-war education act. Like D. H. Lawrence before them, many of these writers concentrated their attention on issues of social class and the consequences of this new working-class empowerment – some with enthusiasm, some with regret and alarm.

As Philip Purser puts it, a working-class 'passport' was almost a necessity in the British cultural climate of the late 1950s and Potter apparently did much to draw attention to his humble roots at university.[3] 'According to his *Isis Idol*', David Walter has written, 'he boiled eggs in a tin kettle rather than dine in Hall, and tried every stratagem to stop his college servant from calling him "Sir"'.[4] While at Oxford he published an article entitled 'Base Ingratitude?' in the *New Statesmen* in which he discussed the personal problems of being a university student from a poorer background.[5] 'A working-class undergraduate', he wrote, '. . . cannot stomach the two languages that sharply divide up the year, the torn loyalties and perpetual adjustments, the huge chasm between the classes.'[6] It was this article which brought Potter his first television appearance, interviewed on Christopher Mayhew's BBC programme *Does Class Matter?* (1958). 'My father is forced to communicate with me almost as it were with a kind of contempt', he explained. 'I never talk about Oxford at home . . . because somehow one would be using a qualitative kind of language.'[7] Unlike the article, however, his views on television made headlines in the national press – perhaps giving Potter his first insight into the power of this relatively new medium. Much to his embarrassment many of the newspapers took a less than favourable view of what they saw as this rather cocky 'scholarship boy'. 'Miner's Son At Oxford Ashamed of Home', declared the *Reynolds News*, 'The Boy Who Kept His Father Secret'.[8]

While still at Oxford Potter also wrote his first book *The Glittering Coffin* (1960), an angry young diatribe about the state of the nation which, like the article, drew heavily on autobiographical experience. '[T]alking about class in highly personal terms', he wrote, 'is a shocking and embarrassing thing for an Englishman to do. There is a kind of pornography about the subject, an atmosphere of whispered asides and lowered eyes.' (Potter, 1960, p.72) In the same year that the book was published he made his first full-length television programme, a documentary entitled *Between Two Rivers* (1960). It centred around the 25 year old Potter returning to his working-class roots in the Forest of Dean, commenting on the changes he saw taking place and describing his own uneasy relationship with its community. As with his earlier television appearance, he would later feel a certain degree of shame and embarrassment about the way the programme had presented his own family, friends and neighbours. While slightly less polemical than the documentary, similar ground was covered in his second book, *The Changing Forest: Life in the Forest of Dean Today* (1962).

It is not surprising therefore that when Potter turned to television drama in the mid-1960s social class became one of his central themes and obsessions. The two *Nigel Barton Plays* dramatised a scholarship boy's painful rise from clever, working-class schoolboy to aspiring and disillusioned Labour politician. In *Stand Up, Nigel Barton* (1965) we see the anguished protagonist trying desperately to balance his working-class roots alongside his newly acquired life at Oxford. Inevitably he ends up satisfying neither community and becomes increasingly isolated from both of them. *Lay Down Your Arms* (1970) took another anxious scholarship boy and explored the inevitable struggle between father and son. 'Nose always stuck in a book', his father complains, 'bloody know all. Get and do some work.'[9] Even *Son of Man* (1969), Potter's ambitious re-writing of the Passion, was criticised for turning Christ into a 'working-class hero'. '*Blessed* are the poor', he declares, '[t]he rich are thieves.' (Potter, 1970, p.45)

Although this preoccupation with class is clearly less explicit in Potter's later work it is still a recurring and discernible theme in nearly everything he wrote. *Traitor* (1971) and *Blade on the Feather* (1980) both explored the reasons why a public schoolboy should want to betray his British middle-class origins by becoming a Soviet spy. Potter's four-part adaptation of Angus Wilson's *Late Call* (1975) centred on an elderly working-class couple failing to adjust to their son's middle-class life style. His adaptation of Thomas Hardy's *A Tragedy of Two Ambitions* (1973) focused on the social embarrassment two brothers feel about their impoverished father. *Pennies from Heaven* (1978) portrayed the working-class Arthur Parker increasingly frustrated by his middle-class wife's obsession with good manners and diction. In *The Singing Detective* (1986) the young Philip's early cleverness brings back echoes of Nigel Barton and his betrayal of class and community, and in *Lipstick on Your Collar* (1993) the class-based hierarchies of Britain in the 1950s are dramatised through Francis, a bungling and naive scholarship boy from the Welsh valleys.

Social class is also linked with the unmistakably 'nostalgic' impulse in Potter's work. Like the very 'scholarship boy' it often portrays, the drama seems to be caught between a rejection of the past and all it stands for, and a longing to return and re-visit an apparently simpler and more communal world. Despite its vibrant mining community the Forest of Dean is portrayed as having a dense rural heart, as natural and as organic as Thomas Hardy's Wessex. In *Blue Remembered Hills* (1979) and *The Singing Detective* it is lovingly evoked, presented as a veritable 'garden of Eden', its children temporarily held within its warm and natural embrace. Working-men's club, village chapel and school exist at the community's heart, a reminder of a culture and a people not yet threatened by the commercial forces of the modern world. Small-minded, parochial and frequently ignorant communities, they are nonetheless symbols of a by-gone age, a time when the scholarship boy sat in mutual harmony with a people and a way of life he would irreversibly learn to despise and reject.

Subsequently, feelings of guilt and betrayal are inevitably associated with this organic 'Eden'. *A Beast with Two Backs* (1968) has a pregnant woman betrayed by her secret lover and battered to death in the nineteenth-century Forest. In *Blue Remembered Hills* it becomes the setting for the brutal death and betrayal of a seven year old boy. In *Hide and Seek*, an escaped Italian prisoner of war sexually abuses a small boy deep in its undergrowth – a scenario later reflected in *Cold Lazarus* (1996). *The Singing Detective* has a young boy secretly watch his mother's sexual betrayal of his father while hidden in a forest dell (see Chapter Five), and in *Pennies from Heaven* the Forest 'Eden' is shattered when its virgin schoolmistress is seduced and betrayed by the randy Arthur. 'I'm not, I hope, a blasphemous man, Elieen', the village headmaster tells her, 'but I . . . think it much, much more likely that it was Adam who offered the fruit to Eve.' (Potter, 1996, p.115)

Such feelings of guilt and betrayal are inevitably linked with the wider issue of social class. In *Stand Up, Nigel Barton* its hero's betrayal of an innocent child in school is later reflected in his guilty feelings towards his own family and working-class roots. *Vote, Vote, Vote For Nigel Barton* (1965) has its protagonist struggling to come to terms with 'selling' his socialist ideals like the latest brand of toothpaste. 'Yours is the worst form of betrayal', his upper-class wife tells him. 'Your own memories tell you clearly enough what politics is about and yet you sneer at ideas, you sneer at ideology . . .' (Potter, 1967, p.98) In *Traitor* the double-agent Adrian Harris tries to come to terms with a life of betrayal. However, while admitting to the charge of 'traitor', he insists, 'to my class, yes, to my country, no, no, not to England'.[10] In *Cream in my Coffee* (1980) we see an elderly husband still struggling to deal with his wife's infidelity before their marriage. Appropriately enough that betrayal is reflected and intensified by the anxieties they both originally felt about their different social backgrounds.

In this chapter I shall explore the issue of social class, paying close attention to the related themes of guilt, betrayal and nostalgia. Potter's protagonists are literally *torn* between 'two worlds', between the past and the present, childhood and adulthood, the innocent and the corrupt, the organic and the commercial. Within this recurrent and simple structure lies an ambiguous and complex cocktail of rage and nostalgia, buried feelings of guilt, disappointment and betrayal waiting ominously to rise to the surface with frequently painful and traumatic consequences. Such issues are central to Potter's early documentary *Between Two Rivers* and two single plays *Stand Up, Nigel Barton* and *Blue Remembered Hills* which illustrate these concerns and introduce us to many of the central themes and techniques at the heart of this dramatic landscape. 'You cannot betray and be comfortable with the betrayal', Potter told Alan Yentob in 1987, 'and it's pointing out or observing or charting, not with any didactic sense but merely observing it, that can give some of the spring and tension in the drama.' (Potter, 1994, p.65) The complex and personal terrain of social class was certainly all the 'spring' and 'tension' needed to launch Potter's early career in television, yet the themes which that obsession originally uncovered would always remain at the very centre of his work as a whole.

IN SEARCH OF A COMMON CULTURE: 'THE DEMOCRATIC MEDIUM'

I once had a dream, maybe a guilty dream, maybe a stupid one, the possibility of a common culture, which still, to some degree, enchants me. The idea that all kinds and condition of people can at the same time be watching the same thing, I always did find a thrilling thought.

Dennis Potter[11]

1956 was a cultural milestone for Britain. John Osborne's *Look Back in Anger* had just arrived at the Royal Court signalling an apparently radical change in English theatre. The play also heralded the era of the so-called 'Angry Young Man', which as well as referring to playwrights like Osborne and Harold Pinter also included novelists like Kingsley Amis, Colin Wilson and John Braine.[12] *Rock Around the Clock* and *Rebel Without a Cause* were released in British cinemas around the country, cementing the growth of American popular culture and the phenomenal rise of the rebellious 'teenager'. Abstract Expressionism arrived at the Tate Gallery and the first stirrings of Pop Art were being felt at the Whitechapel. A group of aspiring young film-makers (Tony Richardson, Karel Reisz and Lindsay Anderson) gave birth to Free Cinema, which hoped to eradicate what they saw as the cosy and conservative attitudes of British cinema. It was also the year of the Suez crisis, when Britain was finally forced to acknowledge its loss of Empire and its rapid and humiliating decline on the world's stage. Prime Minister Eden tried to conjure up the spirit of the war by comparing Nasser with Hitler, but reluctantly conceded to Egypt when US opposition caused a run on the pound.[13] 'You just got to look around, entcha?', Hopper tells the naive Francis in *Lipstick on Your Collar*, set (like its forerunner *Lay Down Your Arms*) in this pivotal year. 'I mean, you can't put your finger on it, but – it's there, definitely there . . . Change!' (Potter, 1993, p.114)[14]

It was in this watershed year that Potter entered Oxford University, aiming to make a career for himself as a Labour politician. Fortunately for this ambitious scholarship boy the late 1950s saw social class high on the agenda of any political or cultural discussion. The Prime Minister Harold Macmillan's claim that 'you've never had it so good' was reflected in the rapid rise in living standards which had encouraged many social commentators to suggest that Britain was fast becoming a 'classless society'. As the working-class were becoming better paid so it was generally assumed that they took on middle-class attitudes and lost political militancy. Some cultural critics, however, were anxious about the long-term effect these changes would have on working-class culture as a whole. The most influential book to reflect these concerns was Richard Hoggart's *The Uses of Literacy* (1957). It would certainly have a profound effect on the young Potter who read it in his first year at Oxford.[15] Like his young protégé, Hoggart was a scholarship boy with ideals from the political left and a genuine fear for Britain's future. In particular, Hoggart saw the spread of American 'mass culture' as threatening the 'organic' properties of traditional working-class life. 'We are moving towards the creation of a mass culture', Hoggart wrote, '. . . the remnants of what was at least in part an urban culture "of the people" are being destroyed . . . the new mass culture is in some important ways less healthy than the often crude culture it is replacing.'[16]

As well as Richard Hoggart, the young Potter was undoubtedly influenced by the critic (and later academic) Raymond Williams. Both Williams and Hoggart had taught on the Workers' Educational Association (WEA) which, founded in 1903, was set up in an attempt to bring education to working people. Williams must have seemed a particularly inspiring figure for Potter, coming from a Welsh working-class village where his father worked as a railway signal man. In particular, it was Williams' notion of a 'common culture' which seems to have caught his young imagination. Social inequality, according to Williams, had divided British society so radically over the centuries that communication between the classes was no longer possible or conceivable. He proposed, however, the notion of a 'common culture' as a means through which society could learn to share a 'common experience' and continue to develop and survive.[17] Soon Potter would apply Williams' notion to a new and exciting medium. 'The dream or fantasy of a common culture was once as real to me as the tongue in my mouth', he would later write, 'and television (one national channel) came to me at virtually the same time, salted with the guilt of rising through all the suffocating layers of the English class system, just when I was first able to measure what I had lost and what I had gained.'[18]

The idea that television could provide the vehicle for a 'common culture' was by no means exclusive to Potter. In particular, there was much talk of it being the most 'democratic' medium. According to the television playwright David Mercer, the traditional theatre was 'a consumer object for a restricted audience – a middle-class, theatre going audience – whereas in television 15 million people can, at least, switch on for free, and if they want they can switch off. You can't get more democratic than that.'[19] Central to this notion was the belief that television drama could offer a new and radical 'theatre of the people'. Donald Wilson, writing in 1960, argued that 'under our very noses a national "theatre" has developed. . . . For many of these people television is the only theatre they have ever known or ever will know.'[20] It was certainly a concept Potter himself would enthusiastically embrace. As he told Paul Madden in 1976, television seemed to offer him a means of addressing the two worlds he now precariously occupied:

> Given my background (a miner's son who went to Oxford, who'd felt the terrors and pulls and pushes of class, then the kind of unease that everybody feels at some time, who's had an elitist education) and my experience in television journalism, it was inevitable that I would make my mark, if mark's the right word in television. Television seemed to me the most democratic medium. I thought that if I wanted to write both for my parents and the people I grew up with, and the people I was now moving amongst, there was only one medium capable of that, and that was television, and that's still the case. It cuts across the lines, the hierarchies inherent in, for instance, print culture.[21]

Potter could not have entered British television at a more exciting period in its early history. The arrival of commercial TV in 1955 (introduced by the Television Act of 1954) brought about enormous changes in its development and conception. In particular, television drama was beginning to embrace what the American screenwriter Paddy Chayefsky famously termed 'the marvellous world of the ordinary'.[22] Before the 1960s BBC drama produced mainly adaptations, already approved by West End audiences or else derived from the classics or the best-seller lists.[23] This dependence on classic theatre and literature fitted in with the BBC's Reithian legacy (Lord Reith was Director General of the BBC from 1922–38) which aimed to bring 'culture to the masses'.[24]

In a strategy to distinguish itself from its competitor, however, commercial television sought to move away from the theatrical classics of the past. It was with this in mind that ABC (or ITV as it was to become) brought in Sydney Newman, a highly successful producer from Canada's NBC network to make a series of original and contemporary dramas under the title of *'Armchair Theatre'*.[25] Under Newman's influence, there followed a distinct shift in the class address of British television drama. The regional and working-class settings of plays such as Alun Owen's *No Trams to Lime Street* (1959) and Harold Pinter's *A Night Out* (1960) reflected a new realism in British television drama which tended to distinguish itself from the middle-class preoccupations of the English theatre. As Newman would later put it, 'I said we would have an original play policy with plays that were going to be about the very people who owned TV sets – which is really the working-class.'[26] It certainly offered a stark contrast to the middle-class paternalism of the BBC whose 'Sunday Night Play' (in direct competition with 'Armchair Theatre') still tended to transfer stage plays to the screen.

Sydney Newman produced 48 single plays for *'Armchair Theatre'* in 1959 which ABC networked live every Sunday night. Scheduled to follow the huge audience attraction of *Sunday Night at the London Palladium* this new drama series was soon securing a large section of the television audience – frequently in the region of 12 million viewers.[27] Although, as Stuart Laing points out, a survey of its productions for 1959–60 shows that less than a quarter of its output was actually depicting the life of ordinary people, 'Armchair Theatre' still marked a significant shift in the content and production of television drama in Britain.[28] Such large audiences certainly gave writers a new platform for their work. Harold Pinter estimated that it would take a 30 year run of his play *The Caretaker* at the Duchess Theatre to achieve the 16 million audience figure which his TV drama *A Night Out* attracted in one single viewing.[29] With such large audiences and its focus on realistic and contemporary issues many have seen 'Armchair Theatre' as having an enormous influence on British television as a whole. According to the actress Billie Whitelaw, 'No Trams to Lime Street was an absolute watershed in drama, I don't think they realised what they'd started. I mean, because of that things like *Softly, Softly*, *Z Cars* and *Coronation Street* were made, because it became okay to have *ordinary* people going through *ordinary* emotions.'[30]

Unfortunately there were no recordings made of *No Trams to Lime Street*, but a copy of Owen's *Lena Oh My Lena* (1960) still exists. Dealing with a working-class scholarship boy's experiences working in a factory during his summer holidays, it explicitly tackled the issue of social class and social mobility. Characters talked with Northern working-class accents, the young protagonist falling in love with a loud and brash factory girl played by Billie Whitelaw. It was not only in terms of content, however, that this sort of drama was breaking new ground. In the opening scene of the play a lorry drives into a factory forecourt, women are later seen working on a noisy factory floor, and a crowded coffee bar produces a chaotic and busy meeting place for Lena and her new admirer. While long tracking shots gave the impression of depth and space, the greater fluidity of the cameras generally liberated it from television drama's theatrical inheritance. As the television critic Philip Purser remembers, 'the first thing I noticed about "Armchair Theatre" was this physical, geographical aspect that had three dimensions. Things opened up, you looked down through long rooms and out the other end, people walked across a patio or something like that, or out into a yard where a lorry was loading. It was a new *spectrum* of television drama.'[31]

The BBC finally responded to 'Armchair Theatre' by simply 'poaching' Newman from ITV in 1964 and offering him the job of running a similar series of plays for them. The result was 'The Wednesday Play' which heralded the so-called Golden Age of British television drama. Although, as John Caughie points out, 'it was the BBC which eventually reached its Golden Age in the 60s, it was ITV which scared them into it'.[32] The series itself was seen as reflecting the recommendations of the 1962 Pilkington Committee. Richard Hoggart was a member of the committee which tried to promote the *serious* value of the BBC against the 'tawdry' and 'trivial' programming of the commercial service. According to the Pilkington Report, '[m]any mass appeal programmes are vapid and puerile, their content often derivative, repetitious and lacking in real substance'.[33] Jumping on the band-wagon originally conceived by '*Armchair Theatre*' the BBC argued that '*The Wednesday Play*' was actually providing a serious social service, tackling difficult and contentious topics. Hugh Greene, the BBC's Director General argued in 1962 that 'people had to be shown the unpleasant side of life. One must get away from the middle-class "Who's for tennis?" type of drawing-room drama to show the problems of poverty, lack of housing and what have you'.[34]

Encouraged by the Pilkington Committee, 'The Wednesday Play' proceeded to make a series of hard-hitting and controversial dramas. The producer Tony Garnett even quoted from the report in the *Radio Times* during its third season. 'It is one of these key series', he wrote, 'in which "broadcasting must be willing to make mistakes; for if it does not, it will not make discoveries".'[35] Indeed, 'The Wednesday Play' soon acquired a reputation for its gritty, realistic and contemporary portrayal of urban life, with plays like *Cathy Come Home* (1966) and *Up the Junction* (1965) attracting considerable media attention.[36] As the director Ken Loach has since explained, 'the audience were much more innocent at that time. . . . There were two channels . . . the group I was with had a regular slot, week after week, so you could build up an audience and make an impact.'[37] '*The Wednesday Play*' would certainly spawn some of the biggest names in British television drama with writers like Alan Plater, Jim Allen, Jeremy Sandford, David Mercer, John Hopkins and directors like Philip Saville, James MacTaggart, John Glenister, Gareth Davies and Ken Loach all working for the series. 'A Wednesday night without a *Wednesday Play* on BBC1', Potter wrote in 1968, 'is a bit like a pork sausage without an irritating but reassuringly authentic lump of white gristle buried somewhere beneath the skin.'[38]

It was within this exciting and innovative atmosphere that Potter himself began working as a television dramatist in 1965. No doubt the atmosphere of '*The Wednesday Play*' must have suited his own particular obsessions and creative talents, while his background in current affairs, journalism and politics helped to give him a unique and powerful voice. Despite his working-class credentials it was actually Roger Smith, a friend from Oxford (and the best man at his wedding) who first approached Potter about writing for the series. Reluctantly encouraged to turn a novel he was working on into a television play he wrote *The Confidence Course* for the series in 1965 and was quickly commissioned to write another. Above all, the series provided young inexperienced writers like Potter with the opportunity to experiment with the medium, not only in terms of content, but also in terms of structure and style. As Tony Garnett remembers, '[t]he import-ant thing was, we always used to say to a writer, "Okay, go off and do it, and please forget you've ever seen a television play, if you can. That's the first thing. Don't take any models or precedents, and just make the force of the idea and what you want to say dictate how it's going to be done".'[39]

This is not to say there was no form of censorship in opera-tion at the BBC. *Vote, Vote, Vote for Nigel Barton* was famously withdrawn from transmission by Sydney Newman because of its portrayal of British party politics. Apparently, in one heated exchange of views, Newman asked Potter if it was his intention to 'shit on the Queen?'[40] Encouraged to address subjects such as politics and social class, and with a censorship battle already behind him, Potter soon acquired a reputation for being one of a new breed of controversial television playwrights. In total he wrote nine single plays for the series before its title was dropped, becoming 'Play for Today' in the early 1970s. Although he did write for commercial television during this period it was 'The Wednesday Play' where Potter really established his name and reputation, the series granting him the opportunity to express his own passionate obsessions on what was commonly becom-ing known as the theatre of the people. 'There is no other medium', he would write, 'which could virtually guarantee an audience of millions with a full quota of manual workers and stockbrokers for a "serious" play about class. To know this in advance, when actually getting the dialogue down on paper, is to feel the adrena-line slopping about inside yourself. Television, in short, is exciting – just so long as we use it boldly and imaginatively.' (Potter, 1967, p.21)

Seen in this light, one can see much of Potter's work originat-ing and developing from this early period in British television history. His drama (in particular, its concern with social class) owes much to playwrights like Alun Owen and Clive Exton who paved the way for writers like Potter in the late 1950s and early

1960s. In the following section I will examine three of Potter's early productions, focusing on issues of class and nostalgia and mapping-out its technical and stylistic development. Firstly, I shall offer a critique of *Between Two Rivers*, his early documentary for the BBC which immediately established many of the themes and issues which would resonate through his work over the next 30 years. Not only will it help explain his move away from a more political arena in general, and television journalism in particular, it will also provide important clues to the shape and form his drama would eventually take as whole. In a detailed discussion of *Stand Up, Nigel Barton* I shall then chart both the technical and thematic landscape of his early work, concentrating on the issue of class, the role of memory and the construction of what Potter would later come to call the 'interiorisation process'. Surprisingly, all the major themes and dramatic techniques of his later drama are already apparent in this early single play, themes and techniques which would be maintained and developed throughout his entire career. Finally, I shall examine the award-winning *Blue Remembered Hills*, focusing on its treatment of class, childhood and nostalgia, while keeping the discussion firmly within the context of the single play.

BETWEEN TWO RIVERS (1960)

> That was my first meeting with film cameras and with the BBC at work , as it were – as opposed to television cameras in the studio in the discussion programmes and what have you – and it, well, it fascinated me, the process fascinated me, and the lies fascinated me, and the way in which it failed to deal with what I knew to be there.
>
> Dennis Potter (Potter, 1994, p.63)

After graduating from Oxford, Potter was accepted as a general trainee at the BBC on the 6 July 1959. This was apparently on the recommendation of the then Director-General of the BBC, Sir Ian Jacob, who had been impressed by his appearance on Christopher Mayhew's *Does Class Matter?* He first worked as an assistant to Robin Day on the BBC's current affairs programme *Panorama* where, among other duties, he would make a 15 minute film with David Wheeler (producer) and James Mossman (reporter) about the declining coal industry in the Forest of Dean. Later he would act as a script consultant on *The Book Programme* where he dramatised short sequences from novels such as Kingsley Amis's *That Uncertain Feeling*, John Wain's *Hurry On Down* and Stan Barstow's *A Kind of Loving*.[41] He also worked under Grace Wyndham Goldie in 'The Television Talks Department' for whom he was to make his own documentary at the tender age of 25. Produced by Anthony de Lotbiniere, photographed by Peter Sargent and under the supervision of the influential documentary film-maker Denis Mitchell, *Between Two Rivers* was broadcast on 3 June 1960. Filmed entirely in The Forest of Dean, it centred around Potter's own return to the district after his time away at university.

It is easy to detect the influence of Richard Hoggart's *The Uses of Literacy* on Potter's first full-length piece of television. Like Hoggart's book, the documentary begins with 'The Full Rich Life', a nostalgic portrayal of working-class culture. It then goes on to discuss 'The Uprooted and the Anxious', the problems encountered by the working-class 'scholarship boy'. Finally, it mounts a savage attack on modern 'mass culture' which, it argues, is corrupting and destroying traditional working-class life. Like Hoggart, Potter also foregrounds the autobiographical elements of the debate, thereby re-asserting his working-class heritage while distancing himself from its culture and traditions. As one reviewer at the time put it, the programme seemed 'individual and personal, less concerned with the district as an objective reality than with its impact upon the narrator . . .'.[42]

It begins with a warm portrayal of working-class life seen through the eyes of the narrator as a child, taking us from the chapel to the working-men's club and back to the Potter house for a party. At home we see his father and friends in the parlour singing a rendition of *Painting the Clouds with Sunshine*.[43] With mum playing the club piano and dad a member of the brass band, Potter paints a harmonious and nostalgic picture of village life. This cultural 'Eden' is shattered, however, with the arrival of the education system. 'Soon', he explains, 'I went to the local grammar school in Coleford and almost imperceptibly I began to grow away from this tight and secure world.'[44] As he describes the familiar problems of the scholarship boy, so his commentary becomes increasingly more bitter and personal. 'Even at home with my parents', he concedes, 'I felt the shame-faced irritation with the tempo of a pickle-jar style of living . . .'. Not surprisingly the cultural battle-ground takes place around the traditional enemies of 'high' and 'low' culture. We hear extracts from Byron and Beethoven as he explains the great cultural divide which education inevitably opened up. 'I thought then that this miserable pile of dull villages could not possibly be reconciled with great art, great thought, vital emotions, and classical music.'

On his return from university, however, Potter is suddenly overcome by the harmony and authenticity of the world he had left behind. 'I realise now it was too easy to sense the ugly and restrictive', he explains. We see the cramped interior of a coal mining cottage which now 'seems to convey a *total* way of life'. Like Hoggart, this organic culture is dramatically contrasted with the cheap commercialism creeping into village life. 'The county-style hat, the suede boot and the stiletto heel are all symbols of this self-deception', he explains without a touch of irony. 'Tawdry novelettes make even literacy something to be fouled by the rhythm of the cash register.' The chapel, rugby team, brass band and working-men's club are all under threat from the synthetic and the superficial, the empty values of the acquisitive society. He also mounts, surprisingly perhaps, an attack on television. The excited and animated passions of a live rugby crowd are contrasted with the passive and dormant faces of people watching a match on television. Like Hoggart, he also criticises the 'juke-box boys' who hang around the village cafe-bars discussing Elvis. Finally he concludes, '. . . we want our daughter to know something of this land between the two rivers. To see it before it's beaten down by the world of pop . . . seventeen inch screens and *Double Your Money*.'[45]

Potter was, however, far from happy with the way the documentary turned out. In particular, he was ashamed of the way it had portrayed his own family, friends and neighbours. 'I was embarrassed by the tenderness of them', he later explained, 'and therefore the embarrassment had to be expressed in rhetoric and the rhetoric was phoney, because rhetoric usually is. . . .' (Potter, 1994, p.63) From this, one can sense just how intrusive and manipulative Potter must have felt his own portrayal of the Forest of Dean had been. Perhaps he discovered to his cost that documentary could not offer a transparent window on the world any more than a piece of fiction. As Arthur Schlesinger has put it, '[b]oth are created by editing and selection. Both, wittingly or not, embody a viewpoint. The fact that one eschews and the other employs professional actors becomes in the end an economical detail. And the relation of any film to reality depends, not on the amateur standing of its elements, but on the artistic vision of those who must put the elements together.'[46]

The problems implicit in *Between two Rivers* are all the more surprising when one considers that it was made under the supervision of Denis Mitchell. Mitchell's documentary work included *Teenagers* (1955), *In Prison* (1957) and *Morning in the Streets* (1959) which were well known for their realistic view of everyday life. In particular, Mitchell pioneered the use of the tape-recorder to record the voices of real people. One of the chief components of his approach was to dispense with authorial narration altogether. 'The idea was we'd have no narration at all', he has explained, '... And if anyone was being interviewed there was no interviewer heard.'[47] This technique was not employed, however, by Potter who dominates the programme in his off-camera narration and personal appearances. Consequently the realism of the Mitchell technique is forsaken for a polemical essay set to pictures and music. The village and the villagers cease to be important by themselves, acting only as a backdrop to the narrator's rhetorical speeches.

In particular, Potter's intrusive and relentless commentary denies the people filmed the ability to speak for themselves. His voice-over patronises the very community and culture he professes to be celebrating. Indeed, there is the sense that he was settling some old scores, publicly attacking a community who had once dared to identify him as different. One can also sense, however, a desperate need to gain its acceptance, deliberately glorifying its past and presenting himself as the guardian of some national treasure. Walking towards the camera with his swept-back hair, swish mackintosh and pullover, talking in what sounds suspiciously like received pronunciation, he immediately strikes the pose of an *outsider*, adopting a superior and implicitly condescending view of his subject. He sounds more like a visiting *anthropologist* than someone who claims to love and respect the community to which he once belonged. 'Well, I was lucky', he explains in his direct address to camera, 'I *did* get away. By a process of examination and accident I got to Oxford and was able to relax and spread myself in what seemed a far more fertile and richer world than the Forest of Dean.' In 1960 Mitchell was making an African trilogy called 'The Wind of Change', the third documentary of which was entitled *Between Two Worlds*. It was about the contrast between a group of Masai tribesmen and one of them who had left to become a student teacher. Its title, theme and perhaps even the conception of its subject were clearly reflected in Potter's own portrayal of British working-class life.

Potter himself would later take full responsibility for the way the programme finally turned out. Perhaps, however, the cumbersome and bulky technology of the time was partly to blame for its artificial and contrived appearance. 'You made a film like that with a vehicle the size of a London bus to do the sound, and a vast Mitchell camera and lights everywhere', De Lotbiniere has since explained, 'so how could anyone be natural?'[48] It marks, however, a turning point in Potter's career, and a move away generally from the factual worlds of journalism, current affairs and politics. As he later told Alan Yentob, the experience of making the programme helped him to appreciate the profound differences between 'fact' and 'fiction':

> it was seeing what it is you're observing, seeing how those scenes with the clapperboard in front of them got turned into that, and seeing what was on either side of the camera and wasn't on the film, and the way that my own voice-over had diminished what this person was saying, or what this person was about to say, which is worse. It taught me how easy betrayal is compared to, using the word in quotes if you like, 'art', which is not concerned with betrayal, and art can not betray in that sense.
>
> (Potter, 1994, p.63)

This distinction between fact and fiction or drama and documentary would prove a crucial one for Potter's development as a writer. Television drama would offer him a means of presenting a highly *subjective* view of the world, rather than trying to create an apparently *objective* portrayal of reality. Indeed, this early disenchantment with documentary realism can be seen as instrumental in his work's later subversion of naturalism as a whole. His pompous and self-righteous approach to the subject must have also forced him to confront the lack of humour and irony in the programme. Beneath its concerned and earnest veneer one can detect the overwhelming arrogance and conceit of its discourse, the assumption that TV viewers were bound to be interested in, fascinated by, a subject which could actually appear very parochial, not to say *boring* to others. Perhaps the humour in his own drama can be dated back to this disappointing experience, as can the intense desire in his later work to give voice to the dreams and feelings of ordinary people. While the self-obsession of the piece would prove an unmistakable strain of his work as a whole, Potter was clearly forced to confront the means by which such matters could be portrayed in an original and entertaining style.

The documentary also introduces us to many of the themes and preoccupations which Potter would later develop throughout his dramatic career. Perhaps, with hindsight, it is easy to trace the sense of guilt and betrayal in his work back to this moment, but one can already detect deep-rooted feelings of shame in the documentary itself. In particular, his own feelings of guilt seem to be transferred onto the 'evils' of 'mass culture', which he blames for destroying traditional working-class life, thereby relinquishing him of his own sense of betrayal. Although his view of mass culture would clearly become more complex and sophisticated, it would remain forever ambiguous and contradictory. The nostalgic vision of childhood and the ominous presence of the 'Fall' (here blamed on the education system) would later take a more profoundly personal and psychological framework in his later work. Biography, rather than simply accepted as factual, would become increasingly problematic and self-conscious. Perhaps most of all, the sense of guilt he was to feel over the documentary itself, and the complex issues of class and betrayal would become central motifs in his entire oeuvre. Clearly these are themes which Potter quickly explored in his early career as a dramatist, and in particular *Stand Up, Nigel Barton*, where his passionate intention to create a new grammar of television drama can be seen as a conscious reaction against the disastrous and humiliating results of this early documentary.

STAND UP, NIGEL BARTON (1965)

Through stream of consciousness and diary form it will lead to interior thought, interior characterisation. Further, it will open 250 years of novels and stories from Defoe to Virginia

Woolf, allowing television to draw ideas from a mainstream of English creative life rather from a naturalist backwater.

Troy Kennedy Martin, 'Nats Go Home: First Statement of a New Drama For Television' (1964)[49]

Stand Up, Nigel Barton was originally broadcast on 8 December 1965 as part of the BBC's drama series '*The Wednesday Play*'. Its companion piece, *Vote, Vote, Vote for Nigel Barton*, followed it exactly a week later. Both were directed by Gareth Davies and were a huge critical success, immediately establishing its writer as a leading figure in British television. 'With these two plays Dennis Potter moves into the front rank of TV dramatists', Kenneth Eastaugh wrote in the *Daily Mirror*.[50] *Vote, Vote, Vote for Nigel Barton* won an SFTA award in 1966, in the same year the Screenwriter's Guild judged it the 'Best Play of the Year', and in an unprecedented move gave the runners-up award to *Stand Up, Nigel Barton*.[51] 'This exciting new playwright inspired an extra-ordinary good and large cast . . . and some brilliant evocative direction . . .', Julian Holland wrote in the *Daily Mail*.[52] In particular, *Stand Up, Nigel Barton* marked a turning point in Potter's career as a writer. In 1976 he argued that it was a 'better play' than its companion piece 'because I used television techniques with more ease. Up to *Vote, Vote, Vote for Nigel Barton* I was obtrusively thinking, "How do I use television, how do I go from that scene to that scene, using television in the best way?" After that, it became second nature. I've never since had to think about the grammar of television.'[53]

Like his earlier documentary, *Stand Up, Nigel Barton* tells the story of the archetypal scholarship boy. In particular, it brings together three separate narrative threads: his relationship with his working-class family, his school days in a small mining town, and his struggles for acceptance on his own terms as an Oxford undergraduate. His childhood experiences in the village class-room (the original moment of conflict) are brought to us in a series of unconventional flashbacks, the drama continually shift-ing from past to present and from one social class to another. In the village school we first witness Nigel's (Keith Barron) early isolation from his community. 'I remember I remember / The school where I was – torn' (p.33), he tells us in a direct address to camera. His schoolmistress Miss Tillings (Janet Henfrey) only intensifies his predicament with her constant praise and approval. Later, conflict will inevitably arise between Nigel and his coal mining father, Harry (Jack Woolgar) who believes his son has grown ashamed of his working-class roots. 'Clever sod, ent ya?', he lashes out at him, 'I expect they think the sun shines out of your bum down at Oxford.' (p.28) In contrast, his mother (Katherine Parr) is proud of her son, but is confused that he should feel embarrassed by his home. 'It's clean enough here, Nigel', she tells him. 'You could eat off the floor.' (p.74)

Potter has Nigel's divided loyalties come to a head in two separate episodes which together firmly set up the trajectory of his life. At school he is bullied by Georgie Pringle (Johnny Wade) who mocks and ridicules him for being 'teacher's pet' (p.49). In revenge, Nigel goes back secretly after school and steals the 'class daffodil'. It is an action, however, for which he will later blame the innocent Georgie. Much to the surprise of Nigel, his lie is supported and corroborated by the rest of the class. *'The children sense blood'*, the script explains, *'and start to get nasty'* (p.64). This incident is an early indication of the way Nigel will later seek revenge for the pain and humiliation he suffers for being 'different'. In particular, it is his ability to use and command language (itself, the clearest of all class indicators) which becomes his most effective form of defence. As he explains to Jill, his upper-class girlfriend (Vickery Turner), 'I used to tell lies at school and get off scot free. I found it gave me – a sort of – *power*.' (p.65)

It is this talent for language which Nigel later employs in the Oxford Union where, after taking part in a debate about class, he is asked to appear on a television documentary. Yet the consequences of the programme have clear echoes of his earlier classroom betrayal. 'I was acting it up a bit', he confesses to Jill, 'over-dramatising. I wouldn't mind a job on the old telly, see' (p.70). Once again, then, Nigel protects and promotes himself at the expense of others.[54] He betrays and uses his own mother and father as he betrayed and used the innocent Georgie. Anxiously watching the programme with his parents at home he is forced to confront the extent of his treachery:

NIGEL [*on TV*]: . . . Yet I even find my own father looking at me oddly sometimes, waiting to pounce on some remark, some expression in my face. Watching me like a hawk. I don't feel at home in either place. I don't belong. It's a tightrope between two worlds, and I'm walking it.
HARRY: You bloody liar, Nigel! [*He is addressing the screen.*]

pp.72–3

The troubles of the working-class scholarship boy was hardly an original topic in the mid 1960s. As already mentioned, Hoggart had covered similar ground in *The Uses of Literacy* in a chapter entitled 'Unbent Springs: A Note on the Uprooted and the Anxious'. 'For such a boy is between two worlds of school and home', he wrote, 'and they meet at few points.'[55] In particular, Harry and Nigel's conflict goes back, at least, to D.H. Lawrence's *Sons and Lovers* (1913), with Harry Barton paying more than a passing resemblance to Lawrence's Mr. Morel. Nor was there anything truly original about Nigel's return to his working-class roots. As Alan Sinfield points out, the return of the 'upwardly mobile' son was a familiar scenario in representations of the time.[56] Elements of it can be found in John Osborne's *Look Back in Anger*, Raymond Williams' *Border Country* (1964) and even sociological studies such as Jackson and Marsden's *Education and the Working-Class* (1962). As in Potter's documentary the point of conflict (or reassessment) takes place at the moment of the son's return from the outside world, the point at which the 'two worlds' are suddenly forced to collide.

The dilemma of the 're-visitor' was also a well-known scenario on television by the early 1960s. It was featured in the very first episode of *Coronation Street* (1960) where the young Ken Barlow (William Roache) is seen at home from university and at loggerheads with his working-class family. 'Don't they do this in college then?', asks his father, sensing his son's disapproval, 'I bet they don't eat in their shirt sleeves either.'[57] As Sinfield points out, the theme of the re-visitor is actually reflected in the street's pub name, 'The Rover's Return'.[58] David Mercer's *Where the Difference Begins* (1961) and Alun Owen's *After the Funeral* (1960) also ploughed the same fertile field. Like Williams' *Border Country* both protagonists are forced to return to their roots by the (imminent) death of a parent, bringing the son back to face the family home, and his working-class origins. As with Nigel, the strongly 'Oedipal' clash between father and son becomes the crucial point of confrontation. While the re-visitor is guiltily unable to accept and conform to his father's working-class values, the parent is simply unable to comprehend the cultural and personal gulf which now separates him from his own child. 'If tha's ashamed and embarrassed it's because there's nowt between us', declares the father in Mercer's *Where the Difference Begins*. ' . . . Tha's as far away from me lad as if Tha'd gotten off in one of them sputniks.'[59]

In particular, Potter seems to have been influenced by Raymond Williams' *Border Country*. It is no coincidence, for example, that Nigel's father Harry shares the same Christian name with the father in Williams' novel. In a review of the book in the *New Left Review*, Potter even compared its achievement with his own disappointing documentary. In conclusion he suggests that 'it has made me take stock of my own position'.[60] Above all, it seems that he was forced to reconsider the best way to dramatise the scholarship boy's cultural dislocation. While Mercer's *Where the Difference Begins* and Owen's *After the Funeral* dealt mainly with the present antagonisms encountered by the 'class mobile', Potter's play (like Williams' novel) attempts to show the personal *history* behind the scholarship boy's private dilemma: the mixture of guilt and shame which lies beneath his present predicament. The play's constant shift from past to present and its juxtaposition of different and conflicting social settings (from the Oxford Union to the working-men's club, from an undergraduate party to the small village primary school) subverts the traditional requirements of the linear and chronological narrative. This fragmented disruption of time and place (a technique simply not conceivable in the theatre) forces the audience to see Nigel literally caught between 'two worlds'. Thus the cultural gulf between the classes is heightened by their dialectical relation to one another, and Nigel's childhood betrayals are set and contrasted against the divided loyalties of adult life.

In scene 17, for instance, Nigel is being punished by the university Proctors. 'Now I've done it!' he says in close-up, 'I've really gone and done it.' (p.62) As he lowers his head, however, it becomes apparent that he is now back at school as a child worrying about stealing the class daffodil. Despite their profound differences in time and place, the seamless dissolve between the two scenes suggests the recurrent dilemma of Nigel's personal predicament. A similar dissolve is used at the end of the first scene when Nigel stands and watches his father make his way to work. His profile in the village classroom is superimposed over a freeze-frame of Harry (undoubtedly Gareth Davies' decision) as he walks towards the rain soaked pit-face. Consequently, the social and personal gulf between father and son is temporarily caught in a visual montage which explicitly connects Nigel's past with his present.

This continual connection between Nigel's past and present is most powerfully suggested by Potter's decision that all the children in the schoolroom scenes should be played by *adult* actors – 'imitating childish manners and movements in horribly precise style' (p.31). On one level, it allows the play to dramatise the frightening dimensions of childhood. More importantly, however, it allows Nigel (seemingly unchanged except for short trousers) to re-visit his past, to *re-experience* the crucial moment when he was originally divided from his working-class roots. This, then, is not a straightforward 'flashback' (where Nigel would simply be played by a child actor) but a dramatic means of bringing past and present together, thereby witnessing the dynamics of Nigel's *memory* at work. As Potter explained in the introduction to the play's publication, '"[m]emory" is not the accurate recall of previous events: it is not objective. Past events in our lives are coloured by our own present attitudes, and it was exactly that sort of tension which I wanted to capture in dramatic form.' (p.20). Such a technique encourages its audience to see Nigel's problems as an on-going and continual process. His present and uneasy relationship with his working-class roots is forever shaped and determined by his earlier alienation from a community which both actively encouraged his early cleverness (Miss Tillings) and despised it (Georgie Pringle and others). The psychological complexity of the scholarship boy is thus dramatised by presenting past and present as one continuous dilemma.

Nigel's psychological make-up is not, however, allowed to be presented as a purely *personal* one. While the complexity of his individual problems are clearly foregrounded, the play is also at great pains to present him as an archetype or typical scholarship boy. The characters' tendency to address the camera, for instance, diminishes the naturalism of the play, forcing the viewer to reconsider its attempt to create a portrayal of reality. As the artificiality of the drama is drawn attention to, so the characters themselves cease to be fully rounded individuals. Miss Tillings' direct address to camera in the second scene clearly sets her up as a symbolic figure rather than a believable human being. Her comment to camera that '[c]lever children from common homes like his have to be separated from their – ah – backgrounds. I say nothing controversial' (p.32), presents her as a 'figure-head' for the whole educational establishment. Such a technique highlights her social or political dimensions over her *human* characterisation. As her face 'dissolves' into a bust of Harold Macmillan at the Oxford Union so the political point is even more crudely made (p.32).

Such a technique is clearly reminiscent of Bertolt Brecht's concept of Epic Theatre. As an undergraduate Potter had committed the Labour club at Oxford to putting on Brecht's *The Caucasian Chalk Circle*. By reminding the audience of the play's *artificial* nature, Epic Theatre attempted to force the spectator to confront and study what was being shown, rather than merely empathising with its characters on an emotional level. While Brecht is an undeniable influence it is more likely, however, that the play more closely reflects the ideas and recommendations of Troy Kennedy Martin. In 1964 Martin had declared war on television naturalism in his influential article 'Nats go Home: A New Statement of Television Drama', published in *Encore*.[61] According to Martin, television drama needed to employ the alienation theories of Brecht, Eisensteinian use of montage, the stream of consciousness techniques of novelists like Virginia Woolf, and the non-linear narratives of new wave film-makers like Alain Resnais to create a new grammar of television drama. This new grammar would finally obliterate TV's similarities with the theatre and its naturalistic inheritance.

For Troy Kennedy Martin television drama needed to 'develop new designs leading to maximum fluidity in the studio by doing away with the old box sets and creating acting areas specifically through the use of lighting . . . Sound and Editing'.[62] 'The primary concern of the new drama', he argued, 'must be therefore: to free the camera from photographing dialogue, to free the structure from natural time and to exploit the total and absolute objectivity of the television camera.'[63] Such techniques clearly appealed to the young Potter who had learnt a painful lesson about the limitations of naturalism in his early documentary. Martin's article, however, must have encouraged him that the complexity and subtleties of the novel form (which he had originally been attracted to) could finally be transferred to television. Above all, it was Martin's call to construct 'interior thought' and 'interior characterisation' which would be crucial to Potter's conception of television drama as a whole. Indeed, he responded to Martin's article in 'Reaction' in the following edition. Like Martin, he argued that TV naturalism had to be subverted and replaced by 'a mosaic of objects, details, moods, memories and conversations. Pictures in a real fire. Pictures ablaze.'[64] Later he would pay tribute to

Martin's article in his introduction to *The Nigel Barton Plays* (1967), restating his call that '[a]ll drama which owes its form or substance to theatre plays is OUT'.[65]

Advances in technology also meant that the television dramatist was no longer tied to the Aristotelian unites of time and place which once confined television to a theatre-like performance. The increased use of 16mm filming, much lighter, more flexible cameras and dollies and the use of the VTR (which meant that editing and recording were now possible) gave the writer greater freedom to explore and experiment with the medium. As Tony Garnett has put it, '[a]ll this contributed to several possibilities that have seemed singularly at home on the TV screen rather than on the stage or in the cinema. The interior monologue, the pictures of the imagination, the fantasy life, have come into their own.'[66] Inspired by Martin's article, *Stand Up, Nigel Barton* can be seen as Potter's attempt to use the television technology of the day to create a new grammar for television drama – moving away from the portrayal of *external realities* and presenting the *internal workings* of the human mind. 'I'm much more concerned with interior drama than with external realities', he explained in 1976. 'Television is equipped to have an interior language. Certainly one of the strands in TV drama is that of the interiorisation process, the concern with people's fantasies and feelings about the shape of their lives, and about themselves.'[67] Clearly, Potter's notion of the interiorisation process is reflected in the play's portrayal of Nigel, presenting the audience with an interior monologue through which the personal and social ramifications of the scholarship boy could be portrayed in a new and original way.

Such an approach to television drama has most commonly been referred to as Potter's *non-naturalistic* techniques. Although the term itself is notoriously vague and imprecise, it was fundamental to Potter's belief that television should create a style and grammar of its own. In order to define non-naturalism, however, it is important that one first distinguishes between naturalism and realism. While naturalism is regarded generally as denoting a very detailed illusion of real life, realism does not seek simply to produce a direct or simple portrayal of the real. As Raymond Williams put it, '[n]aturalism was seen as that which merely reproduced the flat external appearance of reality with a certain static quality, whereas realism – in the Marxist tradition, for example – was that method and that intention which went below this surface to the essential historical movements, to the dynamic reality.'[68] Seen in this light, one can see both the drama documentaries of Ken Loach and Tony Garnett and the non-naturalism of Potter's work as an attempt to create a dynamic *realism* in television drama. Whereas Loach and Garnett focused their dramatic approach on the detailed accuracy of description (verisimilitude), Potter's non-naturalistic techniques attempted to subvert the very conventions upon which television's verisimilitude are founded. Techniques such as characters addressing the camera and children's parts being played by adult actors forces the viewer to question the nature of the reality on offer. As Potter himself put it at the 1977 Edinburgh Television Festival:

> The best non-naturalist drama, in its very structure, disorientates the viewer smack in the middle of the orientation process which television perpetually uses. . . . It shows the frame in the picture when most television is showing the picture in the frame. I think it is *potentially* the more valuable, therefore, of the two approaches.[69]

In particular, Potter's non-naturalistic techniques attempt to show the psychological landscape of the human mind rather than offering a faithful or comprehensive version of an external reality. According to Ron Simon, he joins a tradition of artists from novelists like Virginia Woolf to film-makers like Alain Resnais who 'have wanted to approximate the inner flux of the mind, its thoughts and desires, as it interacts with the concrete realities of daily life'.[70] As Potter explained in 1980, 'I hope that they [the plays] are about what goes on in people's heads. . . . The trick is getting that out without actually saying that that is what the characters are thinking. I am happy to break the naturalistic mode. I don't want to show life exactly as it is. I hope to show a little of what life is about.'[71] In this sense, Potter's non-naturalistic techniques are employed in order to create a heightened sense of *realism*; only that dynamic realism is actually more concerned with the *interior* thoughts, memories and fantasies of his character's minds than with the *external* circumstances of their lives.

As in many of Potter's plays, the focus and force of *Stand Up, Nigel Barton* lies in the portrayal of *one* central mind. Through a series of dialectical encounters it dissolves the basic division between past and present so that time and place are seen through the eyes and memories of Nigel alone. Inspired into a rejection of naturalism and documentary realism by writers and critics like Troy Kennedy Martin and aided by the ever-increasing developments in technology, Potter carefully crafted an interior monologue for Nigel's social and personal dislocation. At the play's conclusion, the audience could perhaps understand the psychological roots of Nigel's complex journey, and yet through that understanding be *critical* of his behaviour as a whole. Seen in this light, its title (originally coming from a schoolroom command by Miss Tillings) suggests *Nigel's* moment of judgement has finally arrived. Shown through the intricate and private dimensions of his interior world and memories the audience now has the power to judge *him* in the way he first passed judgement on Georgie and then his own family and class. Clearly Potter's early documentary had forced him to re-assess not only the techniques and conventions of television itself, but also and just as importantly, its methods and morality.

However, the dominant role of its central protagonist means that many of the other characters in the play are weak and clichéd in comparison. As Sinfield argues, such a narrative is usually presented from the point of view of the *re-visitor*, relegating 'family and neighbourhood' to 'their proper supporting role in his story'.[72] Potter's snobbish undergraduates are particularly one dimensional, characters seemingly drawn from the novels of Evelyn Waugh. The self-obsession of the drama, like the documentary, tends to reduce every other character (except the central player) to a marginal position. It is a criticism often levelled against Potter's work as a whole, especially with regards to the portrayal of his female characters (see Chapter Five). Jill, the pill-popping girl-friend, the brutal Miss Tillings and the feckless mother are certainly caricatures, used simply to reinforce different aspects of Nigel's own character and psychological development. His mother, in particular, seems to have no backbone or strength of character at all – reflected in the fact that unlike his father we never learn her first name. When Harry storms out of the house after his son's television appearance, all she can apparently think about is what was on the other channel. 'We missed *No Hiding Place* and all' (p.74), she complains. It is left, of course, to the two *men* to walk to the working-men's club together, but separated by 'a mutual anxiety' (p.75). As with other 'scholarship boy' texts, the relationship between father and son clearly creates much of the drama, but it leaves little room for the portrayal or discussion of any other relationship. Yet, with hindsight, one can see just how important the play is in terms of his work as a whole. For beneath its contemporary and social setting is a drama more concerned with the universal nature of memory and childhood than with the particular struggles of the scholarship boy. Nigel's memories, and the way they impinge on his adult life are perhaps, after all, the real subject of the story.

BLUE REMEMBERED HILLS (1979)

If there is one thing certain about 'the organic community', it is that it has always gone.

Raymond Williams, *Culture and Society*[73]

Blue Remembered Hills was first broadcast on BBC 1 on 30 January 1979 as part of the BBC's drama series 'Play for Today'. This series of single dramas began in the early 1970s, replacing the highly successful '*Wednesday Play*'. While its new title celebrated the contemporary content of the work, it also tended to foreground the ephemeral nature of the medium. 'A play for today. *Just* for today', complains Potter's Christopher Hudson in *Only Make Believe*. 'As tasty as a packet of crisps and just as disposable.'[74] In the 1970s there was, however, still a regular market for the single play and Potter relentlessly continued to pursue many of the same themes and obsessions which had previously fuelled his earlier work. After the success of *Pennies from Heaven* a year earlier (see Chapter Four) he had reached a high point in his career with his plays and adaptations promoted as major television events. On its first broadcast (it has been repeated on several occasions since) the critics saw it as yet another confirmation that he was indeed 'Britain's finest television dramatist'; winning a BAFTA award for its writer in 1980. '*Blue Remembered Hills* was . . . a masterpiece', wrote Richard North in the *Listener*.[75] 'The play was a brilliant, beautifully evocative, vivid and vital picture of childhood . . .', declared Peter Knight in the *Daily Telegraph*.[76] Although it was made some 12 years after *Stand Up, Nigel Barton*, it clearly reflects the development of themes and techniques originally dealt with and formulated in that earlier play.

Shot on film entirely on location in a forest in Dorset the script asserts that the play takes place in 1943 'somewhere in the West Country' (p.41).[77] The language of the children, however, suggests a forest closer to Potter's heart. Seven children (all aged seven) are seen aimlessly roaming the woods, playing soldiers, mothers and fathers and cruelly killing a squirrel before an accident leaves one of them dead. The victim is Donald Duck (Colin Jeavons) an abused child, bullied mercilessly by the other children. In contrast, the burly Peter (Michael Elphick) is the leader of the gang until his position is challenged and overthrown by John (Robin Ellis). The fat Willie (Colin Welland) and the stuttering Raymond (John Bird) are never likely to be contenders for the top position, happy to support whoever happens to be in charge. The plain Audrey (Janine Duvistski) tries vainly to be accepted by Peter, and hopes to be the best friend of the pretty Angela (Helen Mirren) whose main preoccupation seems to be with boys. Finally there is Wallace Wilson whom we never actually see, but whose reputation as 'cock of the class' (p.45) looms large over the proceedings. As this summary of the plot suggests the play is coloured by the complex hierarchical structure of the group and, above all, by the cruel and vicious betrayals of childhood they evoke. Brian Gibson's direction skilfully reflects Potter's script and its eye for the smallest details of childish manners and behaviour.

The play has most frequently been compared to William Golding's *Lord of the Flies* (1954). Potter's children are certainly as cruel, selfish and vicious as Golding's. They fight and bully each other on a regular basis, swapping loyalties with consummate ease. At the end of the play, having locked Donald Duck in a burning barn, they unhappily realise they are responsible for his murder. As in Nigel Barton's classroom betrayal, however, the guilt they feel is quickly concealed and repressed by their collaborated lies. 'We was all together', Willie asserts. 'Miles away!' replies Angela. 'We don't know nothing about it, do us?' (p.84) John agrees. So, like Nigel, they enter a world constructed around their own lies and deceit. As in the earlier play all the children parts are also played by adults. As before, the device clearly dramatises the power and brutality of the children. According to Potter, it seemed 'necessary to use the adult body not only as the magnifying glass but also, however paradoxically, as the seismograph which could more truthfully measure the quakes and tremors of childhood's emotions' (Potter, 1984, p.40). As in Nigel's schoolroom scenes, the technique also foregrounds the memorised aspect of the play. These are, after all, 'blue *remembered* hills', and the device suggests that the action takes place within the cloudy landscape of memory. Potter's own narration at the end of the play suggests an adult consciousness at work. Appropriately enough he reads from A. E. Housman's *A Shropshire Lad*:

> Into my heart, an air that kills
> From yon far country blows
> What are those blue remembered hills?
> What spires, what farms are those?
> That is the land of lost content,
> I see it shining plain.
> The happy highways where I went
> And cannot come again.
>
> pp.84–5[78]

The inclusion of the verse has been felt by many critics to be simply ironic, the brutality of the children (resulting in an innocent death) offers a stark contrast to Housman's romantic picture of childhood innocence. The same verse had already been recited at the end of Edward Bond's screenplay to Nicolas Roeg's *Walkabout* (1973), which seemed similarly ironic in view of the childrens' desperate and arduous journey through the Australian outback.[79] Yet there is a feeling at the end of Potter's play that Housman was actually right in representing childhood as a forsaken world – a world adults still long to retrieve. 'There's an irony about the "land of lost content"', Potter later told Graham Fuller, 'because there is no such land, never can be. And yet there's a yearning to be able to go back and put things right. There is irony in terms of the story, and yet the yearning within the poem is *non*-ironic.' (Fuller, 1993, p.58)

That yearning to return to the 'simpler' world of childhood (despite its violence and cruelty) is clearly evident. Along with the childhood disloyalties, the children's vicious and bitter battles, the play still manages to conjure up a heady nostalgia for a rural England during the Second World War. Lavish shots of wide open countryside create a veritable 'Garden of Eden', while the memories of a 1940s English childhood is triggered through the mention of comics like the *Beano* and *Dandy*, returnable jam jars and cowboy outfits. If their childhood escapades reflect war-time England then it is of a poor, unequal, badly educated and inward-looking nation, yet the children also share an unimaginable amount of freedom (especially by today's standards), grappling in the earth and discovering together a mutual and organic sense of community. Despite their betrayals and cruelties they share a number of moral and social certainties which may offer a glimpse of a more stable and less problematic world than the present. All the children clearly 'know their place' both sexually and socially, the girls play exclusively with dolls and prams, the boys with sticks and toy guns; and while the girls are clearly aiming towards motherhood and marriage the boys look forward to a life in the army and the airforce. It is certainly a long way from the bitter fight for sexual equality and the social discontent of British society in the late 1970s, which saw gender divisions, social class and national identity becoming increasingly unstable.

It is also a world where the alleged evils of the advertising industry have not yet left their aspirational and materialistic impression. Today's media-sophisticated seven year olds would presumably be bored by a day in the countryside with nothing but an old pram and a box of matches (*England's Glory* no less!) as entertainment. The organic setting in the English countryside is also, of course, a stark contrast to the radical post-war rede-velopment of the 1960s which increasingly placed working-class communities into high-rise isolation. Such a portrayal of a 1940s rural childhood is not romantic *per se*, but its contrast with the late 1970s suggests that there was, after all, an innocence of sorts which can never be reclaimed. It may not be perfect, but we wonder with hindsight if their future lives are to be as natural or as vibrant as they are at this precious moment in time.

The nostalgic impulse of the play has, however, been gener-ally played down by critics who, like John Cook, interpret the children's behaviour as evidence of original sin. According to Cook, 'no clear Fall from childhood is depicted . . . the fallen nature of adults is there right from the very beginning in their child selves'.[80] He takes as proof, Willie's biting of an apple in the opening scene, suggesting the 'fallen' world which the children inhabit. Because the play clearly rejects the traditionally roman-tic image of childhood, however, it does not necessarily mean it portrays the children as inherently evil. As we shall see in the following chapter, Potter's work, as a whole, rests on the notion that innocent children are corrupted by the evils of the *adult* world. These children are undoubtedly vicious and selfish, but their natural and organic spirit has not yet been 'broken down' by the menial jobs and unhappy marriages which inevitably lies waiting for them. The escaped Italian prisoner of war (whom we never actually see) suggests an ominous and evil presence lurking outside their small group, not in the children at all. After Donald's tragic death, intense feelings of guilt, betrayal and repression are allowed to penetrate the children's world. Only then are they ready to enter and be accepted by the fallen world *outside* the forest.

Indeed, the play goes to great length to suggest that the children are gradually becoming *corrupted* by their elders and 'betters', rather than being inherently evil at heart. In their childish games they strangely reflect and shadow the adult world, a world which they are gradually learning to perceive yet not fully understand. What the children have in common is a working-class background which is sparse, lacking in love, respect and moral guidance. They have clearly entered the phase in their life when they are beginning to observe and respond to their parents' actions and behaviour, their experiences caught, as it were, between two worlds – a child and adult's. Perhaps that is one of the reasons why the adult actors do not appear totally incongruous in their parts, simultaneously and literally exhibiting – in the disjunction between their childish actions and their adult bodies – the two separate worlds which they are temporarily caught between.

In a game of mothers and fathers the harsh reality of the children's working-class background is clearly played out. 'Hurry up', orders the usually timid Donald in the role of the father, 'I be off up to the *bloody* pub in half a tick. To get *bloody* drunk.' 'You're not coming home stinking of drink at all hours' (p.53), replies Angela in the role of mother. Beneath the game, however, also lurks the realities of Donald's own dysfunctional family. 'Smack her one in the chops', Audrey tells Angela who nurses the doll. 'No, no', Donald instantly replies. 'You can't do that. No smacking. Not in my house.' (p.51) Similarly, the boys ape the events and experiences of the Second World War which they learn about from comics. '"Xpect they'll tie him down on a great big hill of blank ants"', Peter tells Donald about his father. 'That's what the Japs do. It was in the *Champion*.' (p.70) Perhaps, then, the boy's squirrel hunt reflects the hysteria and hatred brought about by the war. Although Peter is the only one intent on killing the poor animal the others join in the fear of being thought a sissy. Once committed, however, the hunt brings up some darker feelings which they are unable to control and instantly regret. An eerie echo of their later 'betrayal' and their own arrival into adulthood:

PETER, JOHN, WILLIE and RAYMOND *immediately close up around the animal, frenziedly kicking at it with their large, hob-nailed, toe-scuffed boots. As they kill the squirrel they giggle and grunt and gasp with shocked awe and excitement. The violent activity stops, abruptly. They stand off a bit, looking at each other guiltily. The wind shifts and sighs in the big oak. A feeling of murder.*

(p.54)

Seen in this light, the play clearly reflects many of the same themes and techniques Potter first tackled in *Stand Up, Nigel Barton*. The children's murder of Donald Duck, like the classroom conviction of Georgie, suggests a community which expresses a hidden and latent violence through the persecution of an innocent victim or scapegoat. Both Georgie and Donald are crucified by a community whose values and morality are based on conformity, prejudice and lies. As in *A Beast With Two Backs* (set in the nineteenth century Forest of Dean) an isolated and introverted community punishes the innocent victim and outsider rather than deal with its own darker sensibilities. However, while such a society is clearly inward-looking, ignorant and vicious, there is nonetheless a discernible feeling of loss associated with it as a whole. Perhaps comparisons can be made between the children's life in the forest and England at the end of the Second World War. Like the children, England too was divided by bitter class or hierarchical divisions. Ignorance, bullying, xenophobia and abuse were not only rife, but simply accepted as a way of life. Yet the cruelty of this community is compensated for a feeling of kinship which is as natural and organic as the forest they inhabit. Donald's death, however, will certainly bring outsiders to this isolated world, disrupting the children's natural community forever. A world of innocence (however brutal) has 'Fallen', and a common and natural culture has been shattered by the guilt, lies and suspicions which will inevitably tear the community apart.

If Potter's characters are caught between 'two worlds', the division between one world and the other inevitably takes place during a moment in childhood – when a natural belief in community is shaken, corrupted and destroyed forever. From that moment his characters are forced to mourn for the 'Eden' they have lost, yet they yearn for a world they know is now no longer obtainable or even desirable. What they yearn *for*, is not so much a return to that world (which was often narrow and restrictive) but to a time when it was the only world they knew – a world which lies forever beyond the cynicism and moral corruption of maturity. His characters are torn between the memories of childhood and the stark realities of adulthood, between one social class and another, between the past and the present – conflicting worlds, linked only by memory, fantasy and imagination.

Like *Stand Up, Nigel Barton*, the play also relies for much of its effect on elements of non-naturalism. While there are no flash backs and the script (unusually for Potter) sticks to a strictly chronological time sequence, the use of adult actors to play the parts of children still proudly continued Troy Kennedy Martin's declaration against television's naturalism. In contrast to the earlier play, however, it does not attempt to portray the inner fantasies of one central protagonist. Yet it does, as a whole, construct a particular (or *English*) memory of childhood – offering a personalised and subjective landscape, rather than attempting to produce a realistic view of an actual world. What these two plays clearly show is the impulse in Potter's work towards the *interior* landscape of the human mind, rather than attempting to portray its *external* realities. While the themes at the heart of his early documentary were to remain (the child's inevitable 'Fall' from their organic origins, the mixture of nostalgia and contempt for that distant past, the difficult and dangerous journey between 'two worlds', and the ambiguous portrayal of mass culture) the factual and naturalistic world of the documentary form would be abandoned forever. Instead, his drama would gradually begin to reflect a 'visionary' kind of writing, one which could celebrate the personal and psychological aspects of human experience.

As we shall discover in the next chapter, Potter's major influences would not come from the theatre or even television drama (where Martin's declaration fell mainly on deaf ears) but from a literary tradition which has its roots deep within British

Romanticism. With the premature death of David Mercer in 1980 Potter was to be one of the few television playwrights who not only remained working within the medium, but also continued to struggle against its dominant forms and structures. For Potter, the *interior* landscape ('what goes on inside people's heads') increasingly became the focus of his work. 'Hemmingway's characters may feel the earth move in their mutual orgasm', he wrote in a preface to *Blue Remembered Hills*, 'but a child can sense it spinning of its axis by the movement of a shadow on the wall.' (Potter, 1984, p.40) Perhaps this image of a 'shadow on the wall' is an apt way to think of Potter's drama, attempting to portray the glimpses and shadowy recesses of the human imagination in the most intimate of domestic settings.

In the process of this chapter I hope to have shown the very roots of Potter's dramatic landscape. In many ways it is shaped by the same forces which first attracted him to the 'democratic' dimensions of the small screen; a need to connect two 'different worlds' and the desire to reclaim or rexamine the communal culture of a mythical past. Those issues are at the heart of these three separate pieces of work, from the guilt-ridden yearning of *Between Two Rivers* and its ambiguous attack on modern mass culture, through to Nigel Barton's personal dislocation and the children's 'Fall' from organic innocence in *Blue Remembered Hills*. As the growing scholarship boy had lost faith in a simple and close-knit Forest community, so England had lost the organic innocence of its past. Mass and folk culture, innocence and corruption, the past and the present are consistently mingled together, producing a complex mixture of betrayal, guilt and an uneasy but always discernible sense of *loss*. While Potter consistently denied the charges of nostalgia, there is an unmistakable yearning to go back and reclaim the past, to rediscover the point where everything inevitably went wrong. And it was in this portrayal of the past that Potter first chose to harness the techniques of non-naturalism. Disappointed and ashamed of his own documentary he began to conceive a form of television drama which could portray the interior dynamics of the human mind, to present what he liked to think of as the sovereignty of the individual. Little wonder then, that his original concern for subjects such as social class and politics were quickly surpassed by a tendency to explore the psychological and even spiritual dimensions of his characters' inner lives. And at the heart of that journey into the self lay the memories of childhood. 'Perhaps we all live in a sort of exile from the lost land of our childhood', he once wrote, '. . . simply and impossibly, with the desire that we could stand where the earth once sang with magic, and look at ourselves as we are now.' (Potter, 1984, p.34)

NOTES

1. Richard Hoggart, *The Uses of Literacy*, Penguin Books, 1990, p.301.
2. Don Taylor, *Days of Vision: Working with David Mercer – Television Drama Then and Now*, Methuen, 1990, p.52.
3. See Philip Purser, 'Dennis Potter', in George W. Brandt (ed.), *British Television Drama*, Cambridge University Press, 1981, p.169.
4. David Walter, *The Oxford Union: The Playground of Power*, Macdonald, 1984, p.157. *Isis* is the Oxford journal which Potter edited while an undergraduate.
5. Dennis Potter, 'Base Ingratitude?' the *New Statesman*, 3 May 1958, pp.261–2.
6. Ibid.
7. Quoted in the script of *Class in Private Life*, programme two of *Does Class Matter?* series, BBC TV, 25 August 1958, included in the BBC Written Archive Centre: TEL1/C/1273/11372.
8. See Dennis Potter, *The Glittering Coffin*, 1960, pp.71–2.
9. Transcribed from a video recording of the play, BBC TV, 1970.
10. Transcribed from a video recording of the play, BBC TV, 1971.
11. Interview with Dennis Potter, *Midweek*, BBC Radio 4, 17 May 1992.
12. The 'Angry Young Man' was, of course, an invention of the media as Harry Ritchie's *Success Stories: Literature and the Media in England 1950–1959* (Faber & Faber, 1988, p.35) has shown, but the label nevertheless served as a symbol of change. While Colin Wilson's *The Outsider* was published in 1956, Kingsley Amis' *Lucky Jim* was actually published in 1954 and John Braine's *Room at the Top* in 1957.
13. See Alan Sinfield, *Literature, Politics and Culture in Post-War Britain*, Basil Blackwell, 1989, p.233.
14. Both *Lay Down Your Arms* and *Lipstick on Your Collar* are set in 1956 at the War Office where Potter himself completed his national service. Unlike the heroes of the two plays, however, Potter had already left the position for university by the time of the Suez Crisis.
15. See Patrick Wright, 'The Last Acre of Truth', *The Guardian* (*Media Section*), 15 February, 1993. No doubt the young undergraduate was thrilled to be seen alongside Hoggart in Christopher Mayhew's *What is Class?* Later, when he became a trainee on *Bookstand* he would

invite Hoggart back to the BBC to be interviewed on the programme. See W. Stephen Gilbert, 1995, p.86.

16. Richard Hoggart, *The Uses of Literacy*, Penguin Book, 1990, p.24.
17. See the conclusion to Raymond Williams', *Culture and Society 1780–1950*, Penguin books, 1971. Like Hoggart, Williams would also be a guest on *Bookstand* while Potter was a trainee.
18. Dennis Potter, 'Downloading', in 'The Television Plays of Dennis Potter', a brochure provided by The Museum of Television and Radio to accompany a retrospective of his work, January 23–May 31 1992. Contributions from John Wyver and Ron Simon are also included.
19. Cited by Francis Jarmen, 'Birth of a Playwriting Man', interview with David Mercer, *Theatre Quarterly*, 3, no. 9, Jan–Mar 1973, p.55.
20. Donald Wilson (introduction and notes), *The Television Playwright: Ten Plays Selected by Michael Barry*, Michael Joseph, 1960, p.18.
21. Interview with Paul Madden, unpaginated programme notes for a National Film Theatre screening of the *Nigel Barton Plays*, November 1976.
22. Paddy Chayefsky was an American television writer who first termed the phrase. *Marty* (1953), starring Rod Steiger, proved that the portrayal of ordinary people could attract both large audiences and high critical acclaim.
23. See John Caughie, 'Before the Golden Age: Early Television Drama', in John Corner, *Popular Television in Britain: Studies in Cultural History*, BFI, 1991, p.26. See also Jason Jacobs, *Early British Television Drama: Aesthetics, Style and Technology*, unpublished PhD, University of East Anglia, 1996.
24. For a more detailed analysis see Carl Gardner and John Wyver, 'The Single Play: From Reithian Reverence To Cost-Accounting and Censorship', *Screen*, Vol. 24, Nos. 4–5, 1983.
25. As George W. Brandt points out, the BBC had already bought 35 dramas from the Canadian Broadcasting Company in 1957, 30 of which were produced by Newman. ABC, however, took the brave step of acquiring Newman himself (Brandt, 1981, p.15).
26. Cited by Gardner and Wyver, 1983.
27. See Howard Thomas (ed.), *The Armchair Theatre*, Weidenfeld & Nicolson, 1959, p.17.
28. Stuart Laing, *Representations of the Working-Class Life: 1957–1964*, Macmillan, 1986, p.149.
29. See Irene Shubik, *Play for Today: The Evolution of Television Drama*, Davis-Poynter, 1975, p. 94.
30. See interview with Billie Whitelaw in *'And Now For Your Sunday Night Entertainment'* (a documentary on *Armchair Theatre*), Channel 4, 8th February 1987.
31. Ibid.
32. John Caughie, 1991, p.36.
33. *The Future of Sound Radio and Television: A short version of the Report of the Pilkington Committee*, Her Majesty's Stationery Office, 1962, p.10.
34. Cited by Francis Wheen, *Television: A History*, Century, 1985, p.115.

Notice the patrician tone of Greene's comments that perhaps compromises the democratic sentiments.

35. Tony Garnett, *The Radio Times*, 27 October 1966, p.38.
36. Such was the controversy over Ken Loach's *Cathy Come Home*, and its depiction of a homeless young mother losing the right to keep her children, that it is often cited as being instrumental in establishing *Shelter*, the charity set up in the 1960s to help the homeless.
37. Interview with Ken Loach by Jeremy Issacs, *Face to Face*, BBC TV, 1994.
38. Dennis Potter, 'The Only Meat Was in the Cookery Class', In My View Column, *The Sun*, 15 February 1968.
39. Interview with Tony Garnet in Roger Hudson, 'Television in Britain: Description and Dissent', *Theatre Quarterly*, April–June 1972, Vol. 2, no. 6, p.19.
40. Cited by Paul Madden, 1967. In the end, though changes were insisted upon, they proved not to be too substantial and its screening went ahead.
41. Ibid., p.88.
42. Hilary Cooke, 'Critic on the Hearth', *The Listener*, 16 June 1960.
43. With an act of perfect symmetry Potter chooses the same song to 'sing' in his 1993 MacTaggart Lecture (Potter, 1994, p.43).
44. All extracts from *Between Two Rivers* were transcribed from a video tape of the original broadcast (BBC TV, 3 June 1960). Conveniently the programme forgets that much of Potter's grammar school career actually took place at St Clement Dane's Grammar School, Hammersmith, London.
45. *Double Your Money* was one of the first British game shows to arrive on commercial television. It was shows such as this – offering cash prizes – which Hoggart and the Pilkington Committe condemned in 1962.
46. Arthur Schlesinger, Jr, 'The Fiction of Fact – and the Fact of Fiction', included in Lewis Jacobs (ed.), *The Documentary Tradition: From Nanook to Woodstock*, Hopkinson & Blake, 1971, p.383.
47. Denis Mitchell, cited by John Corner, 'Documentary Voices', in John Corner (ed.), *Popular Television in Britain: Studies in Cultural History*, BFI, 1991, pp.55–6. According to Corner, such techniques would later influence all manner of film-makers, including the British realist campaigners of the Free Cinema group such as Lindsey Anderson and Karel Reisz.
48. Cited by W. Stephen Gilbert, 1995, p.80.
49. Troy Kennedy Martin, 'Nats Go Home: First Statement of a New Drama for Television', *Encore*, issue 48, March–April, 1964, p.31.
50. Kenneth Eastaugh, *The Daily Mirror*, 16 December 1965. The BBC held questionnaires (based on a sample of 199). It was estimated that the audience for *Stand Up, Nigel Barton* was 12.7% of the population of the UK. ITV at the same time was estimated at 15%. See BBC written archives, Caversham, file: T5/690/1. Its sample of viewers concluded that the writer seemed determined to 'pile on the bad language' and complained about its 'crude scenes'.

51. See Kennith Trodd, 'Preview', *Emergency-Ward 9*, *Radio Times*, 7 April 1966, p.20.
52. Julian Holland, *Daily Mail*, 9 December 1965.
53. See interview with Paul Madden, 1976.
54. 'Long words actually hurt people', Nigel's Labour Party Agent tells him in *Vote, Vote, Vote for Nigel Barton* (Potter, 1967, p.88).
55. Hoggart, 1990, p.296.
56. Alan Sinfield, *Literature, Politics and Culture in Post-war Britain*, Basil Blackwell, 1989, p.266.
57. *Coronation Street* is Britain's longest running television soap opera. Critics originally re-named it 'Hoggart Street' because of its warm portrayal of working-class Northern life.
58. Sinfield, 1989, p.266
59. David Mercer, *Plays One*, Methuen, 1990.
60. Dennis Potter, 'Unknown Territory', *New Left Review*, January–Febuary 1961, p.65.
61. Martin's article may have been partly inspired by experimental BBC dramas such as *Storyboard* (1961), *Studio 4* (1962) and *Teletale* (1963). Certainly figures like Ken Loach, John McGrath and Roger Smith were already pioneering non-naturalistic techniques before Martin's article was published.
62. Troy Kennedy Martin, 1964, pp.32–3.
63. Ibid.
64. Dennis Potter, 'Reaction', *Encore*, 11:3, May–June 1964, p.39.
65. Potter, 1967, p.11.
66. See interview with Tony Garnett in Roger Hudson, 'Television in Britain: Description and Dissent', *Theatre Quarterly*, Vol. 2, no. 6, April–June 1972, p.20.
67. Cited by Paul Madden, 1976.
68. Raymond Williams, 'A Lecture on Realism', *Screen*, 18:1, Spring 1977, p.65.
69. Dennis Potter, 'Realism and Non-Naturalism 2', *The Official Programme of the Edinburgh International Television Festival, 1977*, August 1977, p.37. See also Raymond Williams, 'Realism and Non-Naturalism 1', *The Official Programme of the Edinburgh International Television Festival 1977*, August 1977, p.35.
70. Ron Simon, 'The Flow of Memory and Desire' in 'The Television Plays of Dennis Potter' – a brochure which accompanied the Museum of Television and Radio's retrospective of Potter's work in New York, 23 January–31 May 1992, p.24.
71. Cited by Nicholas Wapshott, 'Knowing what goes on inside people's heads', A Times Profile, *The Times*, 21 April 1980, p.10
72. Alan Sinfield, 1989, p.266.
73. Raymond Williams, 1971, p.252.
74. Dennis Potter, *Only Make Believe*, 1973, BBC TV.
75. Richard North, the *Listener*, 8 February 1979, p.225.
76. Peter Knight, the *Daily Telegraph*, 31 January 1979, p.13.
77. All page references refer to Dennis Potter, *On Television: Waiting For the Boat*, Faber & Faber, 1984.

78. Housman's untitled two verse poem comes from his collection, *A Shropshire Lad*, Harrap, 1940.
79. Potter would later collaborate with Nicolas Roeg on the movie *Track 29* (1986).
80. John Cook, 1995, p.114.

3

Between Good and Evil: Religion and the Romantic Vision

It is not extravagance; it is not mysticism . . . it is but the doing justice to that real and interior spirit of things, which modifies and enlivens the mystery of existence.

Leigh Hunt on William Hazlitt[1]

My characters may be stretched, may be anguished, may be bizarre, may be driven absolutely round the bend. But what they're driven round the bend *about* aren't material things, not even a particular political ideology, although sometimes that might be true. They're trying to be sovereign human beings, sometimes against impossible odds. The dominant motif in nearly all of my work is someone saying, 'God, are you there? And if not, why not?'

Dennis Potter[2]

INTRODUCTION

'When I was a boy', Jack Black declares in *Follow the Yellow Brick Road* (1972), ' . . . I thought God was watching me all the time, every minute of the day.' (Muller, 1973, p.330) As a sick and neurotic adult, however, he desperately prays to God for a 'sign', but receives only the word – *'Slime'* (p.332). This answer is a clear symbol of the painful repulsion he now feels towards an increasingly secular world. Often overlooked by critics, the role of religion and the desperate quest for spiritual salvation is one of the central concerns of Potter's work. Reflecting Modernism's search for meaning in a Godless universe his characters constantly

70

grapple for a form of personal redemption in a world which offers little certainty other than the always 'implacable presence of death itself' (Potter, 1984, p.20). His central protagonists continually turn in desperation to a God who is either missing or simply unable or unwilling to answer. Yet they never truly give up yearning for a 'religious' sense of the universe – a sense they first experienced as a child.

Despite the religious yearning apparent in Potter's work it consistently refused to accept any traditional, organised or orthodox view of the religious experience. 'Religion is not the bandage but the wound', he was fond of proclaiming, suggesting that its role, if it has a role at all, should be in recognising the *horror* of the human condition rather than trying to offer illusory and false reassurances. '[A] religion that doesn't go into the dark side, that isn't concerned with pain, that is something you put on Sunday-best clothes for is of no interest to me whatsoever . . .', he told Mary Craig on *BBC* radio's *Thought for Today* in 1976.[3] As the Revd Donald Reeves put it at Potter's memorial service, he was an 'irritant to those with a secure and comfortable belief in God' and also to the cynical 'lazy agnostics'.[4] A sentiment apparently shared by the Archbishop of York in the late 1980s who defended the sex scenes in *The Singing Detective* (1986) because, in his opinion, it was 'classically Christian Drama'.[5] Certainly there is a 'religious' vision in his work which drives the majority of his plays, novels and screenplays. As Gavin Millar, the director of *Cream in My Coffee* (1980) and *Dreamchild* (1985) has argued, the religious impulse of the drama was usually detectable even in those plays not particularly concerned with spiritual matters at all:

There's no way that you can get away from the strong religious undercurrent, mid current, top current, in his work. Even his ostensibly non-religious work, even when it's just politics there's a certain religiosity about the politics. I think there is a great spiritual thirst there in all his work . . . about his feeling that if God's there then he's not helping much. And he keeps talking about it. Either He's there or He's not there. But he doesn't ignore it.[6]

Much of Potter's work clearly revolves around this longing for spiritual transcendence. Unlike Samuel Beckett's characters who spend their time searching for what is essentially unknown or unknowable, his protagonists occasionally glimpse the vision of a better and holier world in an otherwise barren and secular reality. Salvation, ambiguous and fragile as it is, comes drifting upon the words and melodies of a popular song, set in motion with the arrival of an unexpected stranger or fought out within the agonies and ecstasies of sex. The struggle to see beyond the harsh realities of the physical world permeates the work and provides the dramatic and the religious tensions upon which it ultimately revolves. His leading protagonists all long for a world *other than it is*, where the songs, the television commercials or the simple truths of childhood come true. His drama explores that space between human aspiration and the stark and frequently painful realities of everyday life. It examines the nature and structure of the religious experience, refusing traditional modes of belief, but constantly driven and generated by a furious search for faith in desperate and frequently painful circumstances.

In almost the first line of Potter's debut play *The Confidence Course* (1965), the God-like figure of The Director offers the hope of personal redemption. It is a promise, however, which is ultimately dishonest and conceals a confidence trick that preys on the weak and the desperate. In *A Beast With Two Backs* (1968) the powerful sermons of Ebenezer, the village preacher, ignite the passion of his parishioners and sets them on a trail of vengeance which results in the slaughter of an innocent scapegoat in the form of a performing bear. In *Son of Man* (1969), an earthy and angry Christ subverts the traditional image of Jesus as a mystical incarnation and presents a flawed and ultimately human figure who is plagued by doubts about his own divinity. In *Joe's Ark* (1974) we see a father agonising over his Christian belief in the face of his daughter's imminent death from cancer. *Brimstone and Treacle* reversed the conventional notions of good and evil and explored the moral assumptions and reductive conventions of traditional Christian morality. *Where Adam Stood* (1976) (inspired by *Father and Son* (1907), the autobiography of Edmund Gosse) portrayed a father's attempt to reconcile the scientific discoveries of Charles Darwin with his own literal belief in the Old Testament; and in *The Singing Detective* the evangelical gusto of the hospital's Christian Society is contrasted with the painful search for personal redemption of its cynical and foul-mouthed protagonist Philip Marlow.

A small selection of Potter's 'religious' work follows a similar and consistent pattern and have been labelled 'visitation dramas' by critics.[7] Most often associated with single plays such as *Brimstone and Treacle*, *Angels Are So Few* (1970) and *Schmoedipus* (1974) they are characterised by the arrival of a mysterious stranger into a repressed and sterile home. The motif is, however, evident in much of the work as a whole, and is clearly recognisable as early as his first play, *The Confidence Course*, in which a disruptive stranger claims to be the famous nineteenth century essayist William Hazlitt (a writer who, like the Romantics in general, would have a profound effect on his work – see below). This visitation structure can be glimpsed in *Son of Man* when Jesus first arrives out of the wilderness to confront Andrew and Peter at the shores of the Sea of Galilee. Even in *The Bonegrinder* (1968) and *A Beast With Two Backs* the arrival of an outsider disrupts the normality and everyday perceptions of the visited. The entrance of the Oxford student in *Joe's Ark*, the appearance of the mysterious Daniel Young in *Blade on the Feather* (1980) and the strange and ominous 'Accordion Man' in *Pennies from Heaven* (see Chapter Four) are all suggestive of the same motif. Even the class re-visitor in *Stand Up, Nigel Barton* (1965) ultimately fulfils the same device (see Chapter Two).

The plays, however, which are most associated with this structure are those which take place usually within the confines of a house or a single room and involve no characters other than the stranger and a small family or domestic couple. The morally ambiguous set of circumstances which their visit sets in motion is best summed up by the passage taken from the Bible and quoted at the beginning of *Angels Are so Few* – 'Be not forgetful to entertain strangers; for thereby some have entertained angels unawares' (Hebrews 13:1). Certainly in *Angels are so Few* Michael Biddle (his very name is a corruption of 'Bible') is convinced he is a heavenly messenger. But the visitor is just as likely to be an incarnation of the devil (*Brimstone and Treacle*) or simply a backward and innocent young lad (*Rain on the Roof*). The visitor frequently represents something latent or repressed in the people he visits and usually performs an act of liberating violence or sex which forces the visited to reassess their previously sterile existence. The guilt a middle-aged housewife feels for the baby she once 'abandoned' returns in the form of a mysterious young man in *Schmoedipus*, while the presence of the 'devil' in *Brimstone and Treacle* miraculously causes a brain-damaged girl to regain consciousness.

Such a structure is most evident in Potter's involvement with the single studio play during the 1960s and 1970s. The very form of the visitation drama fitted well into the principally limited space of the television studio which may partly explain the less than successful transition of *Brimstone and Treacle* (1982) and *Schmoedipus* (in the form of *Track 29* (1987)) to the large screen. This simple dramatic structure also helped to keep down the cost of multiple sets, large casts and the use of film (which was often expensive in comparison with video tape). In contrast to a play like *Cream in my Coffee* (1980) (which was shot on film and on location) a visitation play like *Brimstone and Treacle* (with principally two sets, four characters and shot mainly in the studio on video tape) offered enormous economic savings.[8] With their limited use of space and characters these plays had a strong theatrical feel about them, frequently their scripts highlighting the claustrophobic atmosphere of the drama, rather than trying to disguise the play's limiting and restricting dimensions.[9] Indeed, Harold Pinter often employed a similar structure for his stage plays. One thinks, for instance, of the mysterious visitor who arrives in *The Birthday Party* (1958), *The Caretaker* (1960) and *The Homecoming* (1965).

Unlike Pinter, however, whose earlier plays often resulted in evasive and unresolvable conclusions, Potter's visitation dramas frequently appear deceptively simple both in terms of their structure and content. Yet a subtle reversal of binary oppositions (good/ evil, sane/insane, real/imaginary) creates the dramatic tension which forces the viewer to re-examine the means by which their traditional moral and religious perceptions are constructed. One is never sure, for example, if the visitor is real or simply an elaborate fantasy concocted in the minds of the visited. Talking of *Track 29*, Potter said that 'it shares the obsession of that group of plays which has a stranger outside the house. He's going to knock, and you draw him in, but really he's inside your head'.[10] Potter's notion of the 'interiorisation process' would therefore acquire a considerable significance in these early 'religious' dramas, allowing him to continue to portray the *interior* dynamics of his characters' lives and actions. Almost buried beneath overtly sexual and occasionally violent narratives, these dramas offer some of his most morally ambitious, ambiguous and controversial dramatic works.

I shall examine in this chapter a small selection of these visitation dramas in an attempt to locate some of the major 'religious' issues at work. Appropriately this will keep the discussion within the boundaries of both 'The Wednesday Play' and 'Play for Today'; thereby adhering to the historical development of the work as a whole. In particular, I shall concentrate on the contradiction which apparently exists between the drama's profound religious sensibilites and its deep-rooted hatred of organised and ortho-dox religious dogma. Split between the animal and the spiritual, the bestial and the holy, Potter's characters are forced to exam-ine the 'religious' experience, questioning the morality of their private and public lives, causing them to rethink their own reli-gious natures. For it is the spiritual exploration of the self and the 'religious' nature of identity, with all its doubts, feelings of disgust and rejection, which clearly provides the tension upon which so much of his drama ultimately revolves. 'Everything ool be *all right*', says the nine year old Philip Marlow high in the bows of a tree in *The Singing Detective*. 'Won't it, God? Hey? Thou's like me a bit – doesn't, God? Eh?' (Potter, 1986, p.77); and an answer, if it comes at all, arrives only through a long, painful and frequently humiliating process of personal self-discovery.

'THE GLORY AND THE DREAM': THE ROMANTIC VISION

> ... in joy individuality is lost and it therefore is liveliest in youth, not from any principle in organisation but simply from this, that the hardships of life, that the circumstances that have forced a man in upon his little unthinking contemptible self, have lessened his power of existing universally.
>
> Samuel Taylor Coleridge[11]

There seems to have been a significant shift in Potter's religious beliefs during the course of his writing career from the early description of himself as a 'respectful agnostic' to a strong reli-gious conviction by the late 1970s. Indeed, for the early part of his career he was generally perceived as a confirmed atheist.[12] 'I'm not a religious man', he explained in 1969, 'I went to Chapel as a kid, but as soon as I grew up I stopped'.[13] Yet in an inter-view with Colin Morris on *Anno Domini* in 1977 he outlined his belief in what he now regarded as a 'personal loving God'. 'A

God', he said, 'without whom my life, my tensions, my struggles, and that of everyone else seen through my eyes, would be
drained of colour, meaning, purpose.'[14] Potter, however, constantly
distanced his religious faith from any traditional or safe notions
of belief, emphasising his need to question the very nature of
the religious experience. 'Whatever faith I may have or hope to
have, it will be within doubt', he once explained. 'Doubt is
the necessary response of man, at this period of time, to the
awesome claims of religion. But yes, I've changed.'[15]

Potter often reflected in interviews how his own fundamentalist chapel-going background had an enormous influence on
his early imagination.[16] Indeed, many of his central protagonists
share similar formative experiences. 'Chapel three times a week
when I was a lad', Christopher Hudson remembers in *Only Make
Believe*, 'knew this bleeding book', he holds up the Bible, 'like it
was an ache in the ligaments of my memory.'[17] Yet as a young
man Potter's commitment to politics was certainly more prominent than any religious conviction. 'It does not take a religious
man (which I certainly am not) to write in praise of the chapels',
he wrote in *The Changing Forest* (Potter, 1962, p.66). As elsewhere
in his work, the book is filled with Christian allusions and imagery.
The speeches of the Union leaders, he wrote, 'have in their texture
and their finality, an almost biblical ring, echoing with foreboding
ing and familiar words like "doom", "sin", "evil" and "charity"
(p.58). It is certainly a trait he acknowledged in himself, con-
fessing, even then, a tendency towards biblical rhetoric. 'Again,
I repeat, it does not take a religious man to write in praise of
the chapels, but maybe one needs to be a political evangelist.'
(p.66)

How Potter himself came to re-examine the religious side of
his character is best left to the biographies, but this constant struggle for faith is clearly evident in nearly everything he wrote.
Even when God is absent, that absence is felt with a passion and a
fanatical desperation. In *Follow the Yellow Brick Road* Jack Black
is consumed with an overwhelming sense of nausea and depression for his Godless existence. As Duncan Wu has put it, Jack's
'intoxicated expressions of disgust are significant because they
expose not despair but the vacuum left by the absence of belief'.[18]
Even Christ does not appear exempt from such a condition,
explaining that if people 'knew the truth they would gather
on the street corners in order to be sick. Now that would be a

meaningful sacrament.' (Potter, 1970, p.62) 'The world is full of maggots' (Potter, 1984, p.95) declares the desperate father in *Joe's Ark* as he painfully loses his Christian faith, while in *The Singing Detective* the faithless Philip Marlow tells a doctor exactly what he *does* believe in. 'I . . . believe in cholesterol', he explains, 'cigarettes, alcohol, masturbation, carbon monoxide, the Arts council, nuclear weapons, the *Daily Telegraph*, and not properly labelling fatal poisons. But most of all, above all else, I believe in the one thing which can come out of people's mouths. Vomit.' (Potter, 1986, p.40)

These faithless and bitter characters inevitably look back, however, to a time in childhood when they seemed to share a surprisingly close relationship with both Nature and God. They long to return to the rural and spiritual paradise most often associated with Potter's own Forest of Dean – whose very name has more than a passing similarity with Eden. In *Hide and Seek* (1973) Daniel Miller sits high in the bows of a tree in the Forest and sees that 'God was not a word in a book or a gigantic figure in the sky. He saw that God was things, was in and of things, every sort of thing, breathing through them, breathing out of them' (Potter, 1973, p.110). Jack Black recalls a similar moment in childhood when he, God and Nature were temporarily unified; when he saw 'the whole bounce of the landscape in a – a haze of light' (p.363). Occasionally a character may even catch a glimpse (however transitory) of such a visionary moment in maturity. As Jack Barker explains in Potter's only stage play *Sufficient Carbohydrate* (1983), 'I thought to myself – Perhaps it's all going to come back. The wonderful, wonderful belief I had as a child. The *overwhelming* comfort of knowing that Everything Was All Right, because God was there, and God looked after the world, like a gardener would.' (Potter, 1983, p.42)

One can clearly detect in such moments a 'Romantic' element at work in both the language and the description of Nature and God. As in Wordsworth's 'Tintern Abbey' (situated only a few miles from the Forest of Dean) his characters long to recreate that moment when '[w]e see into the life of things', when we feel 'a sense sublime / Of something far more deeply inter-fused. . . .'[19] Like the Romantics, Potter's drama seems to reflect a belief that the child, with almost a visionary clarity, is able to perceive the *living presence* of the natural world and thereby understand the 'universal' nature of experience. As Hazlitt puts it (in an extract Potter has Francis read out in *Lipstick in your Collar* (1993)) his characters yearn '[t]o lose' their 'importune, tormenting, everlasting personal identity in the elements of nature . . .' (Potter, 1993, p.55). Even the bitter and faithless Philip Marlow has a similar yearning. 'I would have liked to have used my pen to praise a loving God and all his loving creation', he tells Dr Gibbon in a rare unguarded moment, 'I would have like to have seen hosts of radiant and translucent angels climbing along spinning shafts of golden light deeper and deeper into the blue caverns of heaven.' (Potter, 1986, p.57)

Yet this vision of Nature and God is inevitably bound up with the Christian and Romantic notion of the 'Fall'. 'Whither is fled the visionary gleam?', Wordsworth asks, 'Where is it now, the glory and the dream?'[20] 'Where does it all go to?' asks Mr Warner, the headmaster in *Pennies from Heaven*. Looking at a child's drawing of a tree he is momentarily entranced. 'It's like a diamond', he explains, 'a tree from The Garden . . . I think they really do see things in a way that . . . they eventually lose. Not only lose, but forget they ever had.' (Potter, 1996, p.116) Such a speech is clearly evocative of the *Genesis* story, with the 'tree' symbolising both the splendour of childhood innocence and yet suggesting the inevitable Fall. According to Wordsworth's 'Ode', '[h]eaven lies about us in our infancy!', but soon 'Shades of the prison-house begin to close / Upon the growing boy. . . .'[21] Christopher Salvensen suggests that the 'prison-house' represents the *body* of the growing boy. The 'bodily sense', he argues, 'comes to intrude on unthinking childhood . . . He begins to become aware of his own body, that vehicle of his self in time.'[22] As in *Genesis*, self-consciousness about the body signals a traumatic and irreversible Fall from Grace.

In *Hide and Seek* the young Daniel Miller is tempted down from his paradisal tree by a voice he mistakenly believes to be that of God. Trusting in 'God', however, he is sexually abused by an escaped prisoner of war. It was 'an innocence', we are told, 'never to be reclaimed, a shock which changed even the ways of looking at the ferns and the foxgloves' (Potter, 1973, p.115). Later the sexual attack itself is described in between extracts from Coleridge's 'The Education of Children'. *Moonlight on the Highway* (1969) has David Peters turn to Al Bowlly's music to escape from the memories of a similar sexual attack. 'He has a longing for an Eden', his psychotherapist explains, . . .' before he reached that

fateful age of ten.'[23] In *The Singing Detective* a boy watches from
a tree as his mother has sex with a schoolfriend's father. *Angels
are so Few* has an 'angel' lose his wings after a sexual assault by
a frustrated housewife, and in *Cold Lazarus* the young Daniel
Feeld is sexually abused in the Forest of Nead. Tragically and
ironically the attack is set to the sounds of the village children
singing *Amazing Grace* in the nearby Chapel.

Consequently, Potter's adult characters are forever trying to
recapture the relationship with God they enjoyed as children before
their traumatic Fall. If the individual could only regain the faculties
of childhood the true splendour of the world would once again
be gloriously revealed. In *Pennies from Heaven* Arthur talks about
'the cotton wool' which sits between him and the world he
inhabits. Once that 'cotton wool' is torn away, however, the
wonder of the natural world becomes wondrously apparent. The
'feelings' of childhood, Coleridge argued, should be carried 'into
the powers of manhood', the 'sense of wonder and novelty with
the appearances, which every day for perhaps forty years had
rendered familiar'.[24] For Hazlitt, this *'creative imagination'* enabled
the human spirit to perceive the objects of the world, 'not as
they are', but in their, 'infinite variety of shapes and combina-
tions of power'.[25] It is a philosophy which was clearly reflected
in Potter's own description of the religious experience. As is
suggested in an interview he gave to John Wyver in 1989:

> Some people have a religious sensibility or yearning and I
> happen to be one of those people. Sometimes I can almost get
> hold of it – as a dream. Grace, justice, mercy, pity, peace –
> they're all names for God in a way. And the achieving of the
> very words and what they represent in human culture is this
> sort of shimmer on the dead materiality and the brutishness
> of the world. There is something awesome in them that if you
> treat with reverence, reverence in the technical sense, you will
> momentarily feel a state of grace perhaps. When those moments
> occupy one they are illuminating and wonderful . . .[26]

This 'Romantic' belief in the power of the 'creative imagination' was clearly apparent in Potter's last interview with Melvyn
Bragg. Diagnosed as suffering from terminal cancer, he explained
that he now saw the world transformed. Echoing the childhood
epiphanies of his own characters, he explained how'. . . the

nowness of everything is absolutely wondrous' (Potter, 1994, p.5). Describing how he saw the apple blossom outside his window, he memorably declared that '[i]t is the whitest, frothiest, blossomest blossom there ever could be, and I can see it' (p.6). For Potter, as for the Romantics, it is the power of the 'creative imagination' to transcend the world around us which enables us to perceive beyond its 'dead materiality'. 'I see God in us or with us', he told Bragg,' ... some feeling why we sing and dance and act, why we paint, why we love, why we make art' (Potter, 1994, p.6).

Through my analysis of the following three single plays I will chart Potter's development as a 'religious' writer, illustrating his work's movement from a 'pessimistic agnosticism', through to a cautious but discernible belief in something beyond and above the purely physical world of the senses. *Son of Man* shows a writer struggling to articulate and recognise his own religious yearnings. Its portrayal of Jesus suggests a man who is uniquely in touch with the transcendental powers of the creative imagination. *Joe's Ark* takes the issue of religious faith and doubt into a contemporary and domestic setting, exploring in particular, how the nearness of death can offer a true and honest insight into a seemingly meaningless and cruel world. Finally, *Brimstone and Treacle* tackles the question of everyday religious faith and morality, taking a glimpse into the dark side of the religious experience and exploring the question of evil, repression and redemption. In this way, I shall show how Potter's work gradually came to accept and portray a profoundly spiritual and Romantic sense of the world, and the means by which it gradually began to develop and explore the complex relationship between faith, doubt and religion. For Potter's characters there is a thin line between good and evil, between the flesh and the spirit, the bestial and the holy, and only by harnessing the creative imagination can the individual finally rise above their *animal* instincts to form a lasting and 'religious' relationship with themselves and the universe they inhabit.

SON OF MAN (1969)

He was an actual man and can therefore share in all that is human; he was not an airy form which beckoned in the clouds, without understanding or wishing to understand what humanly happens to a man. Oh, no, he could have pity over the multitude which needed food, and that in a purely human sense, he who had himself hungered in the wilderness.

Søren Kierkegaard[27]

Originally to be scheduled during Easter week the BBC feared the production of *Son of Man* would cause controversial reactions from the religious community. The transmission date was therefore delayed until after the holiday. For once Potter seemed to be pleased with the BBC's decision. 'I did not want the play shown in what is still called Holy Week and coated over with the sickly piety of religious offerings for Easter', he explained.[28] Pre-empting the later furore over Monty Python's *The Life Of Brian* (1979) and Martin Scorsese's *The Last Temptation of Christ* (1988), the play was still accused of giving a distorted and sacrilegious portrayal of the Messiah. 'Storm over TV Christ' declared the *Daily Mail* on its front page, while the *Daily Mirror* reported that 'Tough Guy Christ Shocks Viewers.'[29] The BBC, perhaps in an attempt to contain the controversy, produced a late night discussion programme exclusively about the play. Simply entitled *Son of Man Reviewed* it gave Potter the chance to discuss the drama with clergymen and critics and defend his interpretation of the New Testament.[30] Describing himself as a 'respectful agnostic', he confessed that he would 'like to believe' and admitted 'yearning for there to be something else'.[31]

Despite the tabloid frenzy, the BBC's own records actually show that the controversy was not shared by the majority of its 4.5 million viewers. Its own 'Audience Survey Report' stated that they received no more telephone calls than were usually expected for an episode of *'The Wednesday Play'*. Indeed, just as many people phoned to complain about the *cheapness* of the production as about the message of the play itself.[32] The recurring criticism was that the desert dunes, rocks and the Sea of Galilee looked like studio mock-ups – which indeed, they were. It was a complaint echoed in most of the reviews which tended to praise the 'bravery' of Potter's script, the quality of the acting and Gareth Davies's fine direction. This, however, was in contrast with the obvious lack of investment in the production as a whole. 'What the BBC's budgeting did to Potter's play was a bit of a crucifixion in itself', commented Stanley Reynolds in the *Guardian*.[33] Shot in three days, on video, entirely in the studio, at a cost of £15,000, the stagy

sets, canvas rocks and studio desert certainly did little to install
the production with any sense of realism. The overall effect is
reminiscent of a school nativity play rather than a piece of high
quality television drama. At times the set shakes and quivers,
almost threatening to fall down, while the Sea of Galilee was, in
fact, made out of glass.[34] Things were probably not helped by
having to share studio space with other television programmes.
Absurdly, the makers of the children's programme *Play School*
lodged a complaint that they had lost precious studio time when
the *Son of Man* production had over-run.[35]

Despite these problems Julian Critchley in the *Times* thought
the play a 'considerable achievement'.[36] James Thomas of the
Express described it as 'one of the most compelling pieces ever
put out by . . . the *Wednesday Play*', while the *Daily Sketch* declared
it to be a 'Gospel of our Times'.[37] 'Potter is perhaps the most
steadily developing television writer', a critic wrote in the *Observer*,
'[i]t has been fascinating to watch his progress from sketchwriting
to an altogether more ambitious platform'.[38] The playwright himself
told the *Radio Times* that he regarded its completion as 'the end
of my apprenticeship as a dramatist, the first play I am pleased
with'.[39] The success of the play (or perhaps the limitations of
the television studio) encouraged Potter himself to adapt the script
for the stage which enjoyed a successful run at the Phoenix Theatre,
Leicester in 1969. Yet, as Philip Purser has pointed out, the play
originally seemed to miss its moment in 1969, apparently not
'revolutionary enough for revolutionaries and not reassuring
enough for believers' – suggesting that a new production was
long overdue, 'away from the stagy sets and backdrops of [the]
studio recording'.[40]

To its credit the production went to considerable efforts to
ensure the historical and religious accuracy of the play. Professor C. F. Evans of King's College, London was the historical
consultant to the production and Father Jim Brand was enrolled
for his religious expertise. Evans provided a six page report which
went into considerable historical details, including the difference
in appearance between Galilee and Jerusalem crowds, while Father
Brand made comments of a more theological nature. Although
Brand criticised Potter's attempt to update the scriptures (he
thought, for example, the parallels drawn between the Romans
and the Russians in Czechoslovakia were a 'bit clumsy') he praised
the writing as a whole, concluding that '[t]here are one or two

brilliant pieces, worthy of T. S. Eliot in his use of antithesis, Jewish idiom and rhythm'.[41] The drama itself is often quoted alongside *The Barton Plays* as one of Potter's most successful earlier productions and won him the 'Allied Craft Award for the Best British Original Screenplay', an award also going to Colin Blakely for his portrayal of Jesus. Despite this, it has since received little attention and can cause problems for critics who, surprised by its biblical setting, are never really sure how it should be discussed and positioned within the Potter oeuvre. Both *The Late Show's* tribute to Potter (broadcast on the evening of his death) and Melvyn Bragg's last interview both chose simply to ignore it in favour of more well-known productions.[42] As Peter Stead has put it, '[m]ore than any other Potter play this is the text that needs to be revisited'.[43]

His twelfth television script and his last '*Wednesday Play*', *Son of Man* was originally broadcast on BBC 1 on the 16 April, 1969. The play itself takes as its story line the journey of Christ from the temptation in the wilderness to the crucifixion, offering a reinterpretation and a re-emphasis of the original biblical text. The controversy surrounding it, however, centred mainly on Potter's depiction of the Messiah as an angry, self-doubting 'working-class hero' who finds the responsibility of his mission a painful and at times completely overwhelming task. His portrayal by the Northern Irish Colin Blakely (Potter had spotted him playing Stogumber in a BBC production of *St Joan*) only added to the earthy conviction of the role. It led Sylvia Clayton in the *Daily Telegraph* to refer to him as a 'harsh . . . hectoring figure who made the Beatitudes seem more like a party political broadcast than a divine revelation', while the *Financial Times* described him as 'a 1969 student neurotic'.[44] There is certainly more than a hint of the hippie activist about him, not surprisingly Andrew (Gawn Grainger) and Peter (Brian Blessed) mistake him for a loony when he first appears to them after his 40 days in the wilderness.

Blakely's aggressive and rhetorical speeches are certainly a long way from the saint-like image of Jesus seen in films such as George Stevens' *The Greatest Story Ever Told* (1965). 'A natural orator', he shakes his fist and shouts his message of love with passion and obvious frustration. 'Use your flaming heads', he tells his disciples furiously slapping his skull, '[t]here are fat men down there rich enough and vain enough to eat off gold plates. And stinking beggars crawling about in the dust for a tiny scrap of

rubbish . . . (p.62)'[45] Set against the Vietnam war, Britain's increasing
troubles in Northern Ireland, Russia's invasion of Czechoslovakia, racial hatred, Third World hunger and impending nuclear
destruction the play is at great pains to suggest the contemporary relevance of his teaching. His explosive attacks on the 'greed.
Extortion. Exploitation. The Killing. The pomp and swagger and
hunger' (p.62), certainly owes as much to Socialist idealism as it
does to any biblical message. '*Blessed* are the poor', he declares,
'for they shall see the Kingdom of Heaven. The rich are thieves . . .'
(p.45). Most memorable of all perhaps is the emphasis Potter
places on Jesus' simple message to 'love thy enemies' (Matthew
5: 43–45). His rejection of an 'eye for an eye and a tooth for a
tooth' echoes Martin Luther King's pacifist belief that 'an eye
for an eye and we all go blind'.[46] It certainly offers a stark contrast to the violent revolutionary spirit which typified the end
of the 1960s. 'Love the man who would kick you and spit at
you', Jesus declares, '[l]ove the soldier who drives his sword
into your belly. Love the brigand who robs and tortures you.
Love your enemies.' (p.43)

It was Jesus' plain and colloquial way of speaking, however,
which provoked the most criticism at the time. One reviewer
complained that 'adjectives like flaming stuck out like electric
light bulbs.'[47] 'Do the working-classes really talk like this?' Father
Brand asked its producer Graeme McDonald in his appraisal.[48]
How accurately Potter caught contemporary English speech
patterns is arguable, but his right to do so is surely not in dispute.
As Winwood Reade wrote in *The Martyrdom of Man* in 1872, 'Jesus
was, in point of fact, a dervish . . . who spoke a rustic patios
and misplaced the *h*, and who was no doubt like other proph-
ets, uncouth in his appearance and uncleanly in his garb'.[49] His
plain way of speaking, however, is only part of the connection
Potter's script forcibly makes between his humble working-class
background and his present teachings. In one memorable scene
he examines a cross with his disciples. As a carpenter by trade
he clearly enjoys the pleasure involved in turning a tree into a
table or chair. The tree, he explains, is provided by God for
humanity to *use* for such aesthetic and utilitarian purposes, but
humanity prefers to make it into weapons of murder, torture
and crucifixion. The scene gives an important and revealing insight
into the mind of a man whose simple message is derived from
his own experience as a working man, rather than any mystical

insight. 'Ach! You should have stayed a tree', he says looking up at the cross, '[a]nd I should have stayed a carpenter.' (p.68)

He even seems unsure whether he really *is* the son of God. His first words, spoken in the wilderness, 'Is it – ? TIME! Is it – me? *Me*?' (p.15) sets a note of self-doubt which is never truly resolved. Indeed, his last words are of a man still desperate for consolation and salvation as Potter chooses to end the play with Jesus' own desperate plea, 'Father! Father! Why have you forsaken me . . . ?' (p.93). The script also has Jesus perform no miracles, further highlighting his significance as a 'son of *man*'. According to Potter, the play was an attempt to get away from 'the Holman Hunt *Light of the World* Christ, or the Catholic Christ, the supra-mystical, risen-from-the-dead Christ' (Fuller, 1993, p.40) and portray him as a man with *human* characteristics and failings. It certainly presents Jesus as a vulnerable figure who is confused, neurotic and obviously in torment. In this respect, as in many others, Potter may have been inspired by Emil Ludwig's *The Son of Man* (1928), an earlier attempt to 'modernise' the story of Christ. According to Ludwig:

> Far from its being my purpose to shake the faith which those who live in Christ have in the divinity of Christ, my aim, rather, is to convince those who regard the personality of Jesus as artificially constructed, that he is a real and intensely human figure. 'Had he never lived', says Rousseau, 'the writers of the gospels would themselves have been as great as Jesus'.[50]

As Potter has Jesus explain, his human characteristics are essential for his God-given role as the communicator between the human and the divine. 'The son of man must be a man', he declares in the play's adaptation to the stage, '[h]e must be all of a man. . . . He cannot be other than a man, or else God has *cheated*.' (p.66) The play, in this sense, is clearly reminiscent of the work of the Danish philosopher and Christian existentialist Søren Kierkegaard, whose works Potter quotes at the opening of *Brimstone and Treacle* (see below). According to Kierkegaard, Christ symbolised the coming together of God and Man and coined the phrase 'God-Man' to express the unique communion between the two. The co-presence of the divine and human constructs a paradox in which Christ was forced to exist and live his life on earth. Granted free-will in his adoption of the human form, the

'God-Man' has to suffer the limitations of human bondage in order that the relevance of the ideal is not limited only to those in possession of 'supernatural' powers. It is for this reason that Kierkegaard emphasised Christ's doctrine of *kenosis* – his voluntary renunciation of certain divine attributes, in order to identify himself with mankind (Philippians 2:6–7). If Christ could not doubt his divine sovereignty then the basis for temptation is denied him. As Kierkegaard puts it, 'Christ will not be God; with an omnipotent resolve he has forced himself into being an individual man, now he must suffer in an entirely real way the miserable impotence of being a poor individual man with humanity's case at heart – and at every moment it is his free resolve which forces him: he has, after all, the power to break through to God'.[51]

Seen in this light, the Jesus portrayed in *Son of Man* is simply an exaggerated version of the majority of Potter's central protagonists. Like Nigel Barton he is torn between two worlds, unable to return to the world of his 'Father', yet tormented by the experiences of his new life. Most of all he is caught between the human and the divine, between the bestial and the holy – only in this case the dialectical struggle is *literal*. In some respects, Jesus is portrayed as a classically Romantic or Byronic figure, a self-tormenting outcast, proudly contemptuous of social norms but suffering from some inner torment and conflict. He talks constantly of joy, exultation and illumination, raging against the view of the world which cannot see beyond its physical limitations. 'Clear away the debris *in front* of your eyes!', he yells at the money changers in the Temple, '[c]lear it away! Away.' (p.75) We see him writhing and moaning on the ground like an epileptic in his communion with the Lord. '*He burns in me!*' he cries, '[t]he Lord God is in my head and in my eyes and in my heart and in my mouth.' (p.68) Yet these moments appear to nourish him and give him a glimpse into the meaning of the world around him, and of his spiritual role in it. In Romantic terms Jesus' communion with the Lord may in fact be seen simply as an intense exchange with what Coleridge referred to as the 'Secondary Imagination'. As Coleridge explains, it is a relationship with God and the holy Spirit which any individual can conduct:

> This elevation of the spirit above the semblances of custom and the senses to a world of spirit, this life in the idea, even in the supreme and the Godlike, which alone merits the name

of life, and without which our organic life is but a state of somnambulism; this it is which affords the sole anchorage in the storm, and at the same time the substantiating principle of all the contradictions of human nature, of the whole riddle of the world.[52]

The *constant* and *painful* struggle between faith and doubt is clearly one of the central concerns of the play, a predicament reflected in all of its major characters, including Jesus himself. Indeed, he vehemently criticises Peter and his disciples for seemingly enjoying their new found faith *too easily*. In contrast, Judas (Edward Hardwicke) is plagued with doubt, despite his instinctive feelings to follow Christ. With no mention of the 40 pieces of silver, he only asks that Jesus give him and the people verification of his divinity. Elsewhere, the struggle between faith and doubt is seen to reside in even the most hardened of hearts. Although the violent and ruthless Pontius Pilate (Robert Hardy) seems repulsed by Jesus' notion to 'love your enemy', he senses the truth of it and witnesses the power of the message on others around him. When he strikes Jesus for declaring that he loves him, he immediately apologises, admitting that it was 'not necessary' (p.92).

It is presumably the play's concern with doubt which has caused some critics like Graham Fuller to refer to it as one of Potter's most 'secular works' (Fuller, 1993, p.38). It can certainly be seen as a humanistic re-writing of the Passion, focusing on the universal power of the Christian message to transcend time and exist independently of its mystical context. Later, however, Potter himself suggested that it may have been revealing a growing interest in spiritual matters, although still uncertain of its nature. 'I wrote the play to see whether there was any residue of religious fervour left in me' he confessed, 'and there is.'[53] In response to its description as humanistic he argued in typical fashion that he regarded 'humanism as one of the minor and less attractive religions'.[54] It certainly shows a mind examining and exploring the intricacies and moral consequences of the Christian message and the painful and eternal struggle for faith. 'It is interesting why I should have wanted to write *Son of Man*', he later explained, 'I wrote it in an almost belligerent frame of mind, in order to put down certain childhood images, chapel-given images. But the very wrestle of doing so inevitably turned me back to the parables, into the challenge and the beauty and glory and pain, and sometimes shoddiness, of the New Testament.'[55]

Like so many of Potter's plays, *Son of Man* is concerned with the *struggle* for faith, rather than the comfort and reassurance offered by religion. It explores the doubt and confusion which occupies the quest for spiritual enlightenment which he saw reflected in Christ's own personal journey. Yet it has a spiritual and Romantic yearning to it which resists the humanist project which seeks simply to deny that there is any power or moral value superior to that of humanity. 'There is faith as well as blood in our veins', Caiaphas tells Pilate, 'religion as well as marrow in our bones.' (p.21) If doubt is the residing theme, then faith is a necessary and inevitable part of that struggle. Without the resurrection, however, the play's conclusion with Jesus hanging tragically on the cross – in darkness and with no sound – seems to offer little hope. Indeed, by all accounts his Father does 'forsake him'. As the credits roll in silence we are clearly meant to wonder if his life (and violent death) has actually brought the Christian message any closer to earth than it was 2000 years before. Granted free-will, Jesus has to chart his own way through the choices between redemption and damnation which every man and woman eventually has to face. Perhaps as a sign of Potter's own growing spiritual awareness he would later add the final line, '[i]t is ACCOMPLISHED' (p.93) when he adapted it for the stage. Despite the doubt, pain and intense struggle of the religious experience, Jesus does finally reach a 'communion' with the Lord which would seem to suggest the direction Potter's work would gradually come to take as a whole.

JOE'S ARK (1974)

> Thus Nature spake – The work was done –
> How soon my Lucy's race was won!
> She died, and left to me
> This heath, this calm, and quiet scene,
> The memory of what has been
> And never more will be.
> William Wordsworth, *Three Years She Grew*[56]

Joe's Ark was Potter's 21st television play to be produced and the third to be broadcast under the BBC title of *'Play For Today'*.

Centred around a young girl's death from cancer, it threatened to be a peculiarly morbid piece of writing even for Potter. As he himself put it, just 'the sort of BBC play, in short, which gives ITV executives a warm glow of instant gratitude and appreciation.' (Potter, 1984, p.20) Perhaps this is one of the reasons why the BBC originally allowed the two-year copyright on the script to expire, having to renew it before it could finally be produced.[57] Yet, according to Potter, this 'chamber drama' possessed elements of humour which the director Alan Bridges, producer Graeme McDonald and the cast were apparently unable to appreciate. At a rare visit to one of the rehearsals, he noticed that 'almost everyone involved seemed intent upon excavating the solemnity rather than the intrinsic comedy of the piece. . . .' (Potter, 1984, p.90) Despite the humour, the play is essentially a serious attempt to tackle the relationship between faith, mortality and human suffering, and as such it is perhaps not surprising that comedy, although preserved, was not Alan Bridges' primary concern.

Despite the playwright's own reservations about the production, critics tended to praise the play's refusal to descend into sentimentality. Philip Purser was clearly moved by 'how truly, how honestly, how understandingly Potter seemed to have imagined the business of dying, not least as it effected the dying one'.[58] Indeed, on Potter's own death, Purser suggested that 'one channel or another fishes it out for replay in addition – or even instead of – the obvious *causes célébres* such as *Brimstone and Treacle*.'[59] Martin Amis' review in the *Listener* at the time was equally laudatory, paying tribute both to the director, his fine cast and Potter's 'marvellously witty and mordant scenes'.[60] 'Calling it *Joe's Ark*', Peter Fiddick wrote in the *Guardian*, 'he summons as the central image the greatest crisis in that rich mythic Old Testament store – the moment when God, in effect, seems to reject his creatures and start again. . . . He may be looking for the universalities, this Potter, but he looks in the earth where his roots are and the result is gripping and human'.[61]

First broadcast on BBC 1 on 14 February 1974, the basic story line of *Joe's Ark* is deceptively simple. A Welsh chapel-going pet shop owner Joe Jones (Freddie Jones) is visited by John (Christopher Guard) a young Oxford student who claims to be in love with his daughter Lucy (Angharad Rees) who, upstairs in her old bedroom, is in the terminal stages of osteogenic carcinoma (cancer of the bone). Lucy reluctantly accepts her visitor and uses him in a last desperate attempt to re-unite her broken family. Her mother is dead and her brother Bobby (Dennis Waterman) is estranged from the family, finding work as a comedian touring sordid working-men's clubs with his girlfriend and assistant Sally (Patricia Franklin). Like all of Potter's visitation dramas, the action takes place primarily within the four walls of the house, divided simply between Joe's noisy and smelly shop and the bedroom of the dying girl.

Alan Bridges certainly captures a long, dark depressing Sunday in the Welsh valleys. With the rain relentlessly pouring down outside, the cramped, cluttered and dimly lit pet shop perfectly reflects the dank and morbid interior of Joe's anguished mind. Lucy's bedroom, cast in shadows, is lit by Dennis Channon like a tomb. Propped up by pillows she lies on her bed, weak and immobile, her black humour barely audible on her faint lips. Even the outside shots of the village streets are isolated, dark and depressing. Meanwhile, the interior of the real and dingy working-men's club, with Bobby and his half-naked girlfriend hopelessly trying to entertain the crowd, does little to lighten up the overall proceedings.

The significance of the pet shop and the torrential rain which continually pours down its windows (until, that is, the death of Lucy) is left in no doubt. We hear the Old Testament story of 'Noah's Ark' recited by the Preacher over the play's opening sequence. 'The world's as bad now as it ever was before the flood' (p.97), Joe later tells the naive student, John. The despair and frustration he feels in the face of his young daughter's imminent death is, indeed, the end of *his* world. It clearly forces him to question and angrily swipe out at his faith and the hell-fire sermons of the village preacher. As Lucy explains to John, '[h]is Christianity survived the death of my mother and the defection of my brother, but not *this*, I think' (p.104). For Joe is an old-fashioned religious man, regularly visiting Zion (the village chapel) and frequently referring to the scriptures. 'Bluebottle maggots and the Bible' (p.115) is how Bobby remembers his childhood.

On the Sunday when John arrives, however, Joe has a violent disagreement with the preacher (Edward Evans) which forces him to leave angrily during the service. Indeed, he first mistakes John for the preacher whom he thinks may have come to make amends. 'I thought you were somebody who I don't want to set foot in this house. Not ever!' (p.96), he tells the naive and nervous student. Later, in a flashback to the morning, we see the preacher giving his sermon. Quoting from The Old Testament he explains how '[t]he imagination of man's heart is evil from his youth' (p.99). This is, however, a concept which Joe can no longer accept in face of the imminent death of his beloved Lucy. 'We are none of us good enough for this earth', the preacher declares, '[w]e all of us lack the holy imagination that could see life as the thrilling wondrous gift that it really is' (p.99). Unable to restrain himself any longer, Joe stands up in Church and shouts '[n]o! That's not true! Not true. . . . You've had your life Daniel. You've lived it . . .' (p.99). Furiously he rushes out of the village chapel leaving the congregation in stunned silence.

This clash between the Preacher and Joe is central to the play as a whole and is clearly meant to symbolise some wider conflict. At its most basic level the argument is between the Old Testament notion of original sin ('the imagination of man's heart is evil from his youth') and a philosophy which believes that humanity can indeed possesses 'the holy imagination to see life as the thrilling wondrous gift that it really is'. The conflict is between a fundamentalist Christianity which sees the individual as inherently sinful and a clearly Romantic view of the world which celebrates the power and sensibility of the human (or holy) imagination. While the preacher's sermon suggests that Lucy is being punished for some inherent sinfulness, Joe cannot accept that his beloved daughter is anything but wholly *innocent*. 'You didn't mess about with her?', he asks John anxiously, '[s]poil her!' (p.118). According to the Romantics, the child is corrupted by society rather than inherently evil. The French philosopher and writer Jean Jacques Rousseau particularly influenced the Romantics with his belief in the natural goodness of man, which is warped by society. 'Let us lay down as an incontrovertible rule', he wrote, 'that the first impulses of nature are always right; there is no original sin in the human heart; the how and why of the entrance of every vice can be traced.'[62] Seen in this light, the play comes to symbolise the struggle between an orthodox religion which interprets human suffering as a judgement from God, and a personal faith which celebrates the power and transcendence of the Romantic imagination.

Indeed, it is not purely coincidental that Lucy shares her name with the child heroine from Wordsworth's *Lucy Poems*, who similarly suffers an early death. For Wordsworth, Lucy appears to symbolise a wise passiveness, a child who has discovered a meditative and reflexive relationship with Nature – 'And hers shall be the breathing balm / And hers the silence and the calm / of mute insensate things'.[63] Appropriately enough, when John first visits Lucy he brings as a gift the fanatical biography of Wordsworth by T. W. Thomas entitled *Wordsworth's Hawkshead*. As John points out in delight the biography took Thompson '*sixty years*' to complete (p.101). Although we hear how Lucy was once consumed with the life and works of both Wordsworth and Coleridge she does not now possess the effort, the time or even the interest to read such a mammoth volume. As she tells her well-meaning visitor, the only thing she now cares about is the 'way carrots taste different from cabbage' (p.102). Lucy's rejection of the Wordsworth's biography in favour of 'cabbage and carrots' may, at first, seem a rejection of the Romantic world of the spirit for the physical or vegetable world of the flesh, but it also suggests an individual who can clearly see the world as it *truly is* – beyond the social and intellectual pretensions of her previous life. Wordsworth's poetry was consumed with the elements of nature which Lucy, in her own absurd way, can now appreciate better than either John or T. W. Thomas' biography, for all its obsession with 'the sort of cakes Wordsworth had for tea' (p.101).

Faced with the closeness of her own death, Lucy acquires a clarity of vision which is no longer distracted by the trappings of human society (symbolised by John, the world of Oxford and Thomas' biography) but is consumed with the *physical* moments of existence which now occupy her day-to-day life. In short, she really does possess the holy imagination which the Christian notion of original sin suggests is beyond human awareness. As we have already seen, Lucy's view of the world would be strangely prophetic of Potter's own when he was diagnosed, like his own character, with terminal cancer. Although her imminent death has forced Lucy to lose her previous engagement with literature and intellectual discussion, she gains instead an ability to perceive the world in its most basic and physical of realities. 'Cabbage and carrots' are not the intellectual and revolutionary concepts she may have encountered at Oxford, but in their own way they are *more* real, *more* solid than all the ideas, books and rhetoric of her university years put together. Ironically she learns to appreciate the fundamental elements of human life (in Romantic terms she may even have formed a renewed communion with the natural world) not through literature or poetry (and certainly not biography!) but through a solitude and introspection forced upon her by illness. Despite the rejection of her father's Christianity, she seems to possess a greater faith and serenity than any other character in the play.

As a result of her illness, Lucy loses interest in the social dynamics of polite conversation and finds that even language itself has become as meaningless as every other human affectation. She rebuffs John's intention to declare his love for her simply as a collection of 'words', and brutally tells him to '[p]iss off' (p.103). Later she will describe words as, '[c]ounters in a game' (p.114), and uses John's misguided devotion to her simply as a means of reaching her brother. In particular, her black humour foregrounds the gulf between the pair and John's insensitivity becomes visibly apparent. He consistently outstays his welcome and, caught up in his own feelings and obsessions, seems ignorant of her pain. Neither does he appear to understand the futility of the situation. Much to his discomfort Lucy continually makes fun about her imminent death. 'I took out life membership of the Oxford Society last year', she declares, '[d]o you think I can reclaim a rebate?' (p.103). She constantly repeats the last words of Edward VII, 'Bugger Bognor', which obviously encapsulates her feelings of frustration and absurdity in a way which he is simply unable or unwilling to understand. Finally he leaves, but only when she reveals her need to 'break wind' (p.105).

In contrast, her brother Bobby (referred to in the script simply as the Comedian) is disillusioned, cynical and makes his living telling obscene jokes in Northern working-men's clubs. He continually swears and verbally abuses everyone including his girlfriend Sally who acts as his 'assistant' on stage. 'I feel like a right tart stuck up there while you dribble on about "the hills and dales"' (p.115) she complains. '[G]et some clothes on, you bloody slut' (p.116), is his typical reaction. Predictably he has rejected his father's Christian beliefs and looks back on his religious childhood with anger and regret. We see him later in a café take out his frustration on a Pakistani cleaner. 'And he can fucking well sweep that up with all the other bloody mess' (p.120) he shouts, throwing his dinner on the floor. Racist, sexist and misanthropic he seems to have no redeeming features at all. Even

Purser admitted to being 'less convinced' by the character, who 'overflowed the excess which swirls through much of Potter's work'.[64] Yet Bobby acts as a necessary contrast both with the dying Lucy and his chapel-going father. He is as obscene and contemporary as Joe is God-fearing and anachronistic. He is, however, as shocked and as distraught as his father is by the news of his sister's condition. Driving home at speed to see Lucy he suddenly asks Sally to marry him. Shocked and astonished, she agrees with little hesitation and perhaps the promise of a new life is embarked upon only moments before his sister's death.

Joe too begins to doubt his Christian beliefs faced with the death of his beloved daughter. At one point he falls to his knees and prays to God in the Welsh language (or as Potter puts it, the 'beleaguered tongue of his childhood' (p.112)). In the published script a translation is provided which reflects Jesus' own torment on the cross. With a reference to Christ's last plea to his Father (which provides the last line of *Son of Man*) Joe begs God to take him instead of Lucy. 'We call out to you as you called out to Your Father! Please, please do not let it happen. Please. Take me instead and all my animals' (p.112). Such a sacrifice explicitly connects Joe's own doubt with that of Christ's. As he tells the preacher in a moment of rage, '[a]nd perhaps Our Lord was forsaken! Perhaps he *was* – have you thought of that!' (p.112). In the pet shop around him he sees only the brute force of instinct and survival. As he tells the Preacher, one 'cichlid' in a tank load of fish and it would '[g]obble them all up in two seconds flat' (p.110). He even suggests that he could kill every animal in the shop if it suited him. 'No, no. You're not a cruel man', the Preacher argues. 'No!', Joe agrees, '[a]nd if I were God, see, I wouldn't do what *He's* doing to our Lucy!' (p.111)

What the play suggests, is that the old fashioned concept of God as a righteous and loving Father-figure is no longer adequate in a world of Darwinian evolution (a conflict later pursued in *Where Adam Stood*) or a society where moral certainty is rapidly disintegrating. If the world has no moral foundation then the death of his innocent daughter is seemingly meaningless to Joe – either God is not there or He simply doesn't care. Lucy's resilience in the face of her own death, however, is finally not dependent on any Christian belief in God's benevolence, but in a personal and private acceptance of her own mortality. Her illness has reduced her world to the smallest of dimensions, but it has also stripped it of the day-to-day banalities which so often come between the individual and God. She sees beyond the structures of any organised religion or education and finds reassurance only in the way the animals in the pet shop seem to accept their own death. 'I think', her doctor (Clive Graham) agrees, 'yes, I think that's one of the very few reasons why I personally believe in – well, God' (p.125).

With the father and son reconciliation at the end of the play, we are granted a final glimpse of hope. Joe's Biblical plea at the beginning to 'let it rain and rain and rain' (p.95) has been suspended. Before mounting the stairs with his newly re-united son he checks that it has stopped. 'I didn't want it to be raining', he tells Bobby. The final close-up of the much abused parrot, 'cocking its head, beautiful. It calls, eyes glittering' (p.131) reminds us further that God's world contains as much beauty as it does sin and tragedy. At this moment, at least, it would appear that some good has come out of Lucy's tragic death. Without her premature death it is arguable that the divide between father and son would have continued indefinitely. It could be argued, of course, that Potter's conclusion is an essentially masculine one. As shall be explored as a whole in Chapter Five the woman is presented as victim, her 'usefulness' only arriving out of this intensely male reconciliation. Lucy symbolises all that the brother and father have lost – their childhood selves destroyed by the inflexible structure of organised religion and the crudities of modern life. Perhaps with her death they are able to glimpse a greater and more significant understanding of their own lives. As Potter explained to Graham Fuller, one is never sure, however, if the reunion at the end of the play is brought about by God or by the cancer. 'That's one of the knots left untied', he argued, suggesting that, in a sense, the two are inseparable from one another. Inverting Cardinal Hume's much quoted comment that he wanted to discover the 'God in cancer', Potter asserted that he was more interested in finding the 'cancer in God' (Fuller, 1993, p.48).

The play differs from *Son of Man*, not only by dramatising the question of the religious experience in a contemporary and less obviously biblical setting, but by moving the question of doubt and despair towards a cautiously more optimistic conclusion. Christianity, it argues, must accept and even embrace the pain and suffering of life or else it is ignoring the very struggle which, as we saw with his portrayal of Christ, grants us our humanity. Above all, the play seems to conclude that even the bleakest of experiences can have a redemptive power at its heart. The father and son reunion at its end offers an ambiguous but nevertheless profound contrast to the conclusion of *Son of Man* which left Jesus hanging desperately in the dark, apparently abandoned by *his* Father. As we see personified in Lucy, the human individual *is* able to harness the holy imagination and see through the trappings of the external world, transcending perhaps even death itself. Out of God can come cancer, but equally cancer itself can bring about something deeper than the human mind is capable of understanding. What is clear, is that Potter's writing was gradually addressing and exploring the religious nature of experience. While refuting the traditional claims of orthodox Christianity, his work continued to examine the power of the human spirit to find a religious sensibility out of the most tragic of all circumstances. It was this same theme which gradually became an overriding concern of his work as a whole, and would provide the basis for one of the most well known and controversial dramas of his entire career.

BRIMSTONE AND TREACLE (1976)

'Tis but one devil ever
  tempts a man,
  And his name's *self.*
    Thomas Lovell Beddoes, *The Bride's Tragedy.*[65]

The controversy surrounding *Brimstone and Treacle* is almost as well known, if not more so, than the play itself. The script was originally sent to the BBC in 1974, accepted and paid for in 1975, Kennith Trodd was assigned producer and Barry Davis was appointed the role of director. It was cast, rehearsed, shot, announced in the *Radio Times* and was due to be screened as part of the 'Play for Today' drama series on 16 April 1976 – the second part of an informal trilogy with *Double Dare* and *Where Adam Stood.* After Bryan Cowgill, the controller of BBC 1, viewed the programme several small changes were recommended and implemented, a later time slot was allotted and an advanced warning to viewers about the programme's content planned.

Cowgill then apparently referred it to the Director of Television Programmes, Alasdair Milne, who immediately withdrew it from the schedule.[66] Writing to Potter, Milne explained his reasons for refusing to transmit the play. Although admitting it was 'brilliantly written and made', he confessed to finding it 'nause-ating'. 'I believe that it is right in certain instances to outrage the viewers in order to get over a point of serious importance', he explained, 'but I am afraid that in this case real outrage would be widely felt and that no such point would get across.'[67]

Potter used his position at the *New Statesman* to address what he saw as this 'brief and insolent letter' in an article entitled 'A Letter to Mr Milne'.[68] What appears to have angered him most is that no discussion surrounding the play, no mention of cuts, re-writes or anything approaching a 'healthy debate', was allowed to take place.[69] If it were to be axed, Potter complained, why not sooner in the production schedule when £70,000 pounds of licence money could have been saved. Most of all, he regretted the loss to the public of what he clearly saw as his best play to date. 'The fast diminishing residue of what was once an almost evangelical passion about the place of drama on the television screen, rather than simpering self-love', he wrote, 'makes me demand that you should be *allowed* to see the play. Unlike Alasdair Milne, I am assuming, of course, that you are grown up and know how to work the off-switch.[70]

Later Milne would write a letter to Trodd saying he had looked at the play again and 'I can only say it always was diabolic.'[71] Potter would later, of course, pounce on Milne's phrase and use it to highlight what he saw as his inability to understand the nature of the work. 'It *was* diabolic', he told Melvyn Bragg, 'it was meant to be' (Potter, 1994, p.22). Trodd remembers seeing Milne as a 'tragic figure, a man with little imagination who went to the theatre no more willingly than did the Queen.'[72] Tension must have been heightened when Milne was appointed Director General just a few years later. It was perhaps one more incident which encouraged Potter and Trodd to set up *Pennies from Heaven Ltd*, their own production company, and eventually 'defect' to London Weekend Television under the encouragement of Michael Grade (see Chapter Four).[73]

Meanwhile *Brimstone and Treacle* was shown on closed circuit at the 1977 Edinburgh Television Festival where delegates were apparently so moved and enraged by its ban that they sent a telegram of protest to Milne.[74] Clive Goodwin gave a lecture on 'Censorship and Drama' at the same festival which suggests that many within the industry were worried by the apparent decrease in artistic freedom overtaking the media in particular.[75] As Mike Hollingsworth and Richard Norton-Taylor point out in *Blacklist* (1988), the mid-1970s saw MI5 (the British Secret Service) direct their attention towards 'subversives in the media'.[76] BBC drama was inevitably an obvious target with its highly publicised assault on social, political and sexual morality. In addition, the Annan Committee was due to report to Parliament in 1977 on the future of broadcasting – always an anxious time for the BBC.[77] The BBC had already turned down *The Naked Civil Servant* (a dramatisa-tion of Quentin Crisp's autobiography) which went on to win many awards for ITV. The verdict of producers was that 'we are in a climate of frightening conformity. Plays which would not have raised an eyebrow five years ago would not be tolerated today. We have capitulated to Mary Whitehouse.'[78]

In 1976 the original television script of *Brimstone and Treacle* was printed in the *New Review* and a year later a stage play of it was produced at the Crucible Theatre, Sheffield, where it was directed by David Leland and starred Christopher Hancock and Ann Windsor.[79] In October and November of 1980 the National Film Theatre ran a retrospective of Potter's work which gave the first public showing of the play, and in 1982 a film version of it was released, directed by Richard Loncraine and starring Sting, Denholm Elliot and Joan Plowright. But it was not until Milne resigned in January 1987, the success of *The Singing Detec-tive* and the arrival of Michael Grade as Director of Programmes, that the BBC finally chose to broadcast the play. A full 11 years after the original ban it was shown on 25 August 1987 during a BBC season of Potter's work. Even then it was accompanied by a special edition of the BBC review programme *Did You See?* in which Ludovic Kennedy discussed it with a collection of critics who pondered on the justification for the BBC's original ban.[80]

Such notoriety has done little to earn the play the serious critical attention it so clearly deserves. As Potter remembers, the newspapers at the time centred their story around headlines such as, 'Devil rapes a helpless young girl'.[81] The feminist critic Germaine Greer remembers being shown a copy of the play in the hope that she would be similarly outraged. However, she remembers enjoying it 'enormously' and has argued that it will probably turn out to be 'the major work, the masterpiece in the end because it's very economical, it's very well proportioned' and 'very subtle about the problem of evil'.[82] When it was finally broadcast in 1987, however, not all the critics were similarly impressed. Although most welcomed its transmission, critics like W. Stephen Gilbert referred to it as 'the most bilious and cynical of Potter's work, a comedy too black for Joe Orton to have contemplated'.[83] Even Potter himself was not excluded from having his own anxieties about the play. As he admitted two years later, '[p]erhaps there was something so rancid or so distorted in the central theme itself that the play did indeed degenerate into an exercise in sickness, a subject for legitimate "outrage".'[84]

Brimstone and Treacle is one of Potter's classic visitation dramas. Like *Joe's Ark*, it revolves around a sick daughter, an over-protective father and an unexpected visitor. Martin (Michael Kitchen) arrives on the doorstep of the suburban household of Mr Bates (Denholm Elliot) and Mrs Bates (Patricia Lawrence), pretending to be a friend of their daughter Pattie (Michelle Newell). Pattie, it becomes clear, has been left mentally disabled by a car accident two years earlier. Encouraging Mrs Bates to leave the young girl completely in his charge Martin rapes her. Later that same night he creeps downstairs to carry out another assault, but is interrupted by her parents. The shock of the assault, however, somehow forces the girl to regain her senses. The play ends with Martin running out into the street and Pattie turning to her father and asking, 'what happened Daddy?' (p.51)[85] Potter argued that this plot, controversial on the surface, was simply an inversion of his previous visitation dramas, suggesting that if the 'neat polite and unctuous young man had been "an angel", the play would not have met with so much trouble.'[86] As it is, Martin is clearly the agent of much *darker* forces. Indeed, he appears to have genuine cloven feet ('the toe-nails are long and claw-like' (p.41)). 'I know a lot about demons, sir!' he tells a passerby, '[d]idn't you smell the sulphur?' (p.32) Apparently, however, Mr and Mrs Bates do not suspect his devilish proportions, although their name's connection with Hitchcock's *Psycho* would suggest that Martin may have finally met his match.[87]

The stifling claustrophobia of the piece is heightened by Barry Davis' direction which perfectly captures the limited and restrictive dimensions of the script. The small, dull suburban living room with its predominately brown and grey colours intensifies this oppressive quality, an isolated standard lamp projecting the only dim light into an otherwise morbid and colourless room. The frequent use of close-ups and head and shoulder shots heightens the *interior* landscape we are meant to be entering, suggesting the whole piece is taking place in the mind of one of its characters, perhaps the guilty and reclusive Mr Bates. Dressed in his red scarf and pullover, Martin provides the only real touch of colour. Later the screen itself is bathed in a red tint as he caresses Pattie's underwear when left alone in her room. Theatrical in its strict studio dimensions, Davis does well, however, to bring a sense of depth, movement and energy to the production as a whole. Occasionally, the living room and its occupants are framed by the camera with Pattie writhing furiously in the foreground, warning them perhaps of a danger only she can sense. Probably the most memorable sequence of all – Pattie being pushed around in her wheelchair by Martin to the sound of *That Old Black Magic* – is not actually described in Potter's original script at all, suggesting that Davis was instrumental, not only in capturing the macabre feeling of the piece, but actually foregrounding it.

Mr and Mrs Bates are one of Potter's bleak suburban couples, repressed, loveless and hopeless. 'I wish someone would plant a bomb here', Bates tells his wife, 'I wish some thick ugly Irish hoik would come and blow us all up . . . starting with you.' (p.35) While she continues to pray and sees signs of life in her disabled daughter, he is sceptical and faithless. 'There is no God. There are no miracles' (p.42), he pessimistically insists. Ironically, however, it is his wife who is responsible for welcoming the devilish visitor into their home, continually defending him in the face of her husband's disapproval. She needs only a small portion of 'treacle', as it were, to swallow his 'brimstone'. A reading further emphasised by the quotation at the beginning of the play which states ironically that 'just a spoonful of sugar helps the medicine go down' – Julie Andrews. Because he talks nicely, is 'good with words' (p.44) and watches *Songs of Praise* (p.39), she ironically concludes that 'the angels must have sent' him (p.44).[88]

Much to her delight Martin frequently complements Mrs Bates on her good taste and refinement. To her instant approval he breaks into a recital of *The Exequy* by Bishop Henry King when he first sets eyes on Pattie.[89] While her husband quite rightly suggests it would be unwise to leave him alone with their young daughter, Mrs Bates immediately jumps to his defence. 'How can a nice young man who speaks like Martin speaks, who says his prayers and (*the clincher*) knows long poems *off by heart* – how can such a person even *think* the things you suggest!' (p.46). Describing Mrs Bates (but with perhaps a wry nod to Mrs Whitehouse) Potter argued that '[h]er God is a creature to be appeased by using correct words, someone who gives or withholds blessing according to syntactical rather than theological rules.'[90] For Martin, however, poetry seems to offer him the perfect *disguise*. Earlier he calls a businessman Samuel Taylor Coleridge. 'Shall we talk about poetry?' (p.31) he asks, in the hope it will impress his intended victim. He is also prepared to take on a religious discourse in pursuit of his evil deeds. He even prays for Pattie at the insistence of Mrs Bates, proving that Satan really can come as a 'man of peace'. However, poetry and prayers are not enough, as Lucy discovers, goodness must be matched with deeds as well as words.

In contrast, Mr Bates is not so easily flattered, but Martin does have some initial success when they get around to the subject of repatriation. 'Send them back to their own countries' (p.49) Mr Bates tells his visitor about the 'blacks' and the 'Irish'. However, when Martin starts talking about transporting them in 'cattle trucks', building 'camps' and using 'C. S. Gas' (pp.49–50) Mr Bates, a member of the National Front, is horrified.[91] In a sense, the young man has simply taken his racist views to their logical conclusions, but it is not a reality the older man is willing to face. 'I thought you wanted to get rid of the blacks . . . ?' (p.50) replies Martin genuinely confused. But Bates, the simple little Englander, cannot understand how his innocent and nostalgic patriotism could possibly produce such extreme consequences. 'All I want is the England I used to know', he confesses. 'The England I remembered as a younger man. . . . I simply want the world to stop just where it is and go back a bit.' (p.50)

Seen in this light, Martin's role becomes surprisingly apparent. Appropriately enough, he plays the role of *devil's advocate*, exposing the repressed and hidden evil which lies at the heart of this family's respectable veneer. This is suggested in the quotation from Kierkegaard given in the opening scene – 'There resides infinitely more good in the demonic man than in the trivial man.'[92] In his own macabre way, Martin (a caricatured symbol of evil) is ironically closer to possessing a Romantic vision of the world than the dull and colourless couple he visits. He is willing to talk of poetry and to pray with evangelical gusto because he (although from 'the other side') will not underestimate the passion and power of the human imagination. In contrast, this repressed suburban couple allow the devil into their home because the trivial nature of their lives has blinded them to the constant and dialectical struggle between love and hate, good and evil. Their bourgeois morality refuses them to acknowledge uncomfortable or ugly truths, they live in a state of emotional denial which makes it easy for Martin to invade and quickly take over their home. The first passer-by he tries to accost is not in the least bothered by social pleasantries. 'I've never met you before', he scoffs, marching off down the road. In contrast, Mr Bates' inability to admit he has never met Martin before, gives the young man enough information to concoct an elaborate story. 'You've forgotten me, haven't you?' he rebukes Mr Bates after deliberately bumping into him. 'Um. No', his victim replies embarrassed, 'um – you must be . . . a friend of Patricia's – ?' (p.32).

Nowhere is this role clearer than in Martin's 'relationship' with Pattie. Through a number of brief and isolated flashbacks we gradually discover that she suffered her injuries after being knocked down by a car. Unknown to her mother, it transpires that she ran blindly into the road after finding her father in bed with her best friend. 'She was a slut!' (p.47) Mr Bates says of Pattie's working-class pal, who ominously played a prostitute in the school play. In fact, according to Mrs Bates, her husband felt '[n]one of Pattie's friends were good enough for her' (p.48). It is an observation which implies an over-protectiveness or even a jealousy which itself could have been sexually motivated. Could this possibly explain why Mr Bates is so frightened of what the visitor may do to his innocent daughter? Could it simply be a physical realisation of his own repressed desires? Moments before the first rape, Martin's words, '[n]ow let Daddy see dem ickle boo-boos' (p.43), may well express some deeper repression locked within the family home. In this sense, Pattie's friend Susan may simply act as a surrogate daughter whom Bates feels he is able to 'abuse' because of her poorer background.

Such a scenario is intrinsically Freudian in its implicit assertion that Pattie's psychological condition or neurosis is the result of unbearable feelings which have been repressed and denied, and forced to remain in her unconscious. Indeed, the doctors say her condition is the result of shock, not the injuries inflicted by the accident. Only by bringing these feelings to the fore (an act ironically brought about by her rape) can she finally be liberated from the symptoms of her neurotic disorder. After witnessing what is virtually the primal scene between her father and best friend, Pattie returns to a child-like condition in which she is totally dependent on her parents. Forced to fight Martin off, however, she remembers the very incident which had originally caused her condition. It is, the play seems to assert, *repression* which causes the greatest misery and becomes a breeding ground for all sorts of evil. As Freud put it, ' . . . the devil is certainly nothing else than the personification of the repressed unconscious instinctual life.'[93] Dramatically speaking, Martin is clearly meant to symbolise the return of the repressed, a physical manifestation of the true evil which lies at the heart of this unhappy, dysfunctional family.

Ironically, however, the evil act brings about a surprisingly good consequence – purging the home of its guilty secret and bringing their daughter back to life. Good *can* emerge from the most painful and apparently evil of circumstances, the play seems to suggest, even the rape of a defenceless young girl. As in Freudian psychoanalysis, the original trauma has to be re-experienced in order that it can be successfully released from the unconscious. Seen in this light, good and evil are not the clear cut moral categories which traditional religious discourse has tended to suggest, but are frequently part of the same dialectical struggle. As Potter put it, '[t]here is, in the end, no such thing as a *simple* faith, and we cannot even begin to define "good" and "evil" without being aware of the interaction between the two.'[94] This struggle, however, is one which lies implicit at the heart of every person, rather than existing *outside* the individual, with say 'the blacks', 'the Irish' or poor working-class families. As Martin warns his audience just before forcing himself onto the defenceless Pattie – 'If-you-are-a-nervous-type-out-there / Switch-over-or-off-for-cleaner-air / But-you-have-to-be-very-smug-or-very-frail / To-believe-that-no man-has-a-horn-or-tail' (p.42). And as Christ himself discovered, it is this *inner* choice between good and evil which actually grants us our humanity, raising us above the purely bestial elements in our nature. 'Animals . . . have no souls', Martin tells Mrs Bates in the stage version of the play, '[y]ou have to be able to choose between good and evil, you see. And for that you have to have a soul.' (p.15)

As with many of Potter's visitation dramas, *Brimstone and Treacle* is an attempt to find a 'religious' sense of the world even in the most desperate and painful of circumstances. However, the difference between this play and his earlier work is the sense that perhaps faith itself is enough to bring about a remarkable and significant change. While it is undoubtedly an evil act which brings about the transformation of Pattie, a 'miracle' does finally take place. At the end of the play the mother's prayers are indeed answered and the child is returned to her parents. Despite the accusations undoubtedly waiting for Mr Bates, in contrast with *Son of Man* and *Joe's Ark*, there is a *complete* family reunion at the end of the play. It is, after all, Mrs Bates' undying faith which actually wins through in the end. As deluded and misguided as she is, her own naive belief that good will finally triumph over evil has prevailed in the face of her husband's sordid and guilty secrets. Perhaps this is the play's final message, that despite the horror and evil in the world there is still an enduring faith which can ultimately conquer all. How ironic that it was a message which Britain's own custodians of moral and religious standards were unable or unwilling to hear.

One can begin to chart the religious sensibility which runs through Potter's work by tracing this growing sense of faith. Among the pain, suffering and evil which his characters inevitably encounter, they desperately turn to an allusive, but nonetheless enduring image of God. Occasionally that 'divine presence', a presence they once felt so intensely in childhood, is briefly glimpsed among the ruins of their lives, not *despite* the pain and suffering which consumes them, but *because* of it. 'If we hunger to know where God dwells in holy grief', Potter once said, 'then we must look to where and how the abused, the weak, the wounded and the desperate ply their lives.'[95] These are the people, like Jesus, Lucy and Pattie, who are *closest* to God, who find salvation and redemption not in the comfortable and respectable environment of an orthodox religion, but in the pain, humiliation and the dark side of the religious experience. In contrast, repression and denial simply dampens the human spirit and suffocates the holy imagination.

At its heart, Potter's work is influenced by a Romanticism which passionately celebrated the powerful and transcendental forces of Nature. Only by harnessing the power of the creative imagination can his characters finally see the world as it truly is. 'The only way to escape these walls around us', declares Casanova in prison, 'is to use the magic in our minds.'[96] It is this magic to which they cling in their seemingly barren and faithless lives – temporarily delivering them above the purely animal or bestial elements in their nature. The young boy who sits high in a tree in *Hide and Seek* and *The Singing Detective* has a innate relationship with God and Nature which will quickly be lost, but the *memory* of that childhood epiphany (and the sense of loss which its absence leaves) is recognisable in almost everything Potter wrote. These visitation dramas have limitations both in their structure and in the comic absurdity which characterises their black and frequently uncomfortable humour. The fairy-tale element to their simple narrative framework makes it difficult for complex theological ideas to be portrayed and sustained successfully. As a result, the 'religious' vision of the work tends to be lost altogether, the audience unable even to detect a recognisable moral structure beneath the plays' obsession with sex, death and human suffering in the extreme. In particular, Potter's preoccupation with the struggle between the *spirit* and the *flesh* made it easy for critics to focus on the controversial elements of the drama, rather than exploring their religious dimensions. But from *Son of Man* to *Brimstone and Treacle* it is possible to detect the growing awareness of a writer increasingly concerned with the psychological dimensions of the human mind, and the spiritual nature of identity.

These three single plays show the complexity and the simplicity of this religious view of the world. While Potter's characters appear to be caught up in long and difficult exchanges with 'God', they still simply yearn to regain the *innocent* vision of the world which they once glimpsed as a child. Like Peter, Joe and Mrs Bates, they still cling desperately to the images of childhood, to the fairy stories and biblical parables which they hope will once again bring comfort and reassurance. But faith is ultimately never simple and his characters also reflect the torment and the doubts which are part of the religious quest. As Potter told Graham Fuller, '[i]n terms of Christianity T. S. Eliot's work shows, in my opinion, that the journey and the doubts and the resistance are more interesting than the arrival, by far' (Fuller, 1993, p.118). These plays are concerned with that journey, asking questions about the nature of doubt, rather than simply reaffirming religious faith, dogma and belief. They are asking difficult questions, refusing to accept the traditional notions by which good and evil, faith and doubt are conceived in religious and moral discourse. Finally, identity itself is not dependent on social class or orthodox religion, but on the moral choices which the subject has to make day by day, minute by minute. Each and every individual (including Christ himself) has been granted free will, and it is this gift, painful and confusing as it is, which ultimately determines their personal sovereignty – that is, to see themselves as *unique individuals*.

NOTES

1. Cited in Roy Park, *Hazlitt and the Spirit of the Age: Abstraction and Critical Theory*, Clarendon Press, Oxford, 1971, pp.67–8.
2. Cited in Alex Ward, 'T.V.'s Tormented Master', An interview with Dennis Potter, *The New York Times Magazine*, 13 November 1987, p.87.
3. This interview with Mary Craig was first broadcast on BBC radio *Thought for Today*, 30 April 1976. Part of it was later published in *The Listener*, 13 May 1976.
4. See Jenny Rees, *The Daily Telegraph*, 2 November 1994.
5. See Alex Ward, 1987, p.87.
6. Taken from *The Late Show: A Tribute to Dennis Potter*, shown on BBC 2, 6 June 1994.
7. See, for example, Adam Barker, 'What the Detective Saw', *Monthly Film Bulletin*, Vol. 55, no. 64, July 1988 and John Wyver, 'A World Where the Songs Come True' (part of the brouchure entitled 'The Television Plays of Dennis Potter' which accompanied a complete retropective of Potter's drama at the Museum of Television and Radio New York) 1992, p.20–1.
8. *Brimstone and Treacle* cost a modest £70,000 to produce in total in 1976. When Trodd and Potter later 'defected' to LWT the budget projections for the three Potter films were £100,000 each. As it turned out the budget rose to £832,000 in total. In order to cut the costs LWT asked Trodd that *Rain on the Roof* (a visitation drama) become a studio play rather than filmed on location. Trodd, however, refused.
9. *Brimstone and Treacle*, for example, was easily transferred to the stage after it was banned by the BBC (see above). A comparison between the scripts shows minor alterations needed to take place. The flash-backs to the car accident, for example, are fully incorporated into the dialogue.
10. Ibid.
11. Cited by Reginald Watter, *Coleridge: Literature in Perspective*, Evans Brothers Ltd, 1971, p.92.
12. See, for example, the *Daily Sketch*, 4 December 1968.

13. Quoted in *The Times,* 7 April 1969, p.6.
14. *Anno Domini,* 'An interview with Dennis Potter by Colin Morris', broadcast on 13 February 1971, BBC 2.
15. Mary Craig, interview with Potter, 1976.
16. In countless articles from the 1960s until his last with Melvyn Bragg, Potter recalled how, as a boy, the local landmarks in the Forest of Dean were literally filled with profound biblical significance. 'Crannock Ponds, by the pit where Dad worked, was where Jesus walked on the water', he told Bragg, 'I knew the Valley of the Shadow of Death was that lane with the overhanging trees' (Potter, 1994, p.22).
17. All extracts from Dennis Potter, *Only Make Believe* (1973) transcribed from the original television play.
18. Duncan Wu, 'Dennis Potter: The Angel in Us', from Ducan Wu, *Six Contemporary Dramatists: Bennett, Potter, Gray, Brenton, Hare, Ayckbourn,* Macmillan, 1995, p.36.
19. Wordsworth, *Poetical Works,* Oxford University Press, 1978, pp.163–5.
20. Ibid.
21. Ibid.
22. Christopher Salvensen, *The Landscape of Memory: A Study of Wordsworth's Poetry,* Edward Arnold, 1965, p.116.
23. Dennis Potter, *Moonlight on the Highway,* 1969. Transcribed from the original television play.
24. Cited by Peter Coveney, *Poor Monkey: The Child in Literature,* Rockcliff, 1957, p.48.
25. William Hazlitt, *On Poetry in General,* 1818. Cited by W.P. Albrecht, *Hazlitt and the Creative Imagination,* University of Kansas Press, 1965, p.63.
26. Cited by John Wyver in 'Arrows of Desire', an interview with Dennis Potter, *New Statesman,* 24 November 1989, p.19.
27. Cited in Paul Sponheim, *Kierkegaard on Christ and Christian Coherence,* SMC Press Ltd, 1968, p.178.
28. Quoted in *The Times,* 7 April 1969, p.6.
29. Brian Dean, 'Storm over TV Christ', *Daily Mail,* 17 April 1969, p.1. Ken Irwin, 'Tough Guy Christ Shocks Viewers', *Daily Mirror,* 17 April 1969, p.2.
30. *Son of Man Reviewed,* 20 April 1969, BBC 1. Discussion of the play with Dennis Potter, clergymen and critics.
31. Cited by Richard Last, the *Sun,* 21 April 1969, p.12.
32. See BBC Written Archives, File No. TX 69/04/02.
33. Stanley Reynolds, *The Guardian,* 18 April 1969.
34. See Graham Fuller, 1993, p. 40.
35. BBC Written Archives.
36. Julian Critchley, 'Considerable Achievement', *The Times,* 17 April 1969, p.14.
37. James Thomas, 'Jesus the Agitator', *Daily Express,* 17 April 1969, p.4. Robert Ottaway, 'This Gospel of Our Times', *Daily Sketch,* 17 April 1969, p.20.
38. Author unknown, the *Observer,* 20 April 1969.

39. From an interview with Dennis Potter by Russell Twisk in *Radio Times*, 10 April 1969.
40. Philip Purser, 1987. In 1995 the Royal Shakespeare Company re-staged *Son of Man* under the direction of Bill Bryden and starring Joseph Fiennes as Christ. It received particularly warm reviews.
41. BBC Written Archives, T5/882/1.
42. See *The Late Show*, 1994 and *Without Walls Special: An Interview with Dennis Potter*, Channel 4, 5 April 1994.
43. Peter Stead, *Dennis Potter*, Seren Books, 1993, p.77.
44. Sylvia Clayton, *Daily Telegraph*, 17 April 1969, author unknown, *Financial Times*, 11 June 1969.
45. For convenience all page references will refer to this published version of the stage play (Potter, 1970) except when there is a difference to the screen version which will be indicated.
46. See Martin Luther King, 'Loving Your Enemies', from Martin Luther King, *Strength to Love*, Hodder and Stoughton, 1964, p.47.
47. Author unknown, *Financial Times*, 11 June 1969.
48. BBC Written Archives, T5/882/1.
49. Winwood Reade, *The Martyrdom of Man* (1872), also cited by John Holmstrom in 'A Dervish', his review of *Son of Man*, *New Statesman*, 25 April 1969 p.596.
50. Emil Ludwig, *The Son of Man*, Ernest Benn Ltd, 1928, p.15.
51. Cited by Paul Sponheim, *Kierkegaard on Christ and Christian Coherence*, SMC Press Ltd, 1968, p.174.
52. From Samuel Taylor Coleridge, *The Friend*, Section Two, Essay Eleven, 1818, Trench, Trubnér & Co Ltd, 1934, p.167.
53. Cited in *The Times*, 7 April 1969, p.6.
54. BBC Written Archives; T5/882/1.
55. Dennis Potter, *The Listener*, 13 May 1976, p.613.
56. Wordsworth, *Poetical Works*, Oxford University Press 1978, p.148.
57. According to Peter Fiddick, untitled, *The Guardian*, 22 March 1976.
58. Philip Purser, *Sunday Telegraph*, 17 February 1974.
59. Philip Purser, *The Daily Telegraph*, 8 June 1994, p.21.
60. Martin Amis, *The Listener*, 9 April 1974, p.250.
61. Peter Fiddick, *The Guardian*, 15 February 1974.
62. Cited by Peter Coveney, 1957, p.8.
63. Wordsworth, 1978, p.148.
64. Philip Purser, *Sunday Telegraph*, 17 February 1974.
65. Cited by Northrop Frye, *A Study of English Romanticism*, Random House, 1968, p.55.
66. See Graham Fuller, 1993, pp.17–18.
67. Cited by Dennis Potter, 'Introduction, 1978.'
68. Dennis Potter, 'A Note for Mr Milne', *New Statesman*, 23 April 1976, pp 548–9.
69. It was the pressure of the *Radio Times* deadline, Milne has since argued, which necessitated an instant decision with no time to consult Potter (see John Cook, 1995, p.93).
70. Dennis Potter, 1976, p.549.
71. Cited by Mihir Bose, 1992, p.107.

72. Mihir Bose, 1992, p.107.

73. Ibid., p.183.

74. See Philip Purser, 1984, p.183.

75. Ibid. Potter also gave a lecture at the festival entitled 'Naturalism and Non-Naturalism'.

76. Mike Hollingsworth and Richard Norton-Taylor, *Blacklist*, Macmillan, 1988, p.116.

77. See Peter M. Lewis, *Whose Media? The Annan Report and After: A Citizen's Guide to Radio and Television*, Consumer's Association, 1978.

78. Cited in 'Banned by the BBC – Then the Show Wins a Top Award for Their Rivals', *Daily Mail*, 27 March 1977, p.6.

79. 'Brimstone and Treacle', *New Review*, no. 26, May 1976.

80. *Did You See . . .? Special: Brimstone and Treacle* BBC 1, 30 January 1987.

81. Dennis Potter, 'Introduction', 1978.

82. Cited in *The Late Show*, 1994.

83. W. Stephen Gilbert, 'The devil rides out', *The Listener*, 20 August 1987.

84. Dennis Potter, 'Introduction', 1987.

85. All page references refer to Dennis Potter, 'Brimstone and Treacle', *New Review*, No. 26, May, 1976.

86. Ibid.

87. In the film version Mrs Bates' Christian name is changed from Amy to Norma, a further nod, if any were needed, to Hitchcock's *Psycho*.

88. *Songs of Praise* is a popular religious programme on British television shown during the Sunday evening 'closed period.' At that time it consisted mainly of a traditional Church service with hymns and prayers.

89. See Margaret Crum (ed.), *The Poems of Henry King*, Oxford University Press, p.68.

90. Ibid.

91. 'The National Front' is an extreme right-wing political organisation which gained a certain popularity and notoriety in Britain during the late 1970s and early 1980s.

92. Like the other quotation it is not cited in the published version of the script.

93. Sigmund Freud, *On Sexuality*, Vol. 7, Penguin Books, 1977, p.214.

94. Potter, 'Introduction' 1978.

95. Taken from *Opinions: Britain in 1993*, 21 March 1993, Channel 4.

96. *Casanova*, unpublished script, BBC, 1973. BBC Television Script Unit.

4

'Banality with a Beat': The Paradox of Popular Culture[1]

Any myth with some degree of generality is in fact ambiguous, because it represents the very humanity of those who, having nothing, have borrowed it.

Roland Barthes, *Mythologies* (1957)[2]

Would someone with a hard face please protect me from those sickly and sugared old tunes? They tinkle-tinkle their simple sweetness and yet somehow complicated accusations out of the most personally demeaning residues of what had seemed to be lost and gone for ever.

Dennis Potter, (Potter, 1994, p.43)

INTRODUCTION

Potter's work throughout his career displayed a profound fascination with the forms and forces of popular culture. Pulp fiction, advertising, tabloid journalism, grade-B Hollywood cinema, radio and television itself became recurrent and increasingly dominant themes in his oeuvre. But it was with popular music – especially the songs of the 1930s and 1940s – that his work has become most associated. In particular, it was the 'lip-synch' device for which his drama is probably most famous. As a result, he has often been portrayed as a great 'promoter' of popular culture, a writer, who in both his work, and his choice of medium, has somehow epitomised the apparent breakdown of 'the great divide' between 'high' and 'low' art. Yet while acknowledging the significance and power of popular culture on the lives and minds of his characters, his drama frequently displayed a curious ambiguity towards pop culture as a whole, simultaneously celebrating and ridiculing its mass appeal and sentimental inflexions.

It takes little knowledge of Potter's work to recognise its continual obsession with the products and moral consequences of contemporary culture. It was clearly evident in his early documentary *Between Two Rivers* (1960) in which he described the hidden dangers of modern mass culture. A critique which he later developed in his second book, *The Changing Forest: Life in the Forest of Dean Today* (1962) which derided the way modern consumerism (including television and popular music) was destroying traditional working-class life. That distaste for mass culture later found expression in his journalism and his early attempts at creative writing. In a sketch entitled 'Mother's Day' for *That Was The Week That Was* (which he wrote with his *Daily Herald* colleague David Nathan) he crudely attacked the banal sentiments of the television commercial. 'What is a mum?', it asked, '[a] mum lives with a dad and 2.4 children in a rented house where the neighbours notice her washing on the line. A mum relies upon secret ingredients and instant cake-mixes. She has kids with dirty teeth who regularly shout, "Don't forget the Fruit Gums, Mum".'[3]

Potter's first television play *The Confidence Course* (1965) highlighted the dangers of high-pressure salesmanship and its tendency to prey on the weakest members of society. The following year *Emergency Ward – 9* (1966) subverted the formulaic conventions of the television soap opera, while *Where the Buffalo Roam* (1966) dramatised an illiterate teenager's obsession with the Hollywood cinema.[4] No longer able to distinguish between reality and the heroic images of the western, its protagonist finally shoots his mother and grandfather before being shot himself by the Swansea police force. Two years later *The Bonegrinder* (1968) portrayed the hidden dangers of England's rapid 'Americanisation' as a whole, while *Paper Roses* (1971) dramatised the immoral and sordid world of tabloid journalism. In *Follow the Yellow Brick Road* (1972) he returned to the blatant and acquisitive banalities of television advertising. Here, however, its deluded and disturbed protagonist appears to find 'spiritual salvation' in their vision of a perfect world.

It is with popular music, however, that Potter's work is probably most associated. One has only to look at the origins of so many of his titles to appreciate its powerful and unmistakable significance on his work, which first came to the fore in *Moonlight on the Highway* (1969). The play centred around one man's obsession with the 1930s crooner Al Bowlly and signalled Potter's increasing interest in popular music as a whole. This preoccupation was later foregrounded in *Pennies from Heaven* (1978) where the 'lip-synch' technique became the vehicle upon which the dreams and personal yearnings of its characters were articulated in song. *The Singing Detective* employed the same device, but unlike Arthur Parker, the pulp novelist Philip Marlow finds neither salvation nor redemption in the popular songs of his childhood. *Lipstick on Your Collar* also employed the same technique, dramatising the influence of American mass culture (heralded by an emerging rock 'n' roll) on Britain in the 1950s.[5] Finally, the posthumous *Karaoke* (1996) explored the repetitive nature of the popular song and its uncanny resemblance with the inevitable predictability of people's lives. 'The music's written and performed by someone else', Daniel Feeld explains, 'and there's this piddling little space left for you to sing yourself but only to *their* lyrics and *their* timing' (Potter, 1996, p.28).

In this chapter I shall examine Potter's use and appropriation of popular culture and music, exploring the way it was conceived and re-contextualised in his work, its seemingly paradoxical relationship with many of the forms and forces it happily (and lucratively) exploited, and the consequences this apparent ambiguity may have for our understanding and interpretation of his drama as a whole. With such a constant preoccupation in his work, one might assume that Potter's treatment of popular culture is easily examined and evaluated. It is an obsession, however, which is surprisingly difficult to assess. While his work originally derided the dehumanising influences of mass culture, there would appear, even in his earliest writings, a discernible fondness towards many of its forms and 'sugary syncopations'. Popular culture, although essentially flawed by its commercial and sentimental nuances, seems to provide an essential role as a contemporary myth-maker – a means by which the working-class, in particular, are able to glimpse the vision of a better and a 'holier' world. It is this very ambiguity which makes it one of Potter's most fertile and revealing of themes.

DREAMS FOR SALE: MASS CULTURE AND ITS CRITICS

> If it is the crime of popular culture that it has taken our dreams
> and packaged them and sold them back to us, it is also the
> achievement of popular culture that it has brought us more
> and more varied dreams than we could otherwise ever have
> known.
>
> Richard Maltby, *Dreams for Sale: Popular Culture in
> the 20th Century* (1989)[6]

For many critics immediately before and after the Second World
War, popular or mass culture was regarded as simply an infe-
rior form of art – either a debasing purveyor of dominant ideology or the commercialising and profit-minded product of modern
mass production. The Frankfurt School (founded at the University of Frankfurt in 1923 and later forced, through the rise of
Fascism, to emigrate to the USA) argued that mass culture
reproduced, endorsed and perpetuated the ideological inequalities of modern capitalism. Heavily influenced by Marxist theories of ideology, critics such as Theodor W. Adorno and Max
Horkheimer, argued that the standardisation of mass culture was
reflected in the minds and perceptions of the masses. 'Listening
to popular music', Adorno argued, 'is manipulated not only by
its promoters but, as it were, by the inherent nature of the music
itself, into a system of response mechanisms wholly antagonistic
to the ideal of individuality in a free, liberal society.'[7]

Despite their profound political differences, the personal psychology and moral individualism favoured by British literary critics
such as F. R. and Q. D. Leavis came to remarkably similar conclusions as their German contemporaries. According to F. R. Leavis,
popular culture dangerously promoted the utilitarian values of
modern commercialism and reflected a society in which material values prevailed. For Leavis, modern industrial society was
in danger of lowering the standards of its aesthetic tastes and
ignoring the 'organic' values of England's past traditions and
culture. These commodities simply lowered the aesthetic standards of contemporary society and demanded from its consumers little or no intellectual involvement. 'Those who in school
are offered (perhaps) the beginnings of education in taste', he
wrote in *Culture and Environment* (1933),' are exposed, out of school,
to the competing exploitation of the cheapest emotional responses,

films, newspapers, publicity in all its forms. . . .'[8] The English novelist and essayist George Orwell came to similar conclusions, particularly in criticising the dangerous influence of American mass culture on British life. In a partly comic essay on 'The Decline of the English Murder' (1946) Orwell blamed the 'Americanisation' of England for a series of cruel and motiveless murders. The 'background' to such murders he argued, 'was not domesticity, but the anonymous life of the dance halls and the false values of the American film.'[9] A scenario reflected perhaps in Potter's own *Pennies from Heaven*.

Following the traditions of Leavis and Orwell, Richard Hoggart's *The Uses of Literacy* (1957) provided a similar critique of modern mass culture. As already discussed in Chapter Two, Hoggart's influential book contrasts an allegedly authentic pre-war working-class culture with the 'shiny barbarianism' of 'the newer mass arts'. For Hoggart, the forces of popular culture, with its sex, advertising, bright plastics, popular songs and cheap literature, were sapping the initiative of the working class and 'unbending the springs of action'. Set in two halves, the book contrasts an older traditional working-class life with the commercialised popular culture sweeping in from America. This 'Candy-Floss World' is epitomised by the 'Juke-box boys' who slouch around the coffee bars listening to the empty and hedonistic sounds on the mechanical record-player.

As John Storey has pointed out, such a critique is based on the notion of a 'cultural Fall' – from healthy culture to corrupt and corrupting mass culture.[10] Hoggart certainly appears to construct a nostalgic 'Eden' out of his working-class childhood of the 1930s, his conception of popular culture constructed on a surprisingly simple binary opposition which presents folk culture as good and mass culture as inherently bad. For Hoggart, this cultural 'Fall' appears to take place in England around the time of the 1950s, epitomised by the arrival of rock 'n' roll and a rapid 'Americanisation' of British life. Before that time, he suggests, there was a British working-class folk culture which was vibrant, organic and *authentic*. 'The Full Rich Life', as he calls it, with its 'charabanc' trips and working-men's clubs were increasingly giving way to a commercialised and Americanised mass culture which no longer had any relationship with the previous culture 'of the people.'[11]

Such a view of popular culture would seem to have striking

similarities with Potter's own. *Between Two Rivers* took a pro-foundly 'Hoggartesque' approach to its subject, contrasting a nostalgic and organic working-class past with the commercial-ised and – mass produced culture which he feared was threat-ening traditional village life. Like Hoggart, Potter's early feeling towards mass culture was clearly negative, criticising both its effect on the working class and the people who apparently con-trolled it. 'The consumer's alleged sovereignty cannot possibly exist under these conditions', he wrote in *The Glittering Coffin* (1960), '[t]he dignity of ordinary people is being swamped by the forces of "admass" – by the advertising agencies and the popular newspapers, by a state of affairs wherein almost all the mass media are in the control of eager, criminally commercial hands.' (Potter, 1960, p.121)

For Potter, England's cultural 'Fall' also appears to take place during the 1950s with the rapid Americanisation of traditional English culture. In *The Bonegrinder*, George King (or 'King George') is an English bank clerk who meets up with (Uncle) Sam Adams, a coarse American tourist who takes over George's home in an early working of the visitation motif. Described by Philip Purser as 'unbelievably vulgar and spiteful', he accused the play of belittling and caricaturing both cultures. 'Dennis Pooter – I mean Potter -', he wrote, 'only hates that poor little Englander because he fears that's what he is himself.'[12] Potter's only stage play *Sufficient Carbohydrate* (1983) also took a swipe at American culture generally. 'This tiny island has no Coca Cola signs', its protagonist Jack Barker proclaims on holiday in Greece, 'no muzak, no hamburgers, not a sniff of cocaine or a single sud of a sodding soap opera . . . It's as though America lived in vain.' (Potter, 1983, p.14).

Yet despite this derision of American popular culture, Potter's work also appears to celebrate many of the forms and possibili-ties of popular culture as a whole. In *Moonlight on the Highway* the Americanised popular songs of the 1930s appear to evoke a nostalgic innocence in contrast with the sexual permissiveness of the 1960s. Set in 1935, the 'lip-synched' performances of the popular songs in *Pennies from Heaven* were also evocative of an older more romantic and innocent world. *Follow the Yellow Brick Road* even explored the glossy images of the television commer-cial and its ability to evoke a kind of religious or spiritual ideal-ism. Although Jack Black's delight in the television commercial is clearly meant to be ironic and *neurotic*, it nonetheless suggests Potter's gradual re-assessment of popular culture generally. For while his work frequently condemned the sentimental superficiality of pop culture, occasionally it appeared to conjure up images of an older working-class tradition – evoking the spiritual memory of a culture no longer in existence. Indeed, such a contradictory relationship with popular culture was hinted at by Potter while still an undergraduate:

> if 'pop' culture is moulded primarily by the economic motive of profit maximization, then it is also shaped in some degree by certain genuine desires and needs. Kenneth Trodd has written that 'I defy anyone who has put in some discriminate listening not to feel that despite the harsh melody of the cash-register, the pre-fabricated sob, the mixture of gold-dust and synthetic treacle, many Pops communicate genuine emotion, and encapsulate the tang, the "atmosphere" of their mood and period to a degree which seems to contradict the shoddiness of their raw materials'. Somehow we are able to discern that a great deal of that which is true and valuable in traditional working-class culture is still reflected in the slicker, cheapened 'pop' culture, however, obliquely, however much like a ray of light sliding through a filthy window.
>
> Potter, 1960, p.121[13]

This image of a ray of light sliding through a filthy window aptly sums up Potter's ambiguous relationship with popular culture. While he clearly despised its commercialised origins, sometimes pop culture could still evoke memories of an older working-class tradition. Like Hoggart, his work tends to look back nostalgically to an English working-class culture which had once provided an organic and powerful form of folk art. As Raymond Williams argued in *The Long Revolution* (1961), popular culture could sometimes offer magical resolutions to problems and situations which were otherwise intractable; offering a form of resistance to dominant modes of thought.[14] As Potter told John Wyver in 1980, 'British popular culture . . . has been sufficiently resilient to all the time push back the more blatant claims of the so-called ruling class in English life. . . . It's . . . like Raymond Williams calling it the Long Revolution. . . . You're saying there is something there which made these changes, which

1. *Blue Remembered Hills* (1979): Audrey (Janine Duvitski) and Angela (Helen Mirren) are literally caught between two worlds.

2. *Son of Man* (1969): Potter's Christ (Colin Blakely) is crucified.

3. *Where the Buffalo Roam* (1966): Willie (Hywel Bennett) and his mother (Megs Jenkins) grapple with the printed word.

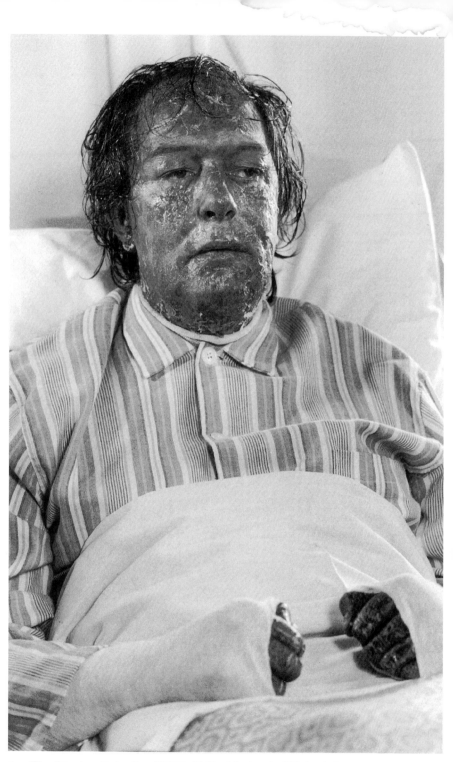

4. *The Singing Detective* (1986): Philip Marlow's (Michael Gambon) loathing of women is physically turned in on himself.

subsisted with the so-called ruling class and must have been entertained by sections of the so-called ruling class.'[15]

Seen in this context, Potter's work paradoxically presents popular culture (despite its banal commercialism) as fulfilling an inherent need within the human subject to transcend the basic realities and inequalities of everyday life. Where once those utopian aspirations and dreams were channelled through an older working-class tradition or through religious or quasi-religious narratives and images, they are now firmly claimed by the commercial forces of contemporary culture. While *Where the Buffalo Roam* clearly displays a 'Leavisite' reaction to an Americanised mass art, *Moonlight on the Highway* and *Follow the Yellow Brick Road* both reveal a writer who was struggling to dramatise the power and relevance of popular culture on the lives and minds of his characters. Finally, in *Pennies from Heaven* I shall discuss Potter's most sustained, detailed and successful exploration of popular music, suggesting ways in which it directly addresses many of the central issues at the heart of the work, and in particular, its complex and inspired portrayal of the continual conflict between mass culture and folk art.

WHERE THE BUFFALO ROAM (1966)

We ... know that movie Westerns and radio and TV programs such as 'The Lone Ranger' ... are by no means enjoyed only by children. ... This merging of the child and grown-up audience means: (1) infantile regression of the latter, who, unable to cope with the strains and complexities of modern life, escapes via *kitsch* (which, in turn, confirms and enhances their infantilism ...) Peter Pan might be a better symbol of America than Uncle Sam.

Dwight Macdonald, 'A Theory of Mass Culture' (1957)[16]

Potter's first explicit dramatic exploration into the influence of popular culture on contemporary life came in his second year as a television dramatist. Following swiftly after the success of the *Nigel Barton* plays and also directed by Gareth Davies, *Where the Buffalo Roam* was first shown on the opening night of the third season of 'The Wednesday Play' on 2 November 1966, and was seen by an audience of around 8.25 million. As the first drama of the series, it was ideally suited to sustain the reputation 'The Wednesday Play' had rapidly established of being bold, imaginative and unafraid of controversy – concerned with, as Tony Garnett put, 'the changing pattern of life today'.[17] Its setting in a working-class district of Swansea, complete with extensive use of location shots, and its treatment of juvenile delinquency and illiteracy was certainly contemporary, and reflected the traditions and the spirit of British social realism both in television and the cinema of the early 1960s.

The play received, however, a mixed response from the critics who detected Potter's attempt at writing a dogmatic morality play. 'It was too often too obvious propaganda which weakened the power of the drama', wrote Kenneth Eastaugh in the *Daily Mirror*.[18] 'Willie', according to Maurice Wiggin in *The Times*, 'was not so much a living person as a lay figure in a manual on how not to bring up a child; an abstract of possibilities, a blueprint of doctrinal theory.'[19] In the *Sun*, Nancy Banks-Smith concluded that 'there were some lumps of uncooked psychology in the play which made it too much like a classic case history'.[20] Only James Thomas in the *Express* praised its apparent non-naturalist techniques, 'a classic example', he wrote, 'of how TV has escaped at last from the conventional confines of the theatre and begun to create real drama for itself'.[21]

Where the Buffalo Roam (its title coming from the cowboy song *Home on the Range*) revolves around the backward and disturbed experiences of teenager Willie Turner (Hywell Bennett). Willie is unable to read and lives with his mother (Megs Jenkins) and grandfather (Aubrey Richards) in a small terraced house in the suburbs of Swansea. On probation for an ominously violent crime, he attends remedial classes and spends his time fantasising he is a cowboy. Willie is the antithesis of the clever Nigel Barton, but like Nigel is forced to be an outsider from the rest of his community, not by his above average intelligence but by an apparently low IQ. We see in flashback the beatings he experienced as a youngster from his now deceased father (David Morrell) who regularly punished the boy for stuttering, and the humiliation at school he encountered from his schoolmistress (Dilys Davies) who mocked and derided the boy's lack of academic competence. Similarly, at remedial classes, he is laughed at for insisting on being called 'Shane'; his cowboy hero from the classic Hollywood Western of the same name. Indeed, Willie seems cut off from society at large, unable to connect with any image other than that on sale at his local Picture Palace. He encounters in town two separate girls who, unable to compete with his cowboy fixation, leave him to dwell on his strange celluloid fantasies. Finally, in a moment of anger and frustration, he shoots his mother and grandfather with what turns out to be a *real* gun, and is later shot himself by the Swansea police force in a western style shoot-out.

The drama itself clearly involves numerous references to popular culture – not least, Willie's retreat into the fantasy of the Hollywood Western. The Country and Western song *Riding down the Canyon* plays over the opening titles, immediately contrasting the reality and the fantasy of Willie's world with the urban austerity of the empty Swansea streets. Although the Western is essentially an American myth it was still an immensely popular genre in England at the time. *High Noon* (1952) and *Shane* (1953) were both classic Western stories, involving a straightforward fight between good and evil. John Ford was still making popular Westerns like *The Searchers* (1956) and Howard Hawks brought the decade to an end with the hugely successful *Rio Bravo* (1959). By the early 1960s films such as *How the West Was Won* (1962), *The Man Who Shot Liberty Valance* (1962) and American television serials like *Rawhide* and *The Lone Ranger* continued to celebrate and mythologise the romantic image of the cowboy.

The play's impressive opening sequence certainly capitalises on the power and familiarity of the Western mythology to a 1960s British audience. We first see Willie dressed as a ordinary young teenager and then (in his reflection in the bedroom mirror) as the traditional western villain, clad all in black, complete with Stetson and gun. The power and apparent reality of Willie's mirror image certainly portrays the extent to which his deluded fantasy has overtaken any notion of the real. As he swings around so we are given a shot of his bedroom as a Western saloon before we witness it as it really is, a cramped box-room adorned with photographs of Hollywood cowboys. Willie is one of Potter's 'torn-heroes', caught between two worlds (Hollywood fantasy/Swansea reality) and therefore, like so many of his protagonists, possesses a double or alter-ego. His mirror reflection displays Willie's deepest desires, his need for escapism and his constant yearning to be other than he is. What is striking about this particular sequence is the rapidity and the quality of the editing.

The constant and fractured cross-cutting between reality and fantasy (interrupted occasionally only by a still of Jack Palance) clearly pays homage to Troy Kennedy Martin's belief that skilful and experimental editing techniques could create a new grammar for television drama – incorporating notions of montage conceived by the Russian film-maker Eisenstein (see Chapter Two).

In terms of its narrative, parallels can clearly be drawn between this single play and John Schlesinger's British movie, *Billy Liar* (1963). As well as sharing a similar name, Schlesinger's Billy escapes the dreariness of his life in a provincial northern town by retreating into a world of fantasy and make believe. Like the opening sequence of Schlesinger's film, the increased commercialism of traditional working-class life is signalled by the theme song of *Housewife's Choice*, a radio request show from the 1960s. As the ominously schizophrenic tones of Petula Clark's *Who Am I?* begins, so Willie makes his way downstairs for breakfast. The popular song is then mixed with a reprise of *Riding down the Canyon* as the deluded teenager stands at the kitchen door with the image of him as a cowboy (riding a horse) superimposed over the shot: the two images (like the two songs) apparently competing for prominence in his head.

Willie's illiteracy has gone completely unnoticed by his family and has to be pointed out to them by his probation officer Mr Jenkins (Glyn Houston). In shock, his Grandfather tells him that he often sees the boy looking in the newspaper. 'The pictures', Mr Jenkins replies in a typically Potteresque swipe at the tabloids, 'some of our newspapers are specifically designed for people who can not read.'[22] Denied a literary heritage, Willie sees the world purely through his *visual* imagination. 'Thursday is brown', he explains to his mother, 'Thursday is a brown sort of colour.' As Mr Jenkins puts it, 'whatever feeds his rather lurid imagination it isn't the *written* word . . . he's one of the few adults left who can look at a neon sign and think it beautiful.' The neon sign, perhaps the most glossy and garish of all the images of mass culture, acquires a beauty only because of the boy's inability to connect with the *written* word. Unable to read (his stuttering as a boy and his highly visual imagination suggests that perhaps he is simply suffering from a form of 'word blindness' or dyslexia) he seeks stimulation in any form he can. In the culturally bankrupt and consumer-ridden world of post-war Britain the lad turns, not surprisingly, to the highly *visual* images of the Hollywood cinema.

Willie's mother buys him a trashy western novella (*Dead Man's Gulch*) in the hope it will inspire him to read. She certainly appears to catch his attention more successfully than his English teacher had achieved with stories of the 'Big Black Bear'. But even at home there appears to be no supervision which can spot and capitalise on the boy's visual imagination. The scene itself is strikingly similar to a sequence in Potter's *Rain on the Roof* (1980) where Billy, another backward young man, is taught to read by a well-meaning but unsuccessful teacher. In both plays it is the boy's tendency towards a highly visual imagination which surprisingly selects a *religious* image to understand and make sense of the words on the page. It suggests an almost natural or organic force which, despite the adult's proficiency in reading, seems denied to them, but open to the illiterate teenager:

WILLIE: 'It', I like 'it.' It's an 'I' and a 'T', innit?
MRS. TURNER: That's right Willie. Oh, it's ever so easy really.
WILLIE: 'It' – that's nice. It's like a man standing outside a church, innit? As you look at it in the book it is. A little man with his hat up in the air standing outside this church with a cross on the top. See?
MRS. TURNER: I never thought of it like that.
WILLIE: No. No, I don't expect you did. Ah, I could learn to read if I wanted to. I don't know what all the fuss is about?

In this way, Potter sets up a juxtaposition between the *visual* and glossy images of popular culture (epitomised by Willie's fixation with the Hollywood Western) and the almost spiritual and organic dimensions of the *written* word, symbolised by the 'man standing outside a church'. As F. R. Leavis argued, the English language was at the heart of Britain's cultural existence and needed to be revived if there was to be any hope for its spiritual, moral and emotional tradition. According to Leavis, the small section of those who could appreciate the language and its finest and artistic use in the great tradition of English Literature had a responsibility to the others to keep the language alive and so keep the 'levelling down' of English culture at bay. 'In their keeping', he wrote, ' . . . is the language, the changing idiom upon which fine living depends, and without which distinction of spirit is thwarted and incoherent. By 'culture' I mean the use of such language.'[23] Like Leavis, Potter's play implicitly refers to a time when there was a pure and organic English community, epitomised by its language, which has been superseded by a corrupt and sinful world; in this case, the cheap, stereotyped and formulaic forces of the American popular cinema. In his first attempt to read Willie glimpses a *spiritual* and *organic* English culture which those who practice a corrupt and debased form of English (epitomised by his mothers' pop radio and his Grandfather's tabloid newspapers) can no longer perceive.

The decline in the pride of the English language and English culture in general, and the spread and influence of popular culture is not, however, restricted to Willie. As he rides on the packed bus through the streets of Swansea (seeing images of himself as the archetypal cowboy through the bus window) a male passenger reads a *James Bond* novel, immersed like Willie, in his own private world of glossy male machismo. Even his English teacher Mr Black (Richard Davies) secretly confesses his own passion for the cowboy film. 'I don't mind telling you', he explains, 'I've seen so many Westerns I could practically draw a street map of Dodge City right here and now.' Indeed, Willie's probation officer seems also to share his passion. 'I suppose it's one of the most potent and evocative myths ever manufactured', he agrees. Inevitably such a classically American and manufactured myth is instantly juxtaposed with a traditional English mythology. 'Knocks Robin Hood into a cock-hat I'm afraid', his teacher reluctantly admits.

Seen in this light, Willie's character dramatises the essentially 'Leavisite' fear for a generation of young men who have lost direction through their complete absorption into the instantaneous and essentially empty landscape of Americanised popular culture. These young men are not simply isolated individuals, but a symbol of England's cultural decline generally. The quintessential American image of the Western cowboy is, of course, a perfect example of the Americanisation and mass production of British culture as a whole. At odds with Leavis, however, Potter equally presents the English cultural heritage (as represented by school and its teachers of English) as consumed by American mass culture as the very children they are supposed to be educating. Willie's final crucified image strapped to a stretcher (as the police carefully lower his dead body from the roof) is a dramatic metaphor which personifies the threat popular culture poses to the organic and pure traditions of England's cultural heritage. For Willie, the American Western provides an alternative world of fantasy where notions of good and evil are clear and uncomplicated, where his own sovereignty as an individual is no longer reliant on acquiring any intellectual or academic skills, but only on his ability to ride a horse and perhaps walk like a man. The shooting of his mother and grandfather and his final demise at the hands of a police shotgun, only heightens our awareness of how superficial and ultimately how dangerous such images can be when they are mistakenly plundered by the vulnerable and the weak as a source of cultural and spiritual identity.

MOONLIGHT ON THE HIGHWAY (1969)

They are not cynical or neurotic; they often indulge their emotions, but are not ashamed of showing emotion, and do not seek to be sophisticatedly smart. I suppose this may be one reason why so many of the older songs are still clung to; they come from a period when it was easier to release the emotions.
Richard Hoggart, *The Uses of Literacy*[24]

Potter re-examined the influence and quality of popular culture in his first extensive exploration into the role of popular music in *Moonlight on the Highway*. It was his eleventh drama for television and signalled an important shift in his relationship with popular culture as a whole. First shown as part of ITV's 'Saturday Night Theatre' series on the 12 April 1969, it was made by Kestrel Productions, an independent television company set up by Tony Garnett, David Mercer, James Mactaggart and Kenith Trodd. Approached by London Weekend Television at the end of 1967, Trodd and Garnett were asked to defect to the other side to counter the success of the BBC's 'Wednesday Play'. When they suggested that they make an autonomous and independent collective, to their surprise LWT agreed. As Trodd later explained, 'they thought they were buying *The Wednesday Play* lock, stock and barrel.'[25] During its short two year run Kestrel produced 17 plays for the new ITV company, including works not only by Potter, but by Jim Allen, Roger Smith and Colin Welland.

Moonlight on the Highway was directed by James MacTaggart

and produced by Kenith Trodd, who until then had worked only with Potter as a story editor for *Emergency Ward – 9*. Broadcast only four days after *Son of Man* it led John Russell Taylor to suggest that out of the two pieces it was 'much more interesting and worthwhile. . . .'[26] In particular, its portrayal of childhood sexual abuse was extraordinarily brave at the time, paying tribute to Potter's refusal to back away from uncomfortable and difficult topics. The issue of abuse and the increasingly important role of popular music would become two of the most important subjects in his work, and here they are combined within a common theme and structure. Although the emotional condition of its protagonist has striking similarities with Philip Marlow in *The Singing Detective* (in particular, his sexual neurosis) the popular songs of his childhood do not actually haunt him in quite the same way (see Chapter Five). Their role is, in fact, much closer to Arthur Parker and his appropriation of their cheap lyrics and catchy melodies as a vision of a better and infinitely more *innocent* world (see below).

Like Willie Turner, David Peters (Ian Holm) is caught between two separate worlds; the sordid and unhappy existence of his day to day life as an unemployed newspaper reporter and an idyllic world of romantic love nurtured and driven by the popular music of his childhood. Indeed, his fascination with the music of Al Bowlly (a 1930's crooner who is often described as the 'English Bing Crosby') is as obsessive and as potentially dangerous as Willie's own western fixation. He publishes the newsletter of the 'Al Bowlly Fan Club' and has converted his home into a shrine for the singer who was killed in the London Blitz in 1941. Anticipating *Pennies from Heaven* we even see David singing along in front of a mirror (complete with his own guitar) to a record of Al Bowlly's *Lover Come Back to Me*. Like Bowlly's music, David's problems seem to date back to his own childhood, in particular, a sexual attack which he suffered as a young boy. As an adult we see him visit a psychiatrist who assesses his condition and sends him away with a prescription for antidepressants. Finally, in a drunken speech (the pills are not meant to be mixed with alcohol) David admits to sleeping with 136 prostitutes. 'Yes! You can't buy love', he joyfully confesses in front of the "Al Bowlly Appreciation Society", 'it's out now. I've said it! I've said it!'[27]

Like many of Potter's male protagonists David appears to have a deep emotional problem with the opposite sex, and seems repulsed and disgusted by the sexual act. 'Love is the sweetest, nastiest, filthiest, violent thing', he explains during his drunken speech. However, when a beautiful young journalist (in 1960's mini skirt and thigh length boots) comes to interview him about his Al Bowlly fanzine, he seems unable to treat her as anything other than a romanticised image in one of Bowlly's songs. 'You're the one he sings about', he tells her, 'if ever there was one.' Confused and a little frightened, she vainly attempts to talk about Bowlly's music. 'But they're so corny', she tells him, unable to appreciate the particular meanings which they obviously suggest to him. Finally he unsuccessfully attempts to force himself upon her, in what looks ominously like attempted rape. Clearly then, David finds it difficult to distinguish between the portrayal of love presented in Bowlly's popular music and the love one experiences in real life. Women for him are either sex objects (prostitutes) or else the idealised romantic heroines portrayed in songs such as *Love is the Sweetest Thing* or *My Melancholy Baby*. Occasionally, however, the split between angel and whore seems to become momentarily blurred.

The key to David's particular sexual problem appears to lie in the play's opening sequence which has him waiting morbidly in the waiting room of a busy hospital. As the camera pans the faces of the mostly elderly patients we are given a glimpse (through voice over) of their thoughts and memories. One man remembers, 'when that bleeding bird's egg broke in me mouth', and an old woman recalls, 'when he asked for the ring back – poor Freddy'. David, however, seems unable or unwilling to remember a deeply buried memory – caught, as it were, in a classic state of denial. 'I do not remember being sexually assaulted by a man with spikey hair and eyes the colour of phlegm when I was ten years old', he speaks in voice over. As Bowlly's rendition of *Moonlight on the Highway* plays over the opening credits, the superimposed image of his father's funeral, the frightening figure of his attacker, and his futile cries as a young abused child, all come back to haunt him. This link between memory and popular music is one which would prove a recurring obsession in Potter's work. It is certainly a theme heightened by the lyrics of this particular Bowlly number.

David's refusal to confront the horrific memories of his childhood sexual attack ('I do *not* remember! No!') is connected with the enormous power of the popular song to bring back the (often repressed) memories of a particular time and place. Ironically Bowlly's music also comes to be associated with a time *before* his traumatic Fall from grace. As Dr Chiltern puts it:

> He has a longing for an Eden. Before the bomb, before the alley, before his father's death, before his mother's dependence. Before he reached that fateful age of ten. The paradisal Eden does not in fact exist. But he dreams that it might have done before the bombs, before the war. The thirties! This singer, this Bowlly is killed by a bomb, he's a thirties figure. He sings of the dreams. He makes sex sound simple. He makes sex sound lovely. Not a bit like sex at all in fact. Note that Peters is only obliquely able to account what is obviously a brutal and traumatic sexual assault by using the words, phrases or titles of schmaltzy songs from an era he can have know nothing about first hand. They were the songs he must have heard on the radio downstairs whist drifting off to sleep.

Dr Chiltern's diagnosis rather aptly explains David's unique appropriation of Bowlly's music. Repulsed by the memories of his sexual attack he retreats into the nostalgic memories of the 1930s, a music he associates with a life before his traumatically awakened sexuality. As Chiltern points out, he unconsciously clings onto the romantic idealism of Bowlly's music as a means of escape from his own emotional and sexual problems. 'All the songs are about love', David explains, 'innocent love, real love. Never about *making* love. Never the wicked things – copulation.' In contrast, he seems repulsed by the popular music of the 1960s which he clearly regards as depraved and sexually explicit. 'Once dreams were possible', he explains, 'that's what the popular songs used to tells us. Now they smash up their instruments on stage. Now they whine and howl through their long hair like a lot of bloody apes.'

Such an appropriation of popular music (despite David's rejection of 1960s rock 'n' roll) suggests that Potter was beginning to recognise popular culture's ambiguous position as an uniquely positive force. While the only suggestion of personal redemption offered to Willie Turner is in the organic images of the English language (the Hollywood Western only providing a violent and perverted wish-fulfilment) here, popular music actually conjures up a temporary but significant state of grace from the inevitable Fall experienced in childhood (see Chapter Three). Such a vision appears to be essentially spiritual in the sense that it provides the glimpse of another reality or 'Eden', a place where the sordid realities of life are briefly forgotten and transcended by a popular medium which refuses to accept the world as it appears. It is this personal yearning for a purer and more innocent world which David seems to glimpse in the songs of Al Bowlly. The sentimental purification of sex, with their romantic promises of a better day and their vision of innocent love (without explicit mention or description of the sexual act) enables him to cope with a life where love is either equated with loss (his deceased father), dependency (his crippled mother) or the intense feelings of shame and disgust he feels about his childhood sexual abuse and his current obsession for prostitutes.

As a result, the play heralds an important shift in Potter's conception of popular culture as a whole. David's ability to harness the forces of popular music reflects a significant movement away from the cultural pessimism inherent in Willie's hopeless condition. Yet why is Potter's conception of Bowlly's music presented at the expense of the music and cultural condition of Britain in the 1960s? Like Hoggart, Potter portrays the popular culture of the 1930s (personified by Bowlly's sentimental tunes) as providing the antithesis to the cultural disintegration of the present day. Unconsciously, David's repulsion from the sexually permissive swinging Sixties forces him to look back to a more vibrant and traditional form of English folk art. Ironically, his sexual neurosis enables him to stay in touch with a form of English culture which has been swamped by the forces of Americanised popular culture – most notably rock 'n' roll. The encounter he has with an elderly patient who confuses Al Bowlly with a man 'who used to keep the eel and pie shop on the Broadway', only further establishes David's pioneering role as an individual desperately trying to keep in touch with an older, more vibrant English culture. Seen in this light, David is able to perceive his current obsession with prostitutes as part of England's wider cultural decline into permissiveness, and his preoccupation with Bowlly's music as a reminder of the cultural 'Eden' he can only dimly remember.

Potter's choice of Bowlly is also significant as he is the English interpreter of what are often originally American tunes. Bowlly's voice ensures that this American mass culture is recontextualised into an English context. It was this tendency to turn American mass culture into a form of English folk art which was also apparent in Hoggart's *The Uses of Literacy*. 'I first heard Paper Doll', Hoggart reflects, 'sung in the red-hot fashion by an American star crooner, and it seemed quite unsuitable for transplantation to Northern England; but two or three years later a local amateur sang it whilst I was in a Hull pub and it had been beautifully translated.'[28] Hoggart is also careful to play down the *commercial* significance of the music. 'Songs that do not meet the requirements', he argues, 'are not likely to be taken up, no matter how much Tin Pan Alley plugs them.'[29] By emphasising the audience's power of discretion and even their ability to translate the songs into their own culture, Hoggart is able to transform what was originally Americanised mass produced art into something more relevant and redeemable. Similarly for David, Bowlly's translation of the American-style crooning, and David's deep emotional investment in the songs, enables them to rise above the level of mass produced Americanised popular culture and be claimed as intrinsically personal and authentically *English*.

Echoing Hoggart, this single play clearly distinguishes between mass culture (made *after* the cultural 'Fall' of the 1950s, epitomised by an Americanised rock 'n' roll) and a form of working-class popular culture (produced *before* the 1950s and epitomised by the English versions of popular songs from the 1930s). Like Hoggart's *The Uses of Literacy*, Potter's drama seems only able to embrace a form of popular culture when it is distinguished from the glossy Americanised culture of the 1960s, and is seen to be a reminder of an older and more organic English culture altogether. The moment of the Fall (both culturally and personally) represents the point at which these two distinct worlds were suddenly divided; a time which can only be reclaimed by a complex and emotionally powerful form of English folk culture. While the songs themselves may appear sugary, commercial and banal they obviously fulfil a very important role in David's natural yearning for a better and more innocent world – a world, that is, before *his* and England's irretrievable Fall from grace.

FOLLOW THE YELLOW BRICK ROAD (1972)

Long live this rubbish which so pleases my eyes, fascinates
my heart, and gives me a glimpse of heaven.

Fereydoun Hoveyda[30]

This fascination with popular culture was further explored and
developed in *Follow the Yellow Brick Road*, produced by Roderick
Graham and directed by Alan Bridges (who also directed *Traitor*
(1971), *Joe's Ark* (1974) and *Rain on the Roof*). It was first broadcast as part of BBC 2's 'Sextet' series and included two renowned
British actors, Denholm Elliot (later to appear in *Brimstone and
Treacle*) and Billie Whitelaw. Like many Potter productions of
this period the play is a macabre comedy which threatens, at
times, to break down completely into farce. The vicious displays
of misogyny by its central male protagonist, its constant preoccupation with sex and God, its comments on television, and the
play's self-reflexive techniques certainly make it an important
Potter drama in any consideration of his work. However, despite
these recurring themes and the quality of its actors the play also
involves some of Potter's most stereotyped characters. As Stanley
Reynolds put it in *The Times*, 'where the play . . . let itself down,
was in the patness of the psychological formulae: the hero was
sexually inadequate; the psychiatrist saw everything as solvable
by a pill; the women saw everything as solvable by sex.'[31] What
is most interesting about the play, however, is the connection it
makes between religious idealism and contemporary culture. It
marked, in particular, a subtle but discernible shift in Potter's
conception and portrayal of popular culture as a whole.

As with David Peters, we first encounter Jack Black (Denholm
Eliot) sitting in the waiting room of a busy hospital to see a
psychotherapist. In an encounter with a lady patient (Ruth Dun-
ning) it becomes clear that Jack (a television actor who has been
reduced to working in the commercials) is under the delusion
that he is taking part in a television play; frequently addressing
the camera and telling it to 'Get off!' (p.321).[32] The narrative is
occasionally interrupted by examples of the absurd television
advertisements he appears in for 'Krispy Krunch' and 'Waggy
Tail Din Din'. Talking with Dr Whitman (Richard Vernon) and
Dr Bilson (Dennis Waterman) it becomes apparent that Jack is
suffering from a form of neurosis which seems to manifest itself

in profound feelings of disgust and despair. These feelings have obviously worsened with the discovery of his wife Judy's (Billie Whitelaw) infidelity with a younger man. As she explains, Jack's feelings of disgust are so profound he finds it impossible to make love with her any longer. Later we see him verbally abuse and kick her before she also confesses to having betrayed him with his agent Colin (Bernard Hepton). Meanwhile Jack confesses his love for Colin's child bride Veronica (Michele Dotrice) who immediately (and to his disgust) invites him to her bed. Finally we witness Jack advertising a new wonder drug which his doctor insists will cure all his problems. 'If Mogabrium had been available two thousand years ago', Dr Bilson explains, 'well I can think of at least one wild man who would have stuck to carpentry.' (p.337)

As this last comment suggests, the play is primarily concerned with issues of a spiritual nature. The secular world of Jack Black (as his name suggests) is devoid of any spiritual warmth or light. In contrast he remembers how as a young lad he felt God was frequently too near. 'When I was a boy', he tells the two doctors, 'I thought God was watching me all the time, every minute of the day.' (p.330) Although Jack's description of God seems as paranoid as his feelings that he is now being followed by television cameras, it suggests that there has certainly been a 'Fall' since childhood (see Chapter Three). Now when he prays to God to grant him a signal or sign the only word which comes into his head is 'Slime' (p.333). This is also the sort of adjective he applies to the television plays he once appeared in, and which he believes he is appearing in now. Written by 'Trotskyites' he insists that the plays are dirty and corrupt (p.323). 'Filth – that's what *oozes* out of these plays', he declares, '[f]ilth of all kinds to mock virtue and to encourage doubt.' (p.324) In an obvious reference to Potter's own *Son of Man* (1969) and *Angels are so Few* (1970) Jack laments the plays' moral and spiritual bankruptcy. 'They turn gold into hay, these people. Angels into whores. Love into a s-s-sticky slime – and Jesus Christ into an imbecile bleeding and screaming on a cross. I hate them. I bloody hate them, and their rotten, festering, suppurating scabs of ideas.' (p.324)

No doubt Jack's hatred of the television play is a reflection of the sort of comments Potter himself had to endure from social commentators like Mary Whitehouse (ominously pre-empting his own dubious title of 'TV's Mr Filth' during the *Blackeyes* debacle

– see Chapter Five). Jack's paranoid speech gives Potter the opportunity to strike out against those critics who seemed unable to
detect the spiritual preoccupations in his own work. Devoid of
any spiritual nourishment, Jack turns instead to the television
commercials as a source of spiritual salvation. Their promise of a
happy and clean world seem incredibly appealing in contrast to
his own feelings of disgust and despair. As he tells the bemused
Dr Whitman:

> JACK: The commercials are *clean*.
> WHITMAN: Clean?
> JACK (*Not listening*): They have happy families in the com-
> mercials. Husbands and wives who love each other . . .
> WHITMAN: But not real husbands and real wives, surely? You
> can't expect – you don't really think that love is so simple or –
> JACK (*Interrupting*): There's laughter and, and, and sunshine
> and kids playing in the meadows. Nobody mocks the finest
> human aspirations. There's no deliberate wallowing in vice and
> evil and and – (*Breaks off.*) No. There's nothing wrong with
> the commercials. Nothing at all!
>
> p.322

Jack's deluded conception of the television commercial could,
in some respects, be seen as suggesting the dangerous consequences of a consumer society; the superficial images of mass
culture infecting the personal dreams and aspirations of the individual. Clearly the television commercials have persuaded at least
one individual that their offer of a care-free existence is a real
and obtainable one. In this context, Jack's faith in their utopian
vision of the world can be seen as parodying the commercialised images of a modern society. Indeed, the title of the play
itself seems to suggest the empty promises of such a world. As
in the film version of *The Wizard of Oz* (1939) the glossy and
colourful 'yellow brick road' only leads to a false and fraudulent 'Wizard', suggesting perhaps that consumerism itself ultimately leads to an empty and superficial goal or even 'God.'
Seen in this light, Jack seems to have completely bought the glossy
allure of mass culture, no longer able to distinguish between reality
and the illusory vision of the world it fabricates. The tacky, muzak
version of 'Follow the Yellow Brick Road' which plays over the
opening and closing credits supporting such a reading.

This disintegration of reality is perhaps also portrayed by Jack's paranoid delusion that a film crew is actually following him around. 'Dear God – the lines I have to deliver' (p.373), he complains to his bewildered doctor. Indeed, it would appear an apt metaphor for a mind struggling to resist the ever increasing forces of media activity on the daily life of the consumer. As Jack occasionally throws insults at the camera, pushing it away from taking extreme close ups of him, we are reminded that the play itself is as artificially produced as the absurd television commercials he appears in; and is subsequently 'selling' something perhaps as superficial and as morally vacuous as 'Waggy Tail Din Din'. At the end of the play, when the camera moves away from Jack's advertisement for 'Mogabrium', it reveals all the electronic paraphernalia of the television studio, further foregrounding the artificiality of the play itself. However, while the character Jack is clearly suffering from a form of pathological paranoia, the fact that Denholm Elliot who plays Jack *is* actually an actor and is also taking part in a television play, can not be completely dismissed. As paranoid as Jack clearly is, ultimately, of course, his belief that he is being followed by television cameras and that his lines are scripted, is undeniably the truth.

This notion that television and advertising are somehow taking over the minds of its consumers was reflected in a variety of cultural critics from the 1950s onwards. Vance Packard's *The Hidden Persuaders* (1957) articulated many of the anxieties surrounding the influence of television and the growth of advertising in the United States. He argued, in chapters such as 'The Packaged Soul?', that '[p]lanes, missiles, and machine tools already are guided by electronics, and the human brain – being essentially a digital computer – can be, too.'[33] Later, critics like Raymond Williams would suggest that advertising needed, however, to provide the consumer with an *emotional* referent in order to sell a *commercial* product. According to Williams, advertising works by attaching an imaginary promise to a material object. Beer, for example, while simply a commodity, is sold on the premise that it is manly or neighbourly. 'The short description of the pattern we have is *magic*', he argued, 'a highly organised and professional system of magical inducements and satisfactions, functionally very similar to magical systems in simpler societies, but rather strangely coexistent with a highly developed scientific technology.'[34]

It is what Williams regards as the *magic* of the advertisement (its emotional appeal) to which Jack is clearly attracted. The utopian world of the television commercial with its happy families and blue skies becomes a veritable refuge from the pain, misery and infidelity in his own life. In this respect, Jack is simply appropriating the commercialised images of a consumer society and ironically using them as a moral and spiritual enclave. As with David Peters, he clings to a form of popular culture as the last vestige of moral decency and decorum in a society of increased sexual permissiveness. As neurotic and deluded as Jack clearly is, the commercials offer him a strangely 'religious' vision in an increasingly secular and promiscuous world: a glimpse of salvation which is perhaps less dangerous than the new antidepressants offered by the smiling Dr Bilson. Similarly, Jack's paranoid belief that he is an actor in a television play suggests that the media has occupied the very private domain of his own subjectivity, yet it may also suggest that the presence of 'God' (that is, 'The Author') is still as apparent to him as it was as a child; he lacks only the religious context to realise or recognise it. In this sense, the absurd commercialism of modern life has forced the religious sense of a world to occupy any vestige of human life it can. As Potter himself put it when later writing about the play:

> I wanted, half mockingly, and with an extremely grudging acknowledgement of what I was myself beginning to understand, to show how the human dream for some concept of 'perfection', some Zion or Eden or Golden City, will surface and take hold of whatever circumstances are at hand – no matter how ludicrous. Even in a future land of Muzak, monosodium glutamate and melamined encounters, the old resilient dreams will insist on making metaphors and finding illumination in the midst of the surrounding dross. There is, then, no place 'God' cannot reach.[35]

However the play is conceived, it is a portrayal of popular culture which shows a subtle but significant shift in Potter's personal perspective. While Willie Turner's fixation with the American cinema was not entirely without some positive dimensions, the only real glimpse of a spiritual renewal lay in the organic images of the words he was tragically unable to read. For David Peters there is the glimpse that the nostalgic longing for a simpler and more romantic form of popular culture could offer personal salvation, but only in an attempt to escape from the sordid and sexually threatening mood of the swinging Sixties. For Jack, however, that glimpse of 'God' is found in the most cheapened and absurd forces of popular culture – the television commercial. While Potter's earlier drama tended to dismiss the relevance of so-called mass art, one can slowly detect the gradual (if reluctant) realisation that popular culture could become the site of some greater and more noble struggle than his work had originally conceived. Eventually there came a growing appreciation of the complexity and sophistication of mass art – a begrudging acknowledgement for the power of its alternative and seductive mythologies.

Despite Potter's own reservations about modern critical theory it is a view of mass culture which is perhaps reflected by contemporary cultural studies. Although we must be careful not to overemphasise Jack's appropriation of the television commercial, the play shows a subtle shift from the conception of audiences as cultural dupes, passively consuming popular culture, to the notion of *audiences-as-producers*, actively producing their own meaning. In other words, Jack's reading of the television commercial enables him to *resist* its dominant ideological forms, and produce his own interpretation. Power does not come only from above, but is also exercised from below – by the consumer. Adapting the ideas of the French theorist Michel Foucault, John Fiske argues that '[t]elevision participates in both these modes of power-pleasure. It exerts the power of surveillance, revealing the world, spying out people's secrets, monitoring human activity, but an integral part of this power is the resistance, or rather resistances, to it.'[36] In his own deluded way, Jack reconstructs the television commercial for his own purpose – and in doing so, he radically transforms his role from consumer to producer. As such, the play heralds an important change in Potter's conception and portrayal of popular culture as a whole, a change which would later be reflected in one of the most successful television productions of his career.

PENNIES FROM HEAVEN: SIX PLAYS WITH MUSIC (1978)

when the audience at a sentimental film or sentimental music become aware of the overwhelming possibility of happiness, they dare to confess to themselves what the whole order of contemporary life ordinarily forbids them to admit, namely that they actually have no part in happiness. What is supposed to be wish fulfillment is only the scant liberation that occurs when the realization that at last one need not deny oneself the happiness of knowing that one is unhappy and that one could be happy.

Theodor W. Adorno, 'On Popular Music' (1941)[37]

During the 1970s the single television play was gradually being replaced by the series and mini-series. As Carl Gardner and John Wyver have pointed out, the shift was both economic and ideological. A harsher economic environment and the effect of inflation on the BBC's fixed revenue highlighted the importance of 'cost-effectiveness' with regards to television in general and the single play in particular.[38] While the single play always had to start, as it were from scratch, a series could spread its fixed costs over the entire budget for a six or 13 week period. The 'strangeness' of the single play's productions and their unpredictable shifts in style and content, meant that they were also difficult to schedule in a world increasingly obsessed with ratings and advertising revenue. A series could, in contrast, quickly establish and maintain a loyal audience over its neatly timed slot for the relevant number of weeks. Buyers and co-production money from overseas also proved increasingly important and the parochial obsessions of the single play were no longer regarded as economically attractive; unable, that is, to fulfill the needs of a potential foreign audience. Hence the growth in the historical series such as LWT's hugely successful *Upstairs, Downstairs*, Thames Television's *Edward and Mrs Simpson* and the BBC's *The Six Wives of Henry VIII* which attracted a huge response from the USA.

Pennies from Heaven was partly a response to these needs, satisfying the BBC with a historical drama (it is set in England in the mid-1930s) and spreading it over six separate episodes at 90 minutes each: providing a staggering nine hours of original television drama in total.[39] It was these extra pressures which eventually forced Potter and Kenith Trodd to set up their own production company, Pennies from Heaven Ltd in 1979. Pennies from Heaven Ltd (PHF) quickly set up a deal with Michael Grade to produce nine projects for London Weekend Television – six single plays written by Potter, a two-parter by the writer

Jim Allen and a work by an unannounced writer. As it was, only the three Potter plays were produced before LWT withdrew funding because PFH had gone £150,000 over budget.[40] The demise of PFH sent Potter off to Hollywood where a film version of *Pennies from Heaven* was to be made by MGM studios with the director Herbert Ross. Despite proving disastrous at the box-office it brought Potter a reported £125,000 writer's fee, and won him an Academy Award nomination for Best Screenplay (based on material from another medium).

The original television serial, costing £800,000, proved a critical and popular success when it was first shown on British television. Potter picked up the Best Writer's Award while the drama itself won the award for the most Original TV production at the British Academy Awards. Directed by Piers Haggard and produced by Kenith Trodd, the serial was first transmitted by the BBC at weekly intervals beginning in March 1978 and was quickly repeated in three two-part modules during December 1978–January 1979. The serial format seemed to help Potter develop both character and narrative in a way previously unimaginable within the confines of the single play, enabling him to create, what one critic referred to, as 'the televisual equivalent of the serialised Victorian novel'.[41] James Murray in the *Daily Express* called it 'a magical welding together of popular music, trenchant humour, high drama and all the tricks of television technology. It's all so refreshing I think it will galvanise the whole country.'[42]

Set in the mid-1930s, the serial centres around Arthur Parker (Bob Hoskins), a working-class sheet music salesman who is frustrated and unhappy in his suburban marriage to the frigid and middle-class Joan (Gemma Craven). On one of his many trips around the country selling sheet music he meets the 'Accordion Man' (Kenneth Colley) and Eileen (Cheryl Campbell) a virginal school mistresses whom he seduces. Abandoned by Arthur and finding herself pregnant, Eileen loses her job and moves to London in search of work. There she is procured an abortion by Tom (Hywel Bennett), a local pimp who attempts to force her into a life of prostitution. However, through a chance meeting in a London pub Arthur and Elieen are finally re-united and set out on a new life. However the police believe Arthur is responsible for the murder of young blind-girl in a Gloustershire field. Although the crime is actually committed by the Accordion Man, Arthur is finally caught and after a farcical trial is sentenced to death. Mourning his death on Hammersmith Bridge, Elieen is suddenly confronted by Arthur's magical re-appearance. 'Couldn't go all through that wivaht a bleed'n 'appy ending' now could we?' (p.247),[43] he declares at the finale.

As Iain Colley and Gill Davies point out, set in England in 1935, *Pennies from Heaven* takes place at the very origins of the popular culture debate. Leavis, for example, first published *Scrutiny* (his Journal against the mass produced arts) three years earlier in 1932.[44] Indeed, the mid-1930s was typified by enormous cultural changes in Britain – not least, the growth in the production and distribution of popular music, the growing significance of radio and the rapid rise of the record industry. As Paddy Scannell and David Cardiff explain, '[b]efore broadcasting, music did not exist as a unified cultural field. It was scarcely meaningful to speak of music in general. What existed were particular musics – the choral societies, brass and military bands with their competitions and festivals. . . .'[45] By 1928, however, it was estimated that there were more than two and half million record players in Britain and by late 1933 late-night 'dance music' was widely available on the radio. With the growth of radio (five million sets were owned in Britain in 1935, reaching nine million by 1939[46]) widespread musical tastes were also undergoing a fundamental cultural shift. Such changes are reflected, of course, in Arthur's occupation. The rise of professional reproduced entertainment meant there was a gradual decline in the need for his precious sheet-music. As Scannell and Cardiff explain:

> The fears of the musical profession about the impact of the radio on their livelihood were put to the Crawford Committee in 1925. The music publishers claimed that radio was damaging the sale of sheet music. William Boosey . . . was convinced that radio spelt the ruination of publicly performed music, a view he put to the Crawford Committee, adding that those who listened in to the wireless gave up practising or playing the piano.[47]

Pennies from Heaven is caught at the very centre of these cultural changes from an amateur and provincial form of musical entertainment to a professional and mass-produced musical industry. As Arthur tells his wife, '[t]he days of sheet music is numbered, my love. What with the wireless and all – stands to reason, don't

it? People don't make their own entertainment now, do they?'
(p.96). Surprisingly perhaps, Arthur even welcomes the changes
himself. 'I'd rather listen to Lew Stone's band', he explains, 'than
hear some cloth-eared berk murdering the same tune on some
pub piano.' (p.96) Later, he actually fulfils his ambition to own
a gramophone shop, although with disappointing results. In 1935
Arthur is a good 10 years too early to capitalise on the growth
in the ownership of gramophones after the war. Historical hindsight, however, actually confirms his belief in the potential power
of popular music and the million dollar industry it would finally
become. 'Do you know something? You've got no vision', he
tells Joan. 'I can see a – yes, a *whole chain* of record shops.'
(p.155)

The opening episode ('Down Sunnyside Lane') crucially establishes some of the enormous cultural changes taking place in
England just prior to the Second World War. The illustrations
by Tom Taylor which accompany the titles (they are different
for every episode) suggest the rapid commercialisation of contemporary life. Their image of pre-war suburbia, with its underground stations and a seemingly endless line of identical houses
and perfectly manicured streets presents an almost mass-produced
community. This was by no means a new perception of suburbia. It is reminiscent of a number of literary representations such
as George Orwell's *Coming up for Air* (1939). 'You know how the
streets fester all over the inner-outer suburbs', Orwells' George
Bowlling explains, '. . . . Long, long rows of little semi-detached
houses . . . The stucco front, the creosoted gate, the privet hedge,
the green front door'.[48] Arthur and Joan's suburban home is also
a symbol of wider social changes. Arthur is himself from a working-class background (his father was a bricklayer) and symbolises the growth in white-collar workers, and the increased
opportunity for social mobility after the First World War. Joan,
however, is from a lower middle-class background (her father
was a Methodist) and the social differences between her and her
husband are a continual source of conflict. Her constant nag-
ging of Arthur's diction is clearly a cultural battle ground with
his cockney expressions and use of bad language unacceptable
to her petit-bourgeois aspirations. 'Common, am I?', Arthur complains. 'Oh, I knew that from the start' (p.3), Joan concedes.

Like Orwell's George Bowlling, Arthur's social mobility is also
foregrounded by his motor car. His family saloon is the ultimate

symbol of mass produced freedom and affluence and the 'chariot' with which he sweeps the Forest of Dean school teacher off her feet. It is also the means by which he initially wins the approval of her coal-mining family. 'Oh, I see. Got a car, have you – sir?' (p.61), says her brother Dave (Philip Jackson), clearly impressed. Earlier, when Arthur picks up the Accordion Man for the first time, the car again suggests a symbol of economic privilege and freedom. 'I've got my dignity', the tramp insists, '[y]ou haven't got a motor car, though, have you?' (p.9), replies the economically superior and mobile Arthur. And at the end of the serial the stolen car becomes a symbol of economic independence and even sexual freedom as Arthur and Eileen ride away like Bonnie and Clyde into their own doomed escape from economic and sexual repression.

The power and the influence of the media and advertising is also established early on in the serial. Joan indulges in fantasies brought about by glossy images in women's magazines on finding herself alone after Arthur's departure. Their promise to provide the reader with instant feminine charm and conscious attractiveness, certainly tempts Joan to escape from her suburban boredom and emotional repression to dream that she is a famous actress. 'Rising Star, Beautiful young Joan Parker', reads the (fantasised) headline below a picture of her in the magazine as she appears to fall into a dream world as powerful as any of Arthur's. Such is the potency of the fantasy, that when a handsome travelling salesman (Nigel Havers) calls at the door she is easily conned into buying an obviously fraudulent piece of cosmetic equipment. Indeed, to make the connection stronger, it his voice we hear before as the narrator of the magazine, foregrounding the connection between the ideological impulse of the popular press and the economic forces of the market place. The salesman's carefully moulded pitch (like the magazine's) preys on a mixture of vanity and boredom to sell goods which the purchaser simply does not need. Only when Joan innocently mentions that her husband too is a salesman does his well-polished patter momentarily slip.

The magazine and the salesman together suggest the commercial and ideological invasion of the home and the minds of its occupants. Where once the individual was able to reject the forces of the media, the 1930s heralded a time when they would infiltrate the family home through images in magazines, the radio, and through the physical intrusion of the commercial salesman and advertising in general. Joan's gullible belief in the glitzy images of the popular press (later she will fret desperately about the possibility of having bad breath after reading an exaggerated account of halitosis in another of her magazines) portrays the ideological manipulation which the market has placed on the personal beliefs and even physical aspirations of the individual. This portrayal of mass culture as a form of ideological indoctrination is one of the serial's recurrent themes and preoccupations. When the headmaster dismisses Eileen because of her pregnancy she asks him why (despite his 'Romantic' conception of childhood – see Chapter Three) he disciplines the children so harshly. 'So that they can learn enough to keep a job in the pits, Miss Everson', he explains. 'What do they want with visions, or trees shaped like diamonds? Or any memory of the Garden of Eden? (*Sniff.*) Cheap music will do, cheap music. And beer. And skittles.' (p.116)

Cheap music is, of course, the major focus of the serial's concern. The six episodes include over 80 popular songs from the 1920s and 1930s, the majority of which are performed by characters who mime or 'lip-synch' to the original recordings of artists like Sam Browne, Jack Jackson, Elsie Carlisle and Lew Stone and his band. The introduction of each song signals a break from the narrative diegesis as characters (and frequently supporting characters) suddenly begin miming and dancing to a song which clearly has no origin in the film's diegetic world. Although the classical Hollywood musical (reaching its heyday in the 1930s) certainly employed the practice of 'lip-synch' as a technical device, here Potter utilises that *technical* consideration and turns it into an *aesthetic* choice. In contrast to the traditional Hollywood musical, the obvious disjunction between the actor's voice and the voice of the original recording (heightened by male characters often miming to female vocals and visa versa) foregrounds the artificiality of these musical intrusions in a seemingly naturalistic narrative. Although a change in lighting, colour, costumes and props may often accompany a song, they are most strongly characterised by the apparently seamless transition from real space to musical space; that is, from speaking to singing, from walking to dancing.

Clearly such a technique is deliberately self-conscious in its appropriation and dissemination of popular music, and seems to address explicitly the growing influence of mass culture on the lives and minds of Potter's characters. They certainly appear to provide a form of expression for otherwise inarticulate characters. 'It's impossible to explain. It's not the sort of thing you can put into words' (p.67), Arthur declares just before bursting into a rendition of Sam Browne's *Yes, Yes! My Baby said Yes, 'Yes'!* The songs may also provide a glimpse into the ideological construction of its characters. Arthur's break into *The Clouds Will Soon Roll By* at the beginning of the first episode, for instance, can been seen as foregrounding his total immersion into the romantic ideology of the music to escape from his suburban reality and loveless marriage. Similarly, it could be argued that the device itself provides a distancing or alienation effect which, in Brechtian terms, forces the spectator to recognise the forces by which the dominant ideology manipulates Arthur's social reality. For Marxist cultural critics like Theodor W. Adorno, popular music reduced individual spontaneity and produced 'conditioned reflexes'. The uniformity and frozen melodies of these mass produced songs act as a form of hypnotic and effortless release from the listener's 'fears and anxieties about unemployment, loss of income' and 'war' – social ills which were, of course, abundant in the world depression of the 1930s. 'It is catharsis for the masses', Adorno argued, 'but catharsis which keeps them all the more firmly in line.'[49]

Although a few of the songs chosen by Potter do have this ideological manipulation in mind (for example, Paxville's address to a Tory meeting with a rendition of *On the Other Side of the Hill* (episode 5)) the majority of them clearly provide another dimension to Arthur's sordid situation. In particular, the serial suggests that the banality and mass produced quality of the songs can actually be transformed by their individual rendition. The human translation of these mass-produced banalities ironically produces something altogether more sublime. Although, as a whole, it portrays England's decline as symbolised by the forces of mass culture, paradoxically the popular song appears to evoke an almost spiritual glimpse into another reality. The music seems to possess traces of an older and more organic way of life than that represented by the cultural changes sweeping England in the 1930s. Indeed, this connection between the popular song and an older organic English tradition is foregrounded throughout the serial. When Eileen first breaks into a song (a rendition of Elsie Carlisle's *You've Got Me Crying Again*) it replaces the Psalm of David she is reading to the school assembly. The religious context explicitly connects the popular song with an older spiritual tradition. As Potter told Bragg in his last interview, 'I wanted to write about the way popular culture is an inheritor of something else. You know the cheap songs so-called actually do have something of the Psalms of David about them. They do say life is other than it is.' (Potter, 1994, p.19)

It is with Arthur, of course, that the true meaning of the music resides. Firstly, he seems to find a form of *sexual* salvation in the romantic melodies of the popular songs. Unlike David Peters, however, who interprets Bowlly's music as a way to *escape* from sexual permissiveness, Arthur uses the music to *articulate* his carnal desires which are otherwise forbidden by a sexually repressive social system. Married to the frigid Joan he relies on their sugary melodies and trite lyrics to express his frustrated desires. As it is explained in the first episode, all the songs are about 'shagging'. 'They'd stamp it out if they could', he insists, '. . . [t]he people in charge. Them that runs the bloody place.' (p.30) However, the songs also provide Arthur with more than simply an expression of sexual desire. Denied an authentic working-class culture by his marriage into the lower middle-classes, his movement into a North London suburb, and the rise and influence of mass culture generally, he finally turns to the songs he carries in his case as the reminder of an older, optimistic and romantic working-class culture. As he tells the salesmen he meets on the road, '[t]hey're things that is too big and too important and too bleed'n simple to put in all that lah-di-dah, toffee-nosed poetry and stuff, books and that. . . . It's looking for the blue ennit, and the gold. The patch of blue in somebody's eye.' (pp.68–7)

Seen in this light, the lip-synch device, with its subtle subversion of the classical Hollywood musical, can be read as an attempt at bridging the widening gap between folk and mass art. According to Jane Feuer's *The Hollywood Musical* (1982) the genre's illusion of 'non-choreography and non-rehearsals', its setting within an amateur rather than professional context, its emphasis on the folk community, and its use of domestic props in dance routines, tended to create the carefully orchestrated illusion of amateur entertainment. As Feuer puts it, the 'Hollywood musical becomes a mass art which aspires to the condition of a folk art, produced and consumed by the same integrated community.'[50] Potter himself liked to refer to the serial as a home-made musical, a fact greatly misunderstood by the disappointing Hollywood version with its lavish sets and expensive costumes.[51] In contrast, the BBC's song and dance routines are characterised by their comparatively cheap sets, and only the slightest modulations of *mise-en-scéne* to denote a musical break. The character's tendency to revert to their original position after the music – as if the song had never actually interrupted the narrative diegesis – only heightens the amateur illusion and exaggerates 'the aura of spontaneity' which Feuer associates with the classical Hollywood musical. According to Walter Benjamin's seminal essay, 'that which withers in the age of mechanical reproduction is the aura of the work of art',[52] and Potter's drama can be seen as an attempt at retrieving that aura from, as it were, the very mouth of mass production.

The lip-synch device, then, is not so much offering a Brechtian exposure of ideology, but is rather dramatising a time before the cultural Fall of the 1950s and 1960s when mass culture in Britain still apparently seemed to have its roots in an older and more organic working-class tradition. Indeed, Hoggart had already attached a similar significance to the same songs, suggesting that, '[t]hey are vulgar, it is true, but not usually tinselly . . . they still just touch hands with an older and more handsome culture.'[53] Although they are undoubtedly commercialised ('dreamed up', as one character puts it, 'in a back office by a couple of Jew-boys with green eyeshades' (p.70)) they seem to offer him the reminder of a purer and more organic form of folk culture. As we have seen, the serial is actually dismissive of many of the cultural changes brought about by the rise of mass culture and the songs only represent a *form* of mass culture which is reminiscent of something else altogether. Not surprisingly, it is the Accordion Man (a busker of traditional hymns) who finally lip-synchs to *Pennies from Heaven*, which in its very title suggests a unification between the *commercial* and the *organic*. The song itself is transformed by the clumsy, lip-synch performance of the tramp which recontextulaises the song from a professional to an amateur context; while its lyrics present the vision of a Fallen world, and an 'Eden' which can only be re-claimed by the redemptive power of human suffering.

Consequently, Arthur and Eileen (who share, of course, the initials of their Christian names with the first sinful couple) symbolise a modern *Fall* – England's organic paradise sacrificed at the hands of a rapid consumerism. The Christian framework is also reflected, of course, in the Accordion Man's rendering of hymns such as *The Old Rugged Cross*. As Colley and Davies point out, he will apparently set up and play '[w]herever two or three or p-preferably four busy streets *intersect*' (p.11), an intensely Christian image.[53] Representing Arthur's alter-ego (Joan mistakes the Accordion Man for her husband at one time) his amateur rendition of the hymns offer a musical and cultural connection with Arthur's popular songs. While Arthur finds a glimpse of spiritual redemption in the popular music of the 1930s, the Accordion Man is a constant reminder of their cultural and spiritual roots. Consequently Arthur's character performs two crucial functions: firstly, as a dishonest and sexually frustrated salesman he is the ultimate symbol of the growing corruption of mass culture, yet his redeemable yearning for a better world (articulated through the songs he carries in his case) re-positions him as a vital link between 'old England' and 'new England' – a corrupt vessel through which an organic world can still be glimpsed.

The Accordion Man's murder of the blind Gloucestershire girl (a perfect vision of a pure and organic innocence) is a warning, however, of what the corruption of England's organic past can produce. Polluted perhaps by Arthur's baser instincts (he longs to take her '*knickers off*' (p.101)) the Accordion Man may be regarded as carrying out the hero's deepest desires, and modern consumerism's darkest and most destructive impulses. Arthur's Christ-like resurrection at the end of the play can be seen as suggestive of the power and resilience of that older culture and tradition. Indeed, the implicit connection between religion and popular culture is finally brought to a fitting climax. His closing words to Eileen, '[t]he song has ended, but the melody lingers on', suggests the power of popular culture as a whole to continue crucial links with the cultural and spiritual traditions of England's past. Seen in this light, Arthur and Eileen's final rendition of *The Glory of Love* provides an appropriate, optimistic and ultimately Christian finale.

In conclusion, one could argue that although Potter was initially critical of popular culture in early works such as *Between Two Rivers* and *Where the Buffalo Roam*, plays and serials such as *Moonlight on the Highway*, *Follow the Yellow Brick Road* and *Pennies from Heaven* revealed a growing appreciation for its more positive and inspirational aspects. While his drama could never completely disguise its original dislike of mass culture, certain forms were gradually privileged because of their ability to help articulate inexpressible dreams and desires. Popular culture, it suggests, could be liberating and inspirational as well as standardised, repetitive and ideological. Such a view can help explain Potter's own ambiguous relationship with pop culture which held both a fear of and fascination for the power of its commercialised and sentimentalised mythologies. Above all, his work gradually came to celebrate its power and, in particular, its ability to offer a form of resistance against dominant ideological practice by conjuring up memories of an older and more organic world – a world before the ideological dictatorship of the mass media had entered and overtaken the homes and minds of its consumers.

This conception of popular culture tends to display the turn which British cultural studies took as a whole in the late 1970s. In particular, Potter's later portrayal of popular culture may be better understood in the light of the theories of hegemony which critics have centred around the writings of the Italian Marxist, Antonio Gramsci. According to Gramsci, there is a perpetual struggle for hegemony which includes a whole hotch-potch of different and contrasting cultural and ideological forces which together fight for supremacy. Consequently, popular culture becomes a site of permanent struggle (what Gramsci terms 'a moving equilibrium'), a space for resistance and adaptation within dominant ideological practice. As Tony Bennett has put it, 'for Gramsci, the part played by the most taken-for-granted, sedimented cultural aspects of everyday life are crucially implicated in the processes whereby hegemony is fought for, won, lost, and resisted – the field of popular culture is structured by the attempt of the ruling class to win hegemony and by the forms of opposition to this endeavour.'[55] Seen in this light, a serial like *Pennies from Heaven* is an attempt to portray that moving equilibrium, to investigate, explore and dramatise the complex and frequently contradictory field of popular culture at the very heart of its historical origins. As Potter would later tell Graham Fuller, 'it was the power of the mythologies, really, that's what I was dealing with.' (Fuller, 1993, p.88)

In particular, Potter's characters are defined by their ability to harness the apparently empty and rootless signs of modern society so that an older and more vibrant culture can be temporarily reclaimed and revived. By recontextualising both their content and context, and by actually reinventing their production and performance, his later work is able to transform mass culture into a form of folk art; thus restoring a human substance into what may appear, at first glance, to be a flat and depthless commodity. Rather than expressing a postmodern sensibility as critics like Ib Bondebjerg and Timothy Corrigan suggest, such a project is essentially modernist in its attempt to return to a moment when a natural world was still intact and retrievable.[56] As Fredric Jameson puts it, 'in modernism. . . . some residual zones of nature or being, of the old, the older, the archaic, still subsist; culture can still do something to that nature and work at transforming that referent.[57] In Potter's drama, as we have seen, that older and more archaic world is still longed for, remembered and ambiguously recalled by the very forces which helped bring about its demise. These privileged and nostalgic forms of popular culture which, despite their commercial and banal syncopations, provide the means by which his characters are able to glimpse, albeit briefly, the vision of a better, holier and more organic world. 'You and your songs', Marlow's wife taunts him in *The Singing Detective*. 'Yeh. Well', he replies, '[b]anality with a beat.' (Potter, 1986, p.196) Banal as they are, for Marlow, as for Arthur Parker, the songs still have a beat to them as vital and as vibrant as any human heart.

NOTES

1. This chapter is an expanded version of my article, 'Banality With a Beat': Dennis Potter and the paradox of popular music', *Media, Culture and Society*, July 1996.
2. Roland Barthes, *Mythologies*, selected and translated from the French by Annette Lavers, Paladin, 1973, p.157.
3. David Frost and Ned Sherrin (eds), *That Was The Week That Was*, W. H. Allen, 1963.
4. The title of *Emergency Ward-9* is a deliberate reference to the long-running British soap *Emergency Ward-10*.
5. At the time of its broadcast Potter argued that *Pennies from Heaven*, *The Singing Detective* and *Lipstick on Your Collar* acted as a form of trilogy, exploring the 1930s, 1940s and 1950s respectively.
6. Richard Maltby (ed.), *Dreams for Sale: Popular Culture in the 20th Century*, Harrap, 1989, p.11.
7. T. W. Adorno, 'On Popular Music', 1941, in John Storey (ed.), *Cultural Theory and Popular Culture: A Reader*, Harvester and Wheatsheaf, 1994, pp.205–6.

8. F. R. Leavis, *Culture and Environment*, 1933, Chatto & Windus, 1964, p.3.
9. George Orwell, *The Decline of the English Murder and Other Essays*, Penguin, 1965, pp.11–12.
10. John Storey, 1994, p.47.
11. See Richard Hoggart, *The Uses of Literacy*, Penguin Books, 1990.
12. Philip Purser, 'Man's Eye View', *Sunday Telegraph*, 19 May 1968. Purser's naming of him as 'Pooter' is a reference to Charles Pooter, the bourgeois and self-important hero of George and Weedon Grossmith's *Diary of a Nobody* (1892).
13. Potter's different spelling of Trodd's Christian name is explained by the fact that Trodd changed its spelling in the 1960s. As well as being a television producer, Kenith Trodd was also the author of the monograph *Lew Stone: A Career in Music*, Joyce Stone, 1971.
14. Raymond Williams, *The Long Revolution*, Penguin, 1961.
15. Dennis Potter in interview with John Wyver, 'The Long-Non Revolution of Dennis Potter', *Time Out*, October 1980, Vol. 548, pp.831–2.
16. Dwight Macdonald, 'A Theory of Mass Culture' in B. Rosenberg and D. W. White (eds), *Mass Culture: The popular arts in America*, Macmillan, 1957. Also included in John Storey, 1994, pp.29–46.
17. Tony Garnett, *Radio Times*, 27 October 1966, p.38.
18. Kenneth Eastaugh, *Daily Mirror*, 3 November 1966.
19. Maurice Wiggin, *The Times*, 6 November 1966.
20. Nancy Banks-Smith, *Sun*, 3 November 1966.
21. James Thomas, *Daily Express*, 3 November 1966.
22. All extracts are transcribed from a recording of the original play, BBC, 1966.
23. Cited by Antony Easthope, *Literary into Cultural Studies*, Routledge, 1991, p.4.
24. Ibid., p.163.
25. Kenith Trodd, 'In at the Birth and Death of Kestrel Productions', interview by Ann Purser, *Stage & Television Today*, 25 June 1970, p.15.
26. John Russell Taylor, *Plays and Players*, Vol. 16, No. 9, June 1969, p.12.
27. All extracts are transcribed from the original recording.
28. Hoggart, 1990, p.161. Interestingly *Paper Doll* would later appear in *The Singing Detective*.
29. Ibid., p.159.
30. Fereydoun Hoveyda on the film director Nicolas Ray. Cited by John Caughie, *Theories of Authorship: A Reader*, BFI, 1981, p.13.
31. Stanley Reynolds, *The Times*, 5 July 1972, p.12.
32. All page references refer to the published script of *Follow the Yellow Brick Road* in Robert Muller (ed.), *The Television Dramatist*, Elek, 1973.
33. Vance Packard, *The Hidden Persuaders: An introduction to the techniques of mass-persuasion through the unconscious*, Penguin, 1960, p.196.
34. Raymond Williams, 1980, p.185.
35. Dennis Potter, Introduction, 1978.

36. John Fiske, *Television Culture*, Routledge, 1992, pp.314–5.
37. Adorno, included in Storey, 1994, p.213.
38. See Carl Gardener and John Wyver, 'The Single Play: From Reithian Reverence To Cost-Accounting And Censorship', *Screen*, Vol. 24, Nos. 4–5, 1983, pp.114–123.
39. Potter later insisted that he was 'given' six episodes by the BBC as a way of apology for the banning of *Brimstone and Treacle* in 1976.
40. For a full account of Potter and Trodd's involvement with LWT see 'Cream Without Coffee' from Mihir Bose, *Michael Grade: Screening the Image*, Virgin Books, 1992, pp.103–121.
41. Michael Ratcliffe, review of episode 1, *The Times*, 8 March 1978, p.9. The serial was also highly successful in terms of rating figures with around 12 million viewers tuning into the last episode.
42. James Murray, 'Brave New World for Dennis', *Daily Express*, 10 February 1978, p.12.
43. All page reference refer to Dennis Potter, *Pennies from Heaven*, Faber & Faber, 1996.
44. Iain Colley and Gill Davies, 'Pennies from Heaven: Music, Image, Text', *Screen Education*, No. 35, 1980.
45. Paddy Scannell and David Cardiff, *A Social History of British Broadcasting, Vol 1, 1922–1939: Serving The Nation*, Basil Blackwell, 1991, p.182.
46. See Antony Easthope, 1991, p.115.
47. Paddy Scannel and David Cardiff, 1991, p.205.
48. George Orwell, *Coming Up For Air*, Secker & Warburg, 1971, p.13.
49. Adorno, included in Storey, 1994, p.213.
50. Jane Feuer, *The Hollywood Musical*, Indiana University Press, 1982, p.3.
51. As Potter told Graham Fuller, 'the very brilliance of the musical numbers destroyed the reason for their being there. They didn't come out of the characters, they didn't come out of their heads.' (Fuller, 1993, p.111)
52. Walter Benjamin, 'The Work of Art in the Age of Mechanical Reproduction', in Walter Benjamin (translated by Harry Zohn) *Illuminations*, Fontana/Collins, 1970, p.223.
53. Hoggart, 1990, p.163.
54. See Colley and Davies, 1980, p.72.
55. Tony Bennett, 'The Turn to Gramsci', from Tony Bennett, Colin Mercer and Janet Woolacott (eds), *Popular Culture and Social Relations*, Open University Press, 1986, p.xv.
56. See Ib Bondebjerg, 'Intertextuality and metafiction: Genre and narration in the television fiction of Dennis Potter', in Michael Skovmand, Kim Christian Schroder (eds), *Media Cultures: Reappraising Transnational Media*, Routledge, 1992, p.167 and Timothy Corrigan, *A Cinema Without Walls: Movies and Culture After Vietnam*, Routledge, 1991, pp.179–193).
57. Fredric Jameson, *Postmodernism or The Cultural Logic of Late Capitalism*, Verso, 1991, p.ix.

5

Mothers and Mistresses: Women, Sexuality and the Male Unconscious

The 'psychical fantasy of woman' is Lacanian shorthand for a process whereby women are split into two types, good and bad, mother and whore, and idealized and denigrated accordingly. The fantasy is meant to be as universal and transhistorical as the symbolic order itself; for by splitting women into two types the man is able to situate himself as subject.

Teresa Brennan (1993)[1]

I think the dichotomy between angel and whore . . . is an exaggeration or a sharpening of a common perception. And it may be that out of my own sexual psychology it is a particular temptation to me. In some of my earlier work I wouldn't have known what I know now. How do I know it? Partly through ageing, but mostly because, and this is a shocking thing to say, the first waves of feminist polemic and perception were actually revelations to me.

Dennis Potter (1989)[2]

INTRODUCTION

In *Follow the Yellow Brick Road* (1972) the anxious and betrayed protagonist Jack Black expresses his personal alienation in a rather shocking and explicit manner. 'The whole world', he tells his psychiatrist, 'can be reduced to a hairy lump between a woman's legs (*Hiss.*) *That* stinking hole!' (Muller, 1973, p.326)[3] He denounces his unfaithful wife as a 'bitch on heat', a 'filthy mucking whore' and a 'sex sodden little slut' (p.343). In *The Singing Detective* (1986)

Marlow screams out a list of obscenities at his estranged wife when she first visits him in hospital. 'You disgusting tramp! Nicola! You two-bit, rutting whore! . . . you heartless bitch! . . . Who are you opening your legs for now you . . . stinking bag of filth!' (Potter, 1986, p.84). And in Potter's first novel *Hide and Seek* (1973) – which its central protagonist describes as a 'dirty book, peopled with . . . faithless women with rotting cunts' (Potter, 1973, pp.27–8) – Daniel Miller is crippled both mentally and physically with sexual guilt. 'Women are the root or flesh of the problem', he explains, '[i]t is my attitude to women, or my conduct with them, which provides the rumours, the poison, the imprisonment in an icy room.' (p.80)

This aggression towards the opposite sex frequently culminates in violence. Many of Potter's female characters (Elizabeth in *Schmoedipus* (1974), Pattie in *Brimstone and Treacle* (1976), Linda in *Track 29* (1987), Jessica in *Blackeyes* (1989)) are all victims of rape or molestation. Nigel Barton slaps his upper-class girlfriend 'hard' around the face when she suggests they make love. 'Don't make fun of me, Jill', he complains, '[d]on't be a bitch.' (Potter. 1967, p.44) In *Follow the Yellow Brick Road* Jack slaps and kicks his unfaithful wife. Daniel Miller repeatedly punches his wife in *Hide and Seek*. In *Sufficient Carbohydrate* (1984) Jack gives Lucy a black eye and bruised ribs, and in *Lipstick on Your Collar* (1993) Sylvia is battered and bullied by her violent husband. Such abuse may even culminate in a woman's death. A young pregnant girl is battered and left to die by her secret lover in *A Beast With Two Backs* (1968). The title – coming as it does from Shakespeare's description of the sexual act in *Othello* – neatly sums up the play's underlying themes. In *Pennies from Heaven* (1976), the innocent and vulnerable blind girl Arthur meets in a Gloucestershire field is later raped and strangled by his alter-ego the Accordion Man (see Chapter Four). In *Double Dare* (1976), a prostitute is attacked and murdered by her client. In *Blackeyes* a semi-clad model walks to a watery grave with a list of men concealed in her vagina. And in *The Singing Detective* both Marlow's real mother and one of his fictional female characters are both found dead floating in the River Thames.

It is this explicit and often shocking portrayal of women which has given Potter's plays the unenviable reputation of being darkly misogynist. Addressing these accusations Potter occasionally agreed that in some part they may have been justified. 'If you come up with English working-class male ideas about women', he explained, 'then traces of that – no, more than traces – a lot of that is going to cling to you for a long time.' (Fuller, 1993, p.133) In an interview during the makings of *Blackeyes* Potter admitted that much of his earlier work may have displayed 'misogynist' undertones, but he argued it was a problem he was consciously attempting to confront. 'I think that my later work picks up some of those [feminist] currents', he argued, '[m]aybe it needed more time for them to be digested, that's all'.[4] Such reassurances did little, however, to calm the chorus of disapproval which inevitably surrounded Potter's work for television. Indeed, the critic Mark Steyn has argued that his female leads actually *worsened* during his dramatic career – their 'function degenerating, respectively, from secondary roles to cypher to wank object'.[5]

From his first year as a television dramatist Potter's female characters were frequently discussed in unfavourable terms. 'The women were weird', Nancy Banks-Smith wrote in the *Sun* in her review of *Stand Up, Nigel Barton* (1965), summing up the major female characters as a 'witch, a bitch and a fool'. 'The schoolmistress', she wrote, 'was a nightmare to frighten little girls with. The girlfriend a tart on tranquillisers'.[6] 'What stuck in my mind', wrote Anthony Thwaite of *Angels Are So Few* (1970), 'was the bored Christine Hargreaves prowling restlessly about like a cat waiting for consummation.'[7] 'Chris lumbers hungrily round his typist', wrote John Carey of *Only Make Believe*, 'thawing her with a burly rant like a male chauvinist Pygmalion.'[8]

Closely linked with Potter's representation of women was his work's apparent need to explore and portray the darker side of human sexuality. Even the acclaimed *The Singing Detective* found criticism in some quarters for the scene in which the young Philip Marlow secretly watches his mother having sex. Accusing it of 'gross sexual violence', Mrs. Whitehouse argued that if Michael Grade (the then Head of Programmes at the BBC) thought the scene 'did not offend against good taste and decency, which it is his job to uphold, then he is not fit for the position he occupies.'[9] Grade had been called by its director Jon Amiel to vet the scene the Friday before transmission, but had decided it should not be cut. While he admitted that the BBC had received 50 phone calls of complaint he explained that 'a number of complaints were received after the warning about the explicit scene, but before the sequence was shown'.[10] Undaunted, Whitehouse wrote to the

Prime Minister and the Home Secretary arguing that broadcasting must be brought under the Obscene Publications Act. The
offending scene was also investigated by the Conservative MP
Norman Tebbit's television 'watchdog committee' which warned
that it was considering taking action.[11]

Three years later *Blackeyes* brought almost universal criticism
in its depiction of a beautiful female model and her fight for
personal autonomy. Despite Potter's assurance that the series was
an attempt to *deconstruct* female exploitation, the British press
universally condemned and ridiculed it. Patrick Stoddart summed
up the prevailing mood in *The Times*. 'It will be an Eng Lit A
Level question one day', he wrote, 'Dennis Potter is (a) The greatest
dramatist of the television age; (b) A flawed genius; (c) A dirty
old man; Discuss.'[12] The criticism was apparently taken very badly
by Potter himself, reaching a crescendo when a journalist on *Time
Out* accused him of being crippled in *mind* as well as body.[13]
Lipstick on Your Collar ran into further trouble. 'Nasty Lipstick
smears sex and violence over the screen', declared the political
editor of the *Sunday Times*.[14] Within the same week the Prime
Minister, John Major, had included violence in television drama
as part of the political agenda.[15]

Not all reactions to Potter's work, however, have been so
unfavourable, and many within and outside the industry have
actively defended his drama against accusations of sexual
exploitation and misogyny. Even so-called feminist critics like
Germaine Greer came out strongly at the time of his death to
defend the overall premise of his work. 'There's no point in being
outraged by Dennis Potter', she argued, 'you have to listen to
what he's saying. It's the truth that's outrageous – *not* Dennis
Potter.'[16] In the 1992 Annual Report of the Broadcasting Standards Council the writer Alan Plater similarly defended the writer's
need to examine and explore the darker areas of the human psyche.
As part of a Writer's Guild delegation which met Gerald Howarth
MP, (who was preparing a Private Member's Bill in 1987 aimed
at extending the Obscenity Laws to cover broadcasting) Plater
found much of his time was actually spent defending *The Singing Detective* against people who had only seen edited highlights
of the series provided by Mrs Mary Whitehouse. Plater argued
that Potter merely represented a long line of artists and dramatists for whom the issue of sex and sexuality was a vital and
fundamental element of the drama they produced:

Sex . . . recurs throughout the history of drama and its importance, almost invariably, is in its effect on other people: tragically in Othello, where the sex takes place in the mind of the
protagonists: farcically and off-stage in Feydeau or Ben Travers;
but traumatically and necessarily on-screen in Dennis Potter's
The Singing Detective, where the boy's glimpse of his mother's
extra-marital sexual encounter is a crucial element in a complex,
multi-level narrative.[17]

However, despite the general conception of Potter's drama as
sexually provocative, there is undoubtedly the discernible presence of a Puritan ethic running through much of his work as a
whole. His characters are caught between the bestial and the
holy, longing for the transcendence promised by the sexual act,
yet disgusted by the physical dynamics of the act itself. Entering television in the early 1960s, the time of the 'Lady Chatterley
trial' and on the cusp of the so-called sexual revolution, Potter's
drama was quickly categorised as sexually liberal and progressive. Yet his treatment of sex is seldom as straightforward as many
critics have lead us to believe. Potter's character are sexually
complex creatures, raging and warring against their baser instincts,
often battling furiously with the painful memories of childhood
sexual abuse. While the British press and media have tended to
label Potter as 'TV's Mr Filth', his work consistently portrayed
sex as an intensely problematic, highly complex and profoundly
menacing area of human behaviour. In this final chapter I shall
explore this apparent contradiction, focusing on the psychological structures which determine its vision of women, sex and
masculine desire.

THE PSYCHOLOGY OF LOVE:
PSYCHOANALYSIS AND THE MALE UNCONSCIOUS

Woman is the archetype of the oppressed consciousness: the
second sex. Her biological characteristics have been exploited
so that she has become the receptacle for the alienation all
men must feel; she *contains* man's otherness, and in doing so
is denied her own humanity.
    Juliet Mitchell, *Feminism and Psychoanalysis* (1974)[18]

The disturbing portrayal of women in Potter's drama most often centres around his male protagonists' fear and loathing of sex. In particular, they seem simultaneously driven and disgusted by their own sexual desires. In *Only Make Believe* Christopher Hudson describes the sexual act as 'that empty, milky, sticky, white scream'.[19] Certainly the sexual aftermath is filled with guilt and recriminations. 'Oh, those moments after we had made love', remembers Daniel Miller in *Hide and Seek*, '[t]he gloom that fell upon me was deep enough to make me want to die.' (p.156) In the same novel (in a passage later re-written for *The Singing Detective* (see below)) Daniel graphically describes his general distaste for the sexual act. An act which he explicitly associates with profound feelings of loss, violence and treachery:

> I am disgusted by the thought of spoiled human flesh. Mouth upon mouth, tongue against tongue, limb upon limb, skin rubbing at skin. Faces contort and organs spurt out a smelly stain, a sticky betrayal. The crudest joke against the human race lies in that sweaty farce by which we are first formed and given life. No wonder we carry about us a sense of inescapable loss, a burden of original sin, and a propensity to wild, anguished violence.
>
> Potter, 1973, pp.118–9

Not surprisingly sex and death are close companions in Potter's work. In *Double Dare* an actress/prostitute is strangled after making love with her client. Later he caresses her naked breasts as she lies murdered on his hotel bed. In *Secret Friends* Helen plunges a garden fork in the back of Martin at the moment of his sexual climax. In *Ticket to Ride* (the novel on which it is based) the connection is made even more explicitly. '"Yes" he said, and "Yes!" she said, as they rocked together, and then the pain that was coiled under his physical joy was suddenly much worse.... The blood pumping out of him more forcefully than the semen had done...' (p.184). So profound are these feelings of fear and disgust for the sexual act that often Potter's male protagonists reluctantly visit a psychiatrist or psychotherapist. 'You don't like sex', Dr Gibbon tells his neurotic patient in *The Singing Detective*, '... isn't it clear that you regard sexual intercourse with considerable distaste – or more to the point, with *fear*.' (p.54)

Frequently the sexual problems which obsess Potter's characters can be located in childhood and, in particular, the early relationship with their mother. Most famously in *The Singing Detective* the complex relationship between Philip Marlow and his mother (leading ultimately to her suicide) has a profound effect on his life, his attitude to sex and women in general. In *Moonlight on the Highway* (1969) Dr Chiltern lists an over-dependant mother as one of David's psychic wounds. In *Blue Remembered Hills* (1979) Donald Duck's disturbed behaviour seems to stem from an abusive and promiscuous mother. In particular, the majority of what were defined earlier as visitation dramas centres around an explicitly Oedipal crisis of sorts. The male visitors all behave, at times, like surrogate sons, often regressing to a state of early infancy. In *Angels Are So Few* the childless Cynthia even beds the innocent young angel who visits her. In contrast, the men's relationship with the father is always less than harmonious. Sam kills George in *The Bonegrinder*, Martin battles with Mr Bates in *Brimstone and Treacle*, and in *Rain on the Roof* (1980) Billy slays Janet's arrogant and unfaithful husband with a piece of broken glass.

However, it is in *Schmoedipus* where this Oedipal scenario is most explicit. The title of the play itself is a reference to a joke about a Jewish mother who takes her son to see a psychiatrist. When told he is suffering from an Oedipus complex she replies, 'Oedipus, Schmoedipus, what does it matter so long as the boy loves his mother?'[20] The play itself, another visitation drama, centres around an American youth who claims to be the long lost son of a middle-aged housewife. Although now in his early twenties he behaves like a small child, urging his mother Elizabeth to read him bedtime stories and play childish games. 'I spy with my little eye', he declares, 'something beginning with – B', his hand reaching provocatively toward her breasts. 'Did you ever feed me?' he asks, his mouth resting suggestively near a nipple. What unites these Oedipal dramas, is an anxiety around sexuality which appears to take place around the image of the mother. Apparently unhappy with their adult lives, these visiting young men return to the family home and regress accordingly. As the psychologist Otto Fenichel has put it, '[w]hen the adult person later experiences sexual disappointment, he tends to fall back to infantile sexuality. The result is that the conflicts that raged about his sexuality in childhood likewise become mobilised again.'[21]

The critic needs to be exceptionally careful when applying

psychoanalytical theory to any work of fiction, more often than not it results in dubious attempts at psychoanalysing 'the *author*.' Leaving the issue of the author to one side, however, psycho-analysis may help explain some of the more difficult aspects of Potter's work. In particular, his characters' damaged relationship with their mother seems to result in a form of adult sexual neurosis – a neurosis which can be understood through the application of psychoanalytical theory. According to the psychologist Melanie Klein, the core of the super-ego is established in the child's early relationship with its female parent. The frustrations which it inevitably encounters in receiving complete satisfaction from her results in the child splitting the world into good and bad objects. In cases where the mother imago is damaged (through death, separation or emotional rejection) this split becomes intensified. As a result, the child learns to divide the world into 'extremely bad and *extremely perfect* objects. . . .'[22] Such a framework may help explain the way Potter's male protagonists regard the female sex. Indeed, some critics have applied a similar scenario to the work of the Romantic poets. According to Barbara Schapiro, the unresolved dynamics of the mother and son relationship lies at the heart of Romanticism, and has a profound effect on their portrayal of women:

> The image of the woman, whether she figures as an ideal goddess or a serpentine vampire, a deserted woman or, more frequently, as the ever-maternal Nature, is central to the poetry of the Romantics. The relationship with the woman which the poetry either expresses or implies is rooted psychologically in the relationship with the first woman of all our lives, the mother.[23]

Like the Romantics, Potter's male protagonists do tend to perceive women as either idealised or depraved creatures, to be feared or seduced accordingly. As John Wyver puts it, Potter's women 'are either angels, before they are seduced (before the Fall), or they are whores.'[24] Certainly, his work has its fair share of angels and idealised feminine creatures. Many of his women represent a vision of beauty and loveliness which inspire his male protagonists with a glimpse of possible redemption. They are frequently described as the 'girl in the songs' (see *Moonlight on the Highway*, *Brimstone and Treacle*, *The Singing Detective* and

Karaoke). 'Never thought I'd see an angel', sings Arthur when he first spies the beautiful Eileen in *Pennies From Heaven*. Women, however, can also assume all of the *negative* feelings and psychological neurosis which disturb his male protagonists. From *The Bonegrinder* to *Karaoke*, Potter's work is literally filled with whores, vamps and prostitutes. Indeed, in *Moonlight on the Highway* David Peters actually admits to paying for sex 136 times, while for Daniel Miller in *Hide and Seek* the figure has risen to 156! (Potter, 1973, p.19).

While clearly not explaining all of Potter's women (one thinks of Nicola Marlow in *The Singing Detective* or Joan in *Pennies from Heaven*) the dichotomy between angel and whore is a recurrent feature in much of the work. Eileen in *Pennies from Heaven*, who is undoubtedly one of Potter's strongest and most self-reliant female characters (smarter, braver and certainly more pragmatic than the self-pitying and adulterous Arthur) is literally reduced to the same simple equation. She begins typically enough as the virgin schoolmistress in the Forest of Dean, but after her Fall (Arthur's seduction) she is banished from 'Eden' and forced to live as Lulu, the London prostitute. Indeed, many of Potter's female angels seem too pure for sex altogether, and need to be transformed in some way. Many of his male protagonists secretly fantasise that their wives or partners are whores. Of course, the wish literally becomes true for Arthur, but for Martin in *Double Dare* the desire is translated onto an actress who is indistinguishable from a prostitute (played by the same actress) whom we intermittently see at her trade. In *Hide and Seek*, Daniel Miller confesses to his wife that he can only achieve sexual satisfaction by pretending that she were a 'tart I had picked up in a bar or on the street corner'(p.156).

Psychoanalysis suggests that such a desire originates in the man's inability to enjoy sex with a lover unless she is debased and objectified in some way. His wife, whom he loves and respects, can no longer perform such a function. According to Freud, the 'erotic life of such people remains dissociated, divided between two channels, the same two that are personified in art as heavenly and earthly (or animal) love. Where such men love they have no desire and where they desire they cannot love.'[25] Such a scenario is only too apparent in Potter's work, reflected in the continual conflict between the flesh and the spirit, the bestial and the holy. Women simply become a symbol of this fundamental dichotomy.

They represent both the promise of transcendence (Man's holy imagination) or the threat of castration (man's animal self and other); but rarely an entity in their own right. This tendency to cast woman as other was clearly something Potter himself identified later in his career. Talking of his male protagonists, he told Graham Fuller, '[t]hey blame women because that's the source of their unease and their wistfulness and their sexual tension. That's traditional male language. You blame it on the temptress, in religious culture the unclean vessel. But of course it's coming from the man.' (Fuller, 1993, p.133)

Such a psychoanalytical context is a helpful way to uncover the mechanics by which Potter's construction of women and male sexuality is conceived. Whilst it is advisable not to exaggerate the Freudian dynamics of his work, it is undeniable that many of his male protagonists display a profound and acute fear of both women and sex, and that such a fear is almost always linked with repressed and unconscious feelings originating in early childhood. In my discussion of the following three serials the implications of these ideas will become clearer and more explicit. The ambiguous feelings towards sex and the mother, and the archetypal dichotomy between angel and whore is vividly and controversially portrayed in *Casanova*. The links between misogyny and the role and influence of the mother is uncompromisingly developed through the physical and psychical suffering of Philip Marlow in *The Singing Detective*. Finally in *Blackeyes* the commercial and sexual manipulation by men of women is explored in an explicitly psychological narrative which lays the degradation of female sexuality directly at the hands of its male characters. Such a narrative development suggests an increasingly self-reflexive and self-critical strain in Potter's work, which gradually came to question its own unconscious portrayal of women, sexuality and the male unconscious.

CASANOVA (1971)

On the basis of psychoanalytic theory, we are prepared to derive such forces of overwhelming guilt and punishment – connected with strongly sexual fantasies – from the Oedipus complex. Clearly the endless series (of seduced women) along with 'the injured third person' characteristics of the Don Juan type appear to confirm this analytical interpretation: that many women whom he must always replace anew represent to him the one irreplaceable mother.

Otto Rank *The Don Juan Legend*[26]

Casanova was Potter's first move into the realms of the television serial and was originally broadcast on BBC 2 during November and December 1971. Throughout the 1960s he had concentrated exclusively on the single play which varied in length from 30–90 minutes. *Casanova* by comparison consisted of six separate episodes, lasting fifty-five minutes each and costing a total of £300,000. The serial was not a form, however, which the playwright seemed to accept willingly. Potter was reported to regard this particular series less as six separate episodes than as one six-hour play unfortunately chopped up into segments.[27] It suggests a writer who was reluctantly accepting the new format of television drama in Britain which saw a shift in the 1970s away from the single play towards serials. If the BBC had hoped that *Casanova* was to be a purely historical costume drama (along the lines of the BBC's own *The Six Wives of Henry VIII* or Thames Television's *Edward and Mrs Simpson*) they were to be sadly disappointed. Directed by John Glenister (episodes 1,2,4) with Mark Cullingham (episodes 3,5,6) and produced by Mark Shivas, its historical setting in eighteenth-century Venice did little to prevent Potter from addressing the very contemporary issues of sex and sexuality which inevitably attracted accusations of 'pornography' and 'obscenity'.

Mary Whitehouse was the most prominent of its critics with her charges against it of 'lewdness and gross indecency'.[28] Potter typically responded in fighting form, arguing that Whitehouse was 'an ignorant and dangerous woman' who was 'incapable of grasping the true meaning of the work'.[29] The series itself seemed to attract a mixed reaction from the critics. According to Clive James, Potter's depiction of Casanova had made 'an interstellar vacancy of what history had previously agreed to be an exceptionally interesting mind.'[30] 'What was missing from it', Stuart Hood wrote, 'was any sense of the Casanova celebrated by Luigi Barzini as a man of great gifts. . . .'[31] Not all the reviews, however, were so unfavourable. In *The Times* Barry Norman found it a deeply serious and compelling work. 'Mr Potter is not there to titillate us', he explained, 'but, with luck, to make us think. . . .'[32]

Time, however, seems to have done little to restore its reputation. Hilary Kingsley and Geoff Tibballs' history of British television remembers it simply as 'a succession of actresses in varying states of undress', while the BBC documentary tribute to Potter broadcast at the time of his death failed even to mention it at all.[33]

It was not surprising that given the BBC's preference for historical drama that Potter should be attracted to the Casanova story. Inspired by Giacomo Casanova's posthumously published twelve-volume *Memoirs* (1826–38) it must have seemed an ideal opportunity to address the contemporary fascination with the moral implications of sex and sexuality within a seemingly historical setting. According to Potter, a new translation of Casanova's memoirs came into *The Times* when he was working there as a book critic. Immediately realising the dramatic potential it offered him as a writer he refused to review the journals and even stopped reading them.[34] What Potter presents is a profoundly original piece of television drama which takes up and subverts the mythological status of the Casanova story.

Casanova is, in fact, a crucial and important play in the Potter oeuvre. The constant shifting in flashback, flashforward, fantasy and hallucination makes it one of his most characteristic of dramas. It explicitly confronts the twin themes of sexuality and religion in a manner which both structurally and thematically can compare only with *The Singing Detective*. Indeed, like Philip Marlow, Casanova is literally a prisoner of his past life and towards the end of his confinement even suffers from a dreadful skin condition. 'I have become so reduced in this place', he laments, 'I have reached the essence of myself.' (part 2 p.75)[35] Certainly he appears to suffer from a form of personal crisis which leaves him ill, isolated and spiritually bankrupt. Only the power of memory appears to liberate him from his present condition as he reflects on the details and experiences of his past life. And like many of Potter's characters, Casanova clearly suffers from a troubled sexuality which is in conflict with the religious and moral values of his day. Indeed, his desire to make love to a countless number of women betrays a complex and dangerous form of sexual neurosis. 'I assumed Casanova must have had that thing they biologically refer to as *tristitia post coitum* – the sadness after fucking', Potter has explained (Graham Fuller, 1993, p.70). And it is this insatiable desire for sex and its personal, moral, religious and spiritual aftermath which Potter examines via the Casanova myth.

Spanning a total of nearly six hours *Casanova* tells the story of a sexual compulsive struggling with the obsessive demands of his own insatiable libido, and battling with the strict morality of eighteenth century religious mores. In the first episode, Casanova (Frank Finlay) is thrown into jail for his moral and religious corruption. In his claustrophobic, rat-invested and dehumanising cell, tormented by his ignorant jailer, Lorenzo (Norman Rossington), he begins the detailed reflection of his life. The introspection forced upon him by his incarceration breaks down the power of repression and memories flood back, producing a cathartic and revealing montage of his past life. 'Sounds. Smells. They – carry us back', he tells his irritating cell mate, Schalon (Patrick Newell). 'They remind us. Secretly. Without words. Without warning. They come upon us like – like wolves from the past. Ravening wolves' (part 1 p.56). And it is this Proustian belief in the power of memory and imagination which both torments and enlightens Potter's hero, and sets him struggling blindly towards redemption.[36] Imprisoned for a total of five years he eventually escapes and we see him (in flashforward) exiled in England. In an unrequited obsession for the virginal Pauline (Valerie Gearon) he suddenly reveals to her the evil and treacherous devices by which he has spent his life seducing women. Finally alone, except for his young and lovely nurse, Caroline (Gillian Hills), he dies an old and seemingly broken man.

The actor Frank Finlay, who had played Christ in Potter's *Son of Man* for the stage, was chosen for the lead. Indeed, there are striking similarities between the two roles. Like Potter's Christ, Casanova is thrown into a wilderness where he is forced to search and grope for some form of spiritual awakening and personal redemption. They both suffer from hallucinations and battle with a form of spirituality which is riddled with pain, feelings of doubt and moments of feverish excitement. And like Christ, he is both tortured and liberated by the fundamental choices which create the human condition. 'Freedom', he tells Valenglart (David Swift), '[t]he one thing which makes us human. Or – divine.' (p.4. p.35) It is this *freedom*, both sexual and religious, which the play attempts to address. Incarcerated, he is forced to reflect upon his past life and the nature and consequence of human freedom. Yet in prison, through memory and hallucination, the nature of his own sexuality becomes suggestively darker. Written at the beginning of the 1970s, it implicitly addresses the nature of sexual freedom, and the power of human sexuality to both liberate and imprison the human soul. In the light of the 1960's sexual revolution it explores the consequences of a new and dangerous permissiveness.

It is clear that Casanova adores beautiful women; usually virgins. Before their inevitable seduction every desirable woman he sees is an angel and a vision of purity. Christina (Zienial Merton) whom he meets, chaperoned by her uncle, is like every love-object he encounters, a completely innocent being who appears to represent the virtues he so painfully lacks. 'Christina is . . . *good*', he tells his friend Bragadin (Geoffrey Wincott), '. . . and totally without guile. . . . She doesn't know the meaning of evil or malice. . . . She is an angel. An angel!' (part 1 p.73). 'You have a beautiful body', he tells the virginal Pauline, '[y]our limbs somehow manage to express *grace*, something inside you, something inaccessible to a person such as me . . .' (part 5 p.79). Clearly such images form the basis of his relationship with a large section of the opposite sex. As he remembers seducing Christina, so a montage of images remind us of the endless list of angels he has similarly worshipped and tricked into bed. Yet he seems unable or unwilling to build a lasting and sustaining relationship with any one of the many women he seduces. Although he appears totally besotted by the beautiful and innocent Christina, he refuses to give her any form of emotional and loving commitment. After seducing her by promising his hand in marriage, he quickly introduces her to his friend Carlo in the hope he will take her attentions away from him. 'Novelty', he explains early in episode one, 'is the tyrant of the soul.' (part 1 p.11)

Women, then, offer Casanova an endless challenge, almost as if their very purity and innocence presents some kind of threat. He tells the innocent Pauline of his treacherous ways in a rare moment of self-disclosure. Finally entrapped in his lies she is about to succumb when he pulls himself back. 'Another minute', he confesses, 'and I would have been on top of you, thrusting my way to the only paradise I know.' (part 5 p.83). Yet when that challenge is met (almost *instantly* after making love) his interest fades. He actually refers to this endless pursuit of women as an illness or psychological condition. 'I can't stay long in any one place', he tells Scahlon when they meet in England, 'I can't stay long with any one person. Always I must find new things, new people. New bodies. . . . No, it is a disease, Schalon. A fever.' (part 5 p.49). Indeed, Potter gives us clear indications that

Casanova's obsession with young and virginal women is linked with a profound form of sexual neurosis. In Episode 5 (*Fevers of Love*) he hallucinates that he is visited by a Nun in his cell. Not the 'epitome of gentleness and feminine piety' she at first seems, she acts more like a *whore*. 'No', he insists, when she begins to undress for him, to which the 'Nun' replies '[n]o mother. . . . No sister' (p.9). Unable to control his desires, however, he slowly reaches out to caress her breasts. And as he does, so she lets out a *'shrill, mocking, whorishly contemptuous laugh. . . .'* (pp.9–10).

Such an extreme hallucination would certainly appear to portray some deep-rooted psychosexual condition. The 'Nun's' pun on mother and sister suggests that Casanova's problem with women can be traced back to the earliest of relationships with the opposite sex. Indeed, such a dream or hallucination could be regarded by Freudian psychoanalysis as re-enacting the origins of the male castration complex. As the young male infant originally believes women to possess a penis, Freud argues that the boy's first sight of the *female* genitals (usually his sister's or mother's) produces a fear and horror in the young male child.[37] Subsequently, the neurotic individual may come to regard women in two separate groups; the castrated (the wicked and sexually permissive woman) and the non-castrated (the perfect mother or virgin).[38] When Lorenzo wakes him, Casanova cries, 'all the same – You are all the same' (p.12). Seen in this light, the hallucination seems to portray Casanova's unconscious fear that women are all the same; that is, they are castrated. Even without the aid of psychoanalysis, the hallucination clearly reflects his inability to see women as anything other than sexual objects; unconsciously split between the morally idealised (the Nun) and the sexually corrupt (the Whore).

Such a neurosis would seem to explain Casanova's compulsion to see women either as angels or whores. Women are whores when sexually experienced (that is, their castrated state is emphasised) and are angels when still virginal and sexually inexperienced. As a result, he can only be attracted to young, innocent virgins. This may help explain his form of *tristitia post coitum* which results after seduction in the discovery that women are, in fact, *all the same*. Yet this constant need to re-discover the non-castrated woman forces him to pursue an endless list of virginal seductions. Psychoanalysis has frequently associated such a condition of hypersexuality with deep-rooted feelings for the mother. Freud argues that in early infancy the maintenance of self-esteem is dependent on the child's narcissistic fusion with the female parent. If, however, for some reason, the individual is not willing to forgo his narcissistic perfection in his childhood, the sufferer becomes obsessed with the sexual act as a means of receiving narcissistic supplies and thereby maintaining his self-esteem. The love-object, on the other hand, becomes simply a mother-imago with no character or personality of her own. The sexual act brings no lasting relief and the sufferer's longing for self-esteem forces him to pursue one sexual partner after another.

It is a condition frequently connected with that other legendary seducer of women, Don Juan. As the psychologist Otto Rank has put it, 'the characteristic Don Juan fantasy of conquering countless women, which has made the hero into a masculine ideal, is ultimately based on the unattainability of the mother and the compensatory substitute for her.'[39] Seen in this context, Casanova pursues young and virginal women in the unconscious hope they will provide the narcissistic fusion he once experienced with his mother (before, that is, the arrival of the Oedipal and castration complex). And nowhere is this more evident than at Casanova's death. In Episode 6 (*Golden Apples*), now an old and sick man, he is nursed by the beautiful Caroline. On his death bed, refusing a priest, he asks only one last request. Left alone with Caroline he begs that he be allowed to suck her nipples. With some apprehension the scene ends with her unlacing the ribbons at the front of her dress.

Such a conclusion to Casanova's life seems entirely appropriate. Here the unconscious memory of the narcissistic fusion with the mother is dramatically and graphically portrayed. As a dying man Casanova is once again reduced to a child's dependency on the woman, and his suckling of Caroline's breasts suggests a final and irreversible reconciliation with a completely satisfying mother-imago. In this sense, the threat of castration is finally subverted by Casanova's total regression into a pregenital fusion with the mother. If, as Otto Rank suggests, the 'Don Juan complex' involves the endless search for the 'irreplaceable mother', then this is surely one of its most explicit dramatisations. The reading (by Frank Finlay in voice over) from Virgil, certainly suggests a total fusion with life, death, sex and Nature. The explicit correlation between Caroline's breasts and Virgil's golden apples, suggests a final narcissistic fusion between Casanova and Mother Earth.

'Let the hard oak bring forth golden apples', Finlay reads in voice-over, '[l]et narcissus bloom on the elder. . . .' (part 6 p.110).

Such a reading of *Casanova* may seem exaggeratedly Freudian, but it is undeniable that Potter is here dealing explicitly with the complex issues surrounding the psychosexual dynamics of a compulsive neurotic. Whatever interpretation is offered, it is difficult to ignore the extent to which the serial foregrounds the dark and desperate workings of Casanova's tortured mind. He is a figure obsessed and frequently liberated by beauty in many forms, but he is also a pathological narcissist who is ultimately unable to sustain a lasting and satisfactory relationship with *any* woman. Like so many of Potter's male protagonists, he seems in mourning for some earlier and prepubescent state before the Fall. Although apparently obsessed by the sexual act, the ambiguous nature of that obsession suggests an individual who seeks in women a regressive return to the unresolved sexual dynamics of early infancy. He is haunted and driven by sex, yet unable to see women in any form other than mother or whore.

It could be argued, however, that the drama does little to deconstruct Casanova's neurotic condition, and may even *romanticise* the philosophical struggle of his disturbed psychological state. His view of women as angels and whores appears, on the whole, to be generally substantiated by the drama itself. His long line of seduced women are either so stupid or unbelievably naive that we can hardly blame him for not wanting a committed relationship. At times we may even sympathise with his inability to find a partner who could match his own intelligence and poetic sensitivity. We are prohibited from exploring the workings of a female mind, as Casanova is clearly meant to provide the interior consciousness from which the whole drama is intended to be viewed. The direction certainly portrays the obsessive point of view of its protagonist. When he first sets eyes on Pauline, for example, he is sitting down, his head momentarily in his hands. As he becomes aware of her presence in the room so the camera quickly positions her from his point of view. Slowly moving up from her feet it presents her first as a headless body before finally resting on her face and plunging neckline. In this way, the camera emphasises Casanova's own objectification of women, a perspective which the viewer is continually encouraged to adopt. Similarly, his long line of conquests are brought to us in a recurring montage, their arms outstretched to the camera they offer their bodies and naked breasts as much to the gaze of the viewer as to Casanova himself.

The final shot of Casanova's silhouette standing on the rooftops, a 'sparkling, moon-lit Venice, shining almost like the "Holy City"' (p.110), suggests an image of Christ (or as the script puts it a revolving angel) which seems a touch flamboyant even for Potter's own Romantic sensibilities. The thinker and sufferer is inevitably male, and the woman, an ego ideal through which the man momentarily finds liberation and release. Consequently, the women remain the passive objects of male admiration and fear, sexualised bodies who are easily flattered and seduced or who cling onto their chastity with an almost frigid determination. Ultimately they have no other purpose than to satisfy the man, simply a receptacle for Casanova's own alienation and philosophical suffering. Despite his apparent regret for the life he has left, it is never made clear how much Casanova actually discovers about himself through the passing of his life – which ends, as it begun, with his narcissistic fusion with the female flesh. Finally the image of a dying old man suckling at the breasts of a beautiful young girl is more pathetic than it is heroic.

THE SINGING DETECTIVE (1986)

The darkness that fills the mirror of the past, which lurks in a dark corner or obscures a dark passage out of the oppressively dark city, is not merely the key adjective of so many *film noir* titles but the obvious metaphor for the condition of the protagonist's mind.

Alain Silver and Elizabeth Ward[40]

'This is the piece of work I'd like to remembered for', Potter told *The Times* eight months before the first episode of *The Singing Detective* was even broadcast. 'It goes leagues forward from anything I've written.'[41] In the week of transmission the *Radio Times* devoted its entire front page to the series, complete with a colourful spread and a lengthy interview with its writer inside.[42] Expectations were unusually high, but the reviews did little to deflate the feeling that this was a special television event. It was not long into the series when the critics were unanimously hailing it as a masterpiece of the small screen. In a review of Episode 3 in *The Times* entitled 'Music to my eyes', Nicolas Shakespeare declared that 'a man who can create such a dramatisation of his own life, illness and fantasies – and then transform this into an entertaining exploration of the creative process – is quite simply a genius.'[43] Reviewing the final episode he concluded that it was 'the best thing I have ever seen on television', proving that 'we have only started scratching the surface of what it is possible to do with this medium.'[44] 'There's television and then there is *The Singing Detective*', Hugo Williams proclaimed in the *New Statesman*. 'It's so good your mouth's hanging open.'[45]

Made in association with the Australian Broadcasting Corporation, *The Singing Detective* was first shown in Britain over a period of six weeks on BBC 1, commencing on Sunday 17 November 1986. Since then it has proved Potter's most enduring and successful work. The series also found popularity abroad in countries such as Germany, Sweden and the USA. In the States it was first aired on a few PBS stations in 1988 and was later released onto the big screen in venues such as New York's Public Theatre. A few critics like J. O'Connor of the *New York Times* helped to spread the show's reputation. Vincent Canby's review was accompanied by the headline 'Is The Year's Best Film On TV?' He claimed that Potter had 'single-handedly restored the reputation of the screenwriter, at least in television. He's made writing for television respectable and, possibly, an art.'[46]

Produced by Kenith Trodd and John Harris *The Singing Detective* was Potter's first return to the BBC after his generally disappointing involvement with LWT.[47] Yet despite the successful Potter-Trodd collaboration, the script was initially turned down by directors like Stephen Frears, Richard Eyre, Malcolm Mobrays, Pat O'Connor and was finally directed by the relative newcomer to television, Jon Amiel. Amiel had been a literary manager in the theatre, a story editor in television and had directed only a few television films including BBC 2's *Silent Twins*. Once fired as a director for the Royal Shakespeare Company, Amiel (now a successful film director in America) remembers his first uneasy meetings with Potter, and his belief that certain aspects of the script needed to be re-worked. Even so, he was clearly horrified when Potter took to re-writing the entire six episodes only weeks before shooting. Although Amiel is now quite rightly disappointed that his own input in the production was not fully credited (see Chapter One), he still remembers clearly the sense of excitement he felt on reading

Potter's original script. 'I knew for an absolute certainty, because all my training had been basically in script development . . . that I was reading a masterpiece', he told Joost Hunningher. 'The thought of directing this thing filled me with complete terror and the thought of not being asked to direct it filled me with as much terror.'[48]

The serial is best understood as the sensational continuation of themes and structural techniques which Potter had been pursuing and developing since the early 1960s. It reveals, in particular, a dramatic exploration of the way his work gradually came to confront and even deconstruct its own portrayal of women and sexuality. However, it is telling how many critics managed to ignore the central concern of the drama; that is, one man's painful battle against a cruel and masochistic form of misogyny. Philip Marlow is the dramatic culmination of Potter's sick and Romantic protagonists, who, unlike his predecessors, is forced through illness and psychoanalysis to face up to and cautiously understand the psychological make-up of his own disturbed and tortured sexuality.

Despite the drama's apparently complex techniques and conflicting narrative levels, the structure of *The Singing Detective* is surprisingly simple. Philip Marlow (Michael Gambon) is a patient in a busy hospital ward suffering from an acute case of psoriatic arthropathy. In bed Marlow reluctantly interacts with other patients, doctors and nurses and remembers his childhood during the 1930s. In flashback, we learn that as a boy he once spied on his mother's (Alison Steadman) infidelity and experienced profound alienation from both home and school. We eventually discover that Mrs Marlow committed suicide by throwing herself in the Thames, an action for which he ultimately blames himself. While in hospital he fantasises about his estranged wife Nicola (Janet Suzman) whom he believes is conspiring with her lover, Mark Finney (Patrick Malahide), to steal the rights of the screenplay for his novel, *The Singing Detective*. Marlow also re-writes this detective story in his head and suffers from bizarre and surreal hallucinations. All these separate narrative levels are brilliantly interwoven in a complex dramatic structure which continually intersect and even collide (different characters, for example, are played by the same actor/actress) so that one narrative frame is constantly juxtaposed with the next. With the help of Dr Gibbon (Bill Paterson) Marlow gradually begins to realise how his childhood experiences not only shaped the landscape of his fiction and his fantasies, but has also determined his neurotic view of women and sex. At its conclusion he is finally able to walk out of hospital, accompanied by his wife, and with a better understanding of himself and his past.

One way to understand the drama is to see the whole series taking place, as it were, in the inside of Marlow's head. A hint of the drama's uniquely subjective perspective is given early in the first episode (*Skin*) when the extent of Marlow's psoriasis brings disgusted reactions from the other patients. Although it is clearly impossible for Marlow to have overheard the abusive comments, he seems strangely able to recount their every word to himself. According to the published script 'he imitates *exactly* what he mostly cannot possibly have heard. That is, he lip-synchronise precisely to the real voices' (p.6). Potter's use of the 'lip-synch' term here (usually applied to his characters' habit of bursting into song) clearly suggests the way the drama as a whole is meant to be viewed. We are explicitly directed to see the series through Marlow's authorial perspective. The multiple narrative levels take place from the interior landscape of Marlow's sick mind. The most striking example of this comes in Episode 4 (*Clues*) when Nicola and Mark Finney are planning to steal Marlow's screenplay. 'I know this sounds crazy', Finney tells Nicola, 'I feel almost as though he has made this all up' (p.147). Later they actually talk while providing the appropriate punctuation and stage directions to their speech and movements as if their very thoughts and actions were written in advance. 'I have this awful-', Finney explains, 'I have this awful dash he stops himself comma and all but shudders full stop.' (p.149). What this suggests is that Marlow is the drama's centre of consciousness, and the pivotal focalizer through which every scene and narrative level must be read. The techniques – compelling and complex as they are – are simply a means of delivering what Potter has referred to as his tendency towards 'first-person narrative' (Potter, 1994, p.12).

Marlow is certainly the crucial point at which all the narrative levels clash, occasionally collide and finally connect. He is the narrative centre of the series and every piece of dialogue and direction is seen (sometimes explicitly written) through his eyes. The childhood flashbacks, the detective narrative, the fantasy involving his wife, Mark Finney and the missing screenplay, even many of the apparently naturalistic hospital scenes are clearly meant to be seen through the texture of *his* imagination. In Episode 5 (*Pitter Patter*) the entrance of the mysterious two men from the detective novel into the hospital ward, suggests the extent to which Marlow's perspective is controlling the events. A little later the same two men find themselves literally lost in Marlow's childhood forest and overhear his father calling for his ten year old boy. It is as if they are caught in Marlow's head, trapped within the boundaries of his tortured imagination. There are suggestions of a postmodern subversion of narrative forms (although these two characters actually resemble figures from a Samuel Beckett or Tom Stoppard play) but more importantly they suggest a brilliant continuation of Potter's notion of the inter-iorisation process (see Chapter Two). *The Singing Detective* is, above all, a *psychological* thriller, and its authorial perspective, conflicting generic levels and complex narrative structure is designed to allow the audience an unique insight into the mind of its sick and troubled protagonist.

If we take the detective story first we can clearly see how it gradually reveals Marlow's psychological condition. The patient and the private eye (both played by Michael Gambon) share, of course, the same name (minus the 'e') of the fictional detective created by Raymond Chandler. Amiel's direction, Potter's period dialogue, the chiaroscuro light and shadow and Max Harris's moody music all conspires to produce an effective and convincing pastiche of 1940s *film noir*. As one might expect, Marlow's detective novel (set during the second world war, the time also of his childhood) is populated by *femmes fatales*, prostitutes, spies, traitors and cops. Like Woody Allen's *Play it Again Sam* (1972) (where the neurotic protagonist is guided in his pursuit of women by the ice-cool figure of 'Humphrey Bogart') Marlow's alter-ego is everything the hospital patient is not. The private-eye, complete with raincoat and 'mid-Atlantic, little side-of-the-mouth quips' (p.100), is tough, macho, fit and street-wise. 'OK. OK. So what's the story? Who's the dame?' he asks Mark Binney when assigned to his case. When Binney enquires how he knows there is a woman involved he replies, '[t]here's always a dame. . . . There's always a body, too. I know that. You know that.' (p.50)

It is this generic portrayal of women which makes the *film noir* tradition such an ideal vehicle through which we are allowed to view Marlow's own psychological relationship with the opposite sex. Indeed, critics have identified the role of the duplicitous women and her explicit connections with death and desire as a crucial image of *film noir*. According to Janey Place, '[f]ilm noir is a male fantasy, as is most of our art. Thus woman here as elsewhere is defined by her sexuality: the dark lady has access to it and the virgin does not.'[49] And it is this tendency within the genre which allows Potter to make explicit connections between Marlow's psychological condition and the pulp novel he is writing. The unfaithfulness of his mother and her subsequent suicide will provide the psychological landscape which is literally mirrored by his cheap piece of fiction. Seen in this light, the detective story is simply the fictional representation of Marlow's own deep-rooted fears and desires.

The detective genre also allows Potter to make explicit connections between detection and psychoanalysis. To be 'cured' Marlow has to find out 'who done it?'; the title, aptly enough, of the final episode. When Marlow asks Dr Gibbon why he has gone to the bother of obtaining a copy of his out-of-print novel, he replies that he is looking for 'clues'. Clearly the detective motif represents Marlow's deeper search for the 'clues' to his own neurosis. 'When I grow up, I be going to be – a detective', he declares as a 10 year old boy high in the trees of his beloved forest. 'I'll find out. I'll find out who did it!' (p.77). As Therese Lichtenstein puts it, 'the detective story becomes an allegory for the therapeutic experience . . .',[50] and it is this psychological 'who done it?' which is the true mystery of the narrative. The detective story itself (which involves some form of espionage with both Russian and former Nazi agents) only offers us a greater insight into the mind of Potter's sick and tortured protagonist.

The popular songs provide a similar function. Like the majority of Potter's male protagonists, Philip Marlow clearly suffers from severe repression. As the private-eye puts it, 'I can sing the singing. I can think the thinking. . . . But you're not going to catch me feeling the feeling. No sir.' (p.86) Yet the songs from his childhood force him to confront painfully personal issues. This device is fundamentally different in purpose from the use of songs in *Pennies from Heaven*. Unlike Arthur Parker – for whom the songs evoke a visionary zeal – these popular melodies clearly bring unconscious and disturbing fears to the surface. The majority of the lyrics centre around issues of sexual anxiety and betrayal. *Paper Doll, Blues in the Night, I Get Along Without You Very Well, Do I Worry? After You're Gone, You Always Hurt the One You Love* all centre around troubled relationships and frustrated sexual desire. Nostalgic perhaps in their period orchestration (they importantly allow narrative convergence from hospital to childhood to the detective story) they resonate with disturbing accuracy Marlow's present and past psychology: hence their prominent position in his memories and hallucinations. Even when they are not dealing specifically in matters of a sexual nature, they nonetheless force Marlow to delve deep into his unconscious and repressed desires. *The Teddy Bears' Picnic* accompanies his recollection of his mother's infidelity in the forest ('If you go down to the woods today/ You're in for a big surprise') and *Dry Bones* portrays his feeling of alienation both from his own body and the medical staff at the hospital.

Surprisingly, perhaps, Marlow's illness provides a similar function. To put matters of biography to one side, it is clear that the skin condition fulfils a variety of dramatic functions. Like Casanova's imprisonment, it forces Potter's protagonist to reflect on his past life in a long and painful period of self-discovery. It strips him of his mobility and, in a sense, his masculinity so that he is forced to reconstruct himself as a subject. The 'cracked, scabbed, scaled, swollen, scarlet and snowy white' skin (p.6) provides the perfect (physical) metaphor for Marlow's troubled mind. Indeed, he appears to see his condition as the physical manifestation of some deeper *psychological* disturbance. 'The skin, after all', Dr Gibbon reminds him, 'is extremely *personal*, is it not? The temptation is to believe that the ills and the poisons of the mind or the personality have somehow or other erupted straight out on to the skin.' (p.56) Like Potter's Daniel Miller in *Hide and Seek* (who also suffers from the same condition), the disease is explicitly linked with profound feelings of self-disgust and sexual guilt. 'I visited this nasty ailment . . . upon Daniel Miller', the narrator explains in Potter's first novel, 'in order to show how the guilt or evil in his mind finds physical expression in and on his body. If I had done the things he has done, if I had copulated with whores so indiscriminately and shamelessly, then I too would expect to find some signs on my frame. . . .' (p.49).

It is in the troubled landscape of his childhood that Marlow (and the viewer) is able to locate the roots of his psychological/ biological condition. The childhood flashbacks enable us to connect all the different strands of the narrative together. We first see the nine year old Philip sitting alone high in the bows of a tree in his childhood forest. Amiel's decision to give us a high camera shot above the trees, as we move slowly into close-up, initially grants us a view of the whole landscape as if the boy were simply a part of the natural habitat. And it is from this heavenly perch that Philip recites the Lord's Prayer. When he is taken to London with his mother it is the forest to which he longs to return. 'Where be the trees?' he asks. 'Where be the oaks?' (p.129). In Episode 3 (*Lovely Days*) he observes his mother and Raymond secretly making their way through the undergrowth while perched in his beloved tree. The sight of this illicit couple, however, is responsible for his sudden Fall from grace. Spotting an insect on a branch he mechanically kills it with the ball of his thumb. Turning to the camera he tells us, 'I cont abide things that creep and crawl and . . . I cont abide dirt.' (p.113) In this way, the creeping and crawling of Raymond and Mrs Marlow is explicitly connected with Philip's 'Fall', while their apparently innocent references to biblical imagery connects them with another fallen couple. 'Oh, you dirty *devil*, Ray', declares Mrs. Marlow. 'You don't want no *angel* doost?' he replies. 'Don't think so much of yourself', is the answer. 'There's always another *apple* in the barrel.' (emphasis added – p.112)

As the boy symbolically makes his way *down* the tree to get a closer view, the couple have already begun making love. Meanwhile, the mature Marlow (in a cut to the present) is seen listening to the death of a patient next to him in hospital. As the past and present are intercut, so the sound of the lovemaking is confused with the doctor's attempt to resuscitate the dying man. And when the forest lovers finish their sexual climax so the patient is finally pronounced *dead*. This explicit connection between sex and death reiterates the child's fall from grace. The human body, once a transparent vessel of the natural world, becomes associated with dirt, death and betrayal. In particular, it causes Philip to view sex as something foul and brutal. As the script puts it, '[f]rom the boy's incredulous point-of-view, the love making seems akin to violence or physical attack' (p.113).

This sequence is crucial in understanding not only Marlow's disgust for the world, but also his hatred and fear of sex and women. Back in his childhood classroom we discover just how deeply he has been effected by the incident. Like Nigel Barton, the boy's unhappiness erupts in school where his obvious cleverness is a constant source of embarrassment and humiliation (see Chapter Two).[51] This time, however, the illicit act is one of defecation on the teacher's desk. The explicitly Freudian overtones of the incident links Marlow's witnessing of the primal scene with severe psychosexual disturbance. As Freud puts it:

> If children at this early age witness sexual intercourse between adults ... they inevitably regard the sexual act as a sort of ill-treatment or act of subjugation: they view it, that is, in a sadistic sense. Psycho-analysis also shows us that an impression of this kind in early childhood contributes a great deal towards a predisposition to a subsequent sadistic displacement with the problem of what sexual intercourse ... consists in: and they usually seek a solution of the mystery in some common activity concerned with the function of micturition or defaecation.[52]

It is on this childhood encounter that the whole serial revolves. Firstly, Potter explicitly connects this traumatic incident with the roots of Marlow's crippling illness. Later in the London underground when his mother smacks him, the young Philip reveals his first psoriatic lesion. This 'mark of Cain', as Paul Delany puts it, suggests the psychological dimensions of his illness.[53] Secondly, the incident also appears to have had a profound and lasting effect on Marlow's psychosexual development. His mother's betrayal, and the confusion between sex and violence, not only taints his relationship with women as a whole (most notably his wife) but also determines the way women and sex are presented in his fiction. 'You don't like women. Do you?' Dr Gibbon asks Marlow. 'Let me rephrase that', he continues, 'I'm reasonably sure that you think you *do* like them. That you even think they are – well – capable of being idolized, or – You don't like *sex*.' (p.54) Later, Gibbon reads a passage from Marlow's detective novel to stress the point. It is interesting to note its striking similarity with a description of the sexual act from Potter's own novel, *Hide and Seek* quoted earlier:

> DR GIBBON: Listen to this. A purple passage.
> MARLOW: No. A blue one, I hope.
> DR GIBBON: (*Reads*) 'Mouth sucking wet and slack at mouth, tongue chafing against tongue, limb thrusting upon limb, skin rubbing at skin –'
> MARLOW: Oink. Oink.
> DR GIBBON: ' – Faces contort and stretch into a helpless leer,

organs spurt out smelly stains and sticky betrayals. This is the
sweaty farce out of which we are brought into being –
MARLOW: Oink. Oink.
DR GIBBON: ' – We are implicated without choice in the slippery
catastrophe of the copulations which splatter us into existence
– '

*He half waits for another jeering 'Oink' but it does not come. Without
looking up, he continues to read –*
'We are spat out of fevered loins. We are the by-blows of grunts
and pantings in a rumpled and creaking bed. Welcome.'
He closes the book, looks at Marlow, questioningly.
MARLOW: (*Jeer*) Yeh. The Milk of Paradise.

(p.58)

This passage explicitly connects Marlow's illness, his detective
story and his problems with women in general (and his wife in
particular) with a deep-rooted psychological condition dating back
to an incident in early childhood. Once again, the suggestion
leans heavily towards the role of the mother in Marlow's
psychological condition. At one point Nicola (Marlow's wife)
actually takes Mrs Marlow's place in the forest. As with Marlow's
mother, she lies on her back, her legs astride with an unknown
lover on top, calling to her husband, 'Caught me, have you,
Marlow?' (p.75). Interestingly Mark Binney takes to referring to
Mrs Marlow as, 'my babby, my babby' (p.115) during their illicit
encounter. Elsewhere there are several implicit references con-
cerning this apparent connection between mother and wife. In
hospital the cantankerous George is asked the name of his wife
by a doctor. Surprisingly unable to answer he eventually explains
that she has *no* Christian name. 'Mum, I call her Mum', he tells
the doctor, '[w]hat the bleed'n hell do you think I call her!' (p.73).

It is during a word association exercise with Dr Gibbon that
Marlow is finally forced to confront the intensity of these feelings
towards women and sex. 'Passion', he says to Marlow, to which
his patient's rapid reply is 'pretence'. 'Woman', replies Gibbon,
which Marlow answers with 'Fuck'. 'Fuck' is repeated by the
doctor to which Marlow answers with 'dirt' and then 'death'
(p.177). And it is this contempt of women and fear of sex which
he eventually recognises as the key to his illness. Mrs Marlow's
suicide (she throws herself from the Hammersmith Bridge into
the Thames on learning that her son had witnessed her sexual

infidelity) leaves Marlow blaming himself for her death. As a result, he learns to equate the sexual act with feelings of guilt, fear and betrayal. Noting the erogenous nature of the skin, psychologists have tended to perceive psoriasis as an unconscious form of self-abuse. As Otto Fenichel puts it, 'outbreaks of psoriasis in particular may represent sadistic impulses turned against one's ego.'[54] This suggests that Marlow's illness is, in some respects, a form of unconscious self-punishment inflicted on himself by his own guilt. 'What are you doing here?' his wife finally asks him in hospital. 'Oh, punishing myself', he replies with an ironic smile (p.194).

Like other Potter protagonists, it would seem that for Marlow sexual satisfaction can only really be achieved through the relations with a debased sexual object. 'I'm sorry', he apologies to a prostitute he has just slept with. '. . . It wasn't really me calling you names. I don't mean them. . . . It's nothing personal.' (p.182) And the explicit connection between the novel's portrayal of women and Marlow's own relationship with the opposite sex is deliberately foregrounded. Indeed, much of this conversation has already taken place in Marlow's detective story between Finney and Sonia (the actress Kate McKenzie plays both the fictional prostitute and the real prostitute), suggesting an intimate relationship between Marlow's cheap novel and his own life. The flat is also the same (except for changes in decoration) as Mark Binney's in the detective story, and the one Nicola and Mark Finney are seen in when planning to steal Marlow's screenplay. Mark Binney's name is, of course, taken from the boy whom Marlow finally blames for the school room incident and whose father, Raymond Binney, was Mrs Marlow's illicit lover. In the last episode Marlow's novel and the world of the hospital finally collide in a climatic conclusion. A shoot-out between Marlow and the mysterious two men in the hospital ward ends with Marlow the private-eye finally shooting his creator through the forehead. 'I suppose you could say we'd been partners, him and me', the detective explains. 'Like Laurel and Hardy or Fortnum and Mason. But, hell, this was one sick fellow from way back when. And I reckon I'm man enough to tie my own shoe-laces now.' (p.248)

The overwhelming achievement of *The Singing Detective* is in the way in which it self-consciously deconstructs its own portrayal of women and sexuality. By showing how Marlow's childhood experiences have shaped his relationship with the opposite sex, it reveals the mechanics by which sadistic male fantasies are unconsciously manufactured into the realms of *fictional* representation. Unlike *Casanova*, where the dichotomy of angel and whore is implicitly supported by the protagonist's own obsessive and romanticised view of women, here we are forced to interpret female characters as the product of one man's tortured and disturbed psychology. The profoundly subjective insight into Marlow's childhood, fiction, fantasies and hallucinations offers the spectator the ability to piece together the reasons for his deep-rooted fear of women and sex. The total collapse of the male body forces his own notions of masculinity and subjectivity into crisis. His psychological discoveries finally enables him to re-build and reconstruct both his notion of himself and his sexuality. Accompanied by his long suffering wife, his cautious re-entrance into the outside world suggests a genuine reconstruction of the male ego.

Such a reading of *The Singing Detective* shows just how far Potter's portrayal of women had evolved since *Casanova*. While there is similarly no insight into a female mind, the misogynistic psychology of its central male protagonist is shown to be severely damaged by experiences in childhood. By dramatising how that psychological damage surfaces in both the fiction and the reality of a writer's life, Potter was able to investigate female oppression at its origins within the dynamics of the masculine unconscious. While Casanova goes to his death no nearer to understanding his sexual neurosis than he was as a young man, Marlow is able to acknowledge his disturbed sexuality and in doing so begin to reconstruct himself and his relationship with the opposite sex. The serial's ending also suggests a more cautiously optimistic answer to the problems encountered by Potter's protagonists as a whole. If the crisis of identity is not miraculously resolved, there is certainly cause for some optimism. While critics have tended to dismiss the serial's ending as unrealistically optimistic, it dramatically illustrates the power of the male unconscious to liberate itself from its own misogynist desires.[55] However, the deliberately ironical refrain of Vera Lynn's *We'll Meet Again* suggests a more ambiguous ending. As Marlow must know only too well, he will probably be forced to confront his illness and his problem with women and sex again in the future. The roots of his misogyny may at last be acknowledged and confronted, but there is clearly no suggestion that the ghosts of his past will ever be completely laid to rest.

BLACKEYES (1989)

> In a world ordered by sexual imbalance, pleasure in looking has been spilt between active/male and passive/female. The determining male gaze projects its fantasy onto the female figure, which is styled accordingly. In their traditional exhibitionist role women are simultaneously looked at and displayed, with their appearance coded for strong visual and erotic impact so that they can be said to connote *to-be-looked-at-ness*.
>
> Laura Mulvey (1975)[56]

'There ought to be a public outcry about *Blackeyes*', wrote Gary Bushell in the *Sun*. 'Not because it is too sexy, but because it is a load of old cobblers.'[57] As irreverent as this comment may seem, it rather aptly sums up the reception which Potter's four part serial attracted on its first and only British transmission on BBC 2 during November 1989. *Blackeyes* was seen as Potter's follow up to the dazzling triumph of *The Singing Detective* only three years earlier. Nicolas Roeg (whom Potter had worked with on *Track 29*) came the closest to accepting the job of director, but when he finally pulled out Potter took the brave (some claimed foolish) decision to direct the serial himself. Based on his own complex and multi-layered 1987 novel of the same name, the intricate narrative structure of the series would have posed problems for the most experienced of directors, but was clearly an ambitious project for any directorial debut. Problems with his unstable health and disagreements with his long term producer Kenith Trodd (it was later produced only by Rick McCallum) only exasperated Potter's problems. No wonder it became a project to which he felt obsessively committed. As he told John Wyver a few weeks before its transmission, '[t]his sounds horribly melodramatic – but in a literal way I was willing to perish to do *Blackeyes*.'[58]

It must have therefore come as an enormous shock when *Blackeyes* instantly became Potter's most ridiculed and derided of dramas, with people criticising the BBC for its waste of licence fee money.[59] Even before the screening of the first episode the British tabloids correctly anticipated the onslaught of criticism it was to receive. A two page spread in the *Daily Mirror* asked if it was 'All Clever Stuff – Or Just Dirty, Den?'[60] The broadsheets were no less critical. 'I can't quite shake off this feeling that the only person involved in *Blackeyes* who is wearing less clothes than Gina Bellman is the Emperor Dennis himself', explained Patrick Stoddart in *The Sunday Times*.[61] In the *Listener*, James Saynor called the world of *Blackeyes* a 'Fucking hell', which, he explained, 'might seem an indecorous turn of phrase, but it's fully keeping with Potter's grimacing, flagellatory vision.'[62] Hugh Herbert described it as 'Potter's Peepshow' in the *Guardian*. 'Men', he wrote, 'are likely to cry "Foul!", while women, sensing hand-me-down feminism, are likely to cry, "What do you want, a gold star?"'[63]

Ironically, *Blackeyes* originally began as Potter's answer to charges of misogyny levelled at some of his earlier work.[64] Maurice James Kingsley (Michael Gough) writes a best-selling novel based on the exploits of his niece Jessica's (Carol Royle) experiences as a beautiful model. Jessica, enraged by her passive portrayal in her uncle's book, seeks revenge by attempting to re-write her story. The abuse she feels over the book is mirrored and intensified by the *sexual* abuse she suffered at the hands of Kingsley when she was a child. Meanwhile, we see the fictional Jessica, Blackeyes (Gina Bellman), living out her sordid life as a vulnerable young model. She is manipulated and abused by men, most notably Jamieson (Colin Jeavons) who aids her modelling career in return for sexual favours. Gradually it becomes clear that the possession of Blackeyes becomes the central motif of the story as she is fought over, not only by Kingsley and Jessica, but also by police detective Blake (John Shrapnel) who investigates her death and Jeff (Nigel Planer), a copywriter and aspiring novelist. Finally, Jessica claims revenge on her uncle, not with a literary re-write (she quickly discovers she hasn't the talent!) but with the repeated stabbing of a stiletto heel through his throat. As the serial ends, so Blackeyes finally breaks free of *all* the authorial voices which have constrained her, even, ironically enough, Potter's himself as narrator.

The style of the serial (it was shot on 35mm film and was originally to also be produced into a movie-length version – the BBC initially saw it as a step nearer to gaining big-screen credibility for its drama offerings) suggests the complex narrative structure of the novel. Potter's direction clearly has more in common with European film-making than conventional British television drama, and may have seemed excessively self-conscious for many viewers. Its continual shift from fantasy, reality, flashforward and flashback is heightened by Potter's decision to edit the material into an almost continual montage of sound and vision. Sequences such as Blackeyes' slow walk into the Serpentine in her baby-doll nightdress are repeatedly replayed and intercut within individual scenes, while sounds such as the nursery rhymes, songs and television/radio programmes of Jessica's childhood are allowed to seep in and out (almost imperceptibly) of the main narrative. According to Potter, this deliberately unconventional style of directing and editing fulfilled his need to defamiliarise the traditional mechanics of the cinema. Prompting memories of Troy Kennedy Martin's influential article on television drama (see Chapter Two), he argued that '[f]ilm is totally unaware of what has been going on for most of this century in fiction and literary terminology.'[65] Unlike *The Singing Detective*, however, where the conflicting narrative threads are woven and centred around the memories and imagination of its central protagonist, *Blackeyes* has the viewer cast adrift in a world which (uniquely for Potter) has no central authorial voice or perspective; other than Potter's own ambiguous and disembodied narration.

But it was the indeterminacy of the central figure of Blackeyes herself which confused the critics and viewers the most, and produced the greatest misunderstandings. Blackeyes is (originally at least) simply a figment of Kingsley's sexist imagination. As Potter's opening narration put its, she is as 'plastic, as dead and as demeaning as any standard male fantasy'.[66] Perhaps the very type of female character which Potter himself had been accused of creating in his earlier drama. As a result, she is allowed to display precious little depth of character, is strangely devoid of any emotion and is forced to parade around in bikinis and skimpy underwear. Referring to the original novel Raman Seldon concludes that Blackeyes 'possesses the openness of a sign awaiting the mark of the observer's inscribing gaze.... She is a post-structuralist text totally at the mercy of the reader's pleasure.'[67] Indeed, she clearly acts as a 'floating signifier', simply waiting to be inscribed with characteristics and a personality of her own. As Jessica and Kingsley struggle for possession of her (she is simultaneously Kingsley's fantasy and Jessica's alter-ego) she remains a one-dimensional, fictional character suspended between two (at least) contrasting and opposing narrative worlds.

However, not only was Blackeyes' metaphorical role in the story unclear, but one can see how Gina Bellman's performance could be misinterpreted as simply fulfilling the male spectator's own erotic fantasy.

Through his own voice-over, Potter attempted to illustrate his complicit role (as screenwriter *and* director) in the construction of the narrative. As he told Wyver, 'no matter how "feminist" some of the aspirations might be, the basic fact remains that I am a man making it. So I wanted to bring that ambivalence right to the centre.'[68] According to Potter, his own voice-over was not only meant to *guide* the viewer through the complex and multi-layered story, but also provide a deliberately alienating narra-tive which sought to expose his voyeuristic gaze, while asking the viewer to question the authorial nature and perspective of the piece as a whole. As he told Graham Fuller, it was 'a last-minute, desperate attempt to pull all [the] strands together. Not only were you showing the manipulation within the story, you had this manipulator narrating it. I was hoping that out of that collision, that multiplicity of exploitation and manipulation being demonstrated in an almost explicitly Brechtian way, you would feel the alienation.' (Fuller, 1993, p.113)

Yet such a strategy clearly ran the risk of playing straight into the hands of the media by confirming and foregrounding his controversial status as a sexually explicit playwright. Indeed, the portrayal of Kingsley as the archetypal dirty old man was dangerously close to the tabloid's own construction of 'Dirty Den'. 'I wanted to show you a beautiful woman in an easy, easy sort of way', Potter's voice explains over the opening title sequence, 'but my own yearning sneaked up on me as I hunted her down.' He explains in the second episode that 'lips make the same shape for a spit as they do for a kiss. Blackeyes, my unattain-able love, which is it I'm doing?' In the final scene of the con-cluding episode Potter's complicit role in her story is explicitly confirmed when he, as narrator, desperately tries to claim her once and for all. 'Hey! Blackeyes', Potter's voice-over cries as she finally walks away from the camera. 'Come back. Please, my love. *Please*. Blackeyes, come back to a – a man's world. Don't *you* start re-writing.' Not surprisingly, the audience found it diffi-cult to distinguish between Potter's deliberately ambiguous voice as the narrator (and seemingly the author) and the serial's over-all feminist intentions. The author's own desire for his young and beautiful female character was clearly mistaken for Potter's own dubious interest in Gina Bellman, the actress who played Blackeyes.

Similar ambiguities exist around Potter's direction. Clearly the serial is meant to dramatise the sexual imbalance inherent in conventional cinema (television, literature and advertising) so that contemporary representations of women were exposed as intrinsically biased towards the male perspective. Blackeyes herself is the explicit personification of what the feminist film critic Laura Mulvey refers to as the 'isolated, glamorous, on display, sexualised' heroine; and her male observers (including Potter as narrator) exactly portray the voyeuristic 'male gaze'.[69] Appropriating Freudian and Lacanian psychoanalysis Mulvey argues that the dominant male gaze of classical narrative cinema is designed so as to avert the unconscious threat posed by the female subject. As a result, she is sexualised, fetishised and objectified; her threat finally curtailed. According to Mulvey, '[d]esire, born with language, allows the possibility of transcending the instinctual and the imaginary, but its point of reference continually returns to the traumatic moment of its birth: the castration complex. Hence the look, pleasurable in form, can be threatening in content, and it is woman as representation/image that crystallizes this paradox.'[70]

Seen in this light, *Blackeyes* is an explicitly self-conscious attempt to deconstruct the traditional means by which male creativity has tended to deal with the unconscious threat posed by woman. Yet, like Potter's narration, the camera work was seemingly far too ambiguous for much of its audience. While Potter's narrative attempts to condemn the conventional portrayal of the female figure, his direction seems surprisingly complicit in constructing the traditionally sexist images of conventional cinema and television. The controversial scene from the first episode when Blackeyes strips and performs with a bottle of body lotion for a room full of slavering advertising men, asks the viewer to condemn this exhibitionist role of the woman and the determining and sexualised perspective of the male gaze. Yet the excessive positioning of the camera *within* the audience forces the viewer to adopt the gaze of the *men*. As a result, the traditional construction of the objectified woman and the voyeuristic perspective of the male gaze tends to be maintained and re-affirmed. As Mulvey puts it, a 'woman performs within the narrative, the gaze of the spectator and that of the male characters in the film are neatly combined without breaking narrative verisimilitude.'[71]

Had, for instance, the spectator been allowed to see the scene only from Blackeyes' point of view, the result (and our view of the men) might have been very different. As the critics quite rightly pointed out, it is difficult to see the naked body of a beautiful young actress as a critique of female exploitation when, through its very construction, she is created as an *erotic spectacle*.

Although Germaine Greer has argued that the criticism of the male gaze is implicit in the opening episode, the voyeurism of the serial as a whole undermines this central critique.[72] In the second episode Bellman once again strips for the gaze of both a randy photographer and inevitably the camera. Although the quick movement of the camera away from Blackeyes initially prevents the viewer from adopting a voyeuristic perspective ('I don't think we should compromise here', declares Potter's narration) it quickly re-positions itself with the perspective of the male photographer's gaze; offering the spectator the same erotic spectacle. Potter's narrative insistence when her bra is finally removed, that 'No. I'm looking at her eyes. Her *eyes*!', simply implies a guilty, uncomfortable but complicit voyeurism which itself does little to deconstruct the woman's exhibitionist role. Later in the same episode, the camera moves into an extreme close-up of her face, which again re-affirms her role as passive object of the male gaze. 'Closer. Closer!', implores Potter's narration as the camera moves in. 'The closest I dare. Near enough to kiss her eyelids. Oh, my God I'm making love to her. Is that what I'm doing? Stop it, please.' On the one hand, such implicit criticism of the camera's manipulative and intrusive gaze offers the viewer a means of criticising conventional film and television practice, on the other, it simply re-establishes the voyeuristic separation between, as Mulvey would put it, woman as 'passive image' and the man as 'bearer of the active look'.

Seen in this light, Blackeyes is, in fact, metaphorically blind; she has no look of her own. Her black enigmatic eyes are for being looked *at*, not ironically enough, for *looking*. The authorial perspective (as far as there is one) is of a disembodied male voice which denies her a gaze of her own through its implicit relation to the voyeuristic gaze of the camera. In short, Blackeyes is never allowed to develop beyond her role as a standard male fantasy. This is not surprising when we discover that Jessica is herself unable to write her own story, and it is left to a man, Jeff (an aspiring novelist) to write that story for her. As the 'man who loved Blackeyes' (and a lover of Keats) he seems as unlikely to treat the subject any more objectively than Kingsley. According to Potter's narration, '[p]oor Jeff – even his deepest fantasies are banal. But then he does work in advertising.' Indeed, it is suggested in Episode 3 that he actually observes Jessica/Blackeyes (their homes are identical) from his neighbouring flat. This is all the more ominous when we discover that the novel he is writing is about 'a disappointed, obsessive who cannot stop spying on the young woman who lives next door.' Jessica is ultimately as powerless (perhaps even as one-dimensional) as Blackeyes herself and is as reliant on the male creative perspective as her alter-ego. The revenge she takes on Kingsley, as sweet as it is, does not alter his construction of her past (both in terms of his literary as well as his sexual abuse) and can only free Blackeyes from his distorted narrative; rather than offer the viewer an alternative and radical re-writing.

What becomes clear is that the serial was crucially flawed in the way it attempted to *challenge* or *expose* the sexist imagery which it continually constructs for the viewer. The anger and sadness Blackeyes clearly feels for her sordid manipulation as a model is constantly undermined by a camera and a narration which are complicit in that exploitation. If its feminist landscape appears to suggest striking parallels with the influential essay written by Mulvey in the mid-1970s, then it can also be criticised along the same lines. Many critics have argued that Mulvey's original essay was over-deterministic in its inability to allow any room for the female gaze; the woman defined only as an object of the male unconscious. This is clearly the failure of Potter's serial which, despite its honourable intentions, simply does not allow the alternative perspective of Jessica or Blackeyes to deconstruct its authorial and masculine perspective. As the film critic David Rodowick has put it with reference to Mulvey's essay, 'the question still remains: where is woman's place? Mulvey speaks of a male unconscious but a female unconscious takes place in her analysis only as an absence, a negativity defining castration and the not-masculine, or as a yet unrealized possibility.'[73]

Seen in this light, Potter's drama as a whole never fully liberates itself from the binary structure of the classic and Romantic narrative, which tends to situate woman as *other*; as a negative value to the positive, active and creative male. While the explicitly Freudian nature of his drama allows Potter to trace notions of sexuality and identity to the very root of his characters' experience, it also tends to position women as the product of male fear, desire or both. Although there is a gradually self-conscious and increasingly self-reflexive relation to the female subject (reaching its most explicit portrayal in *The Singing Detective* and *Blackeyes*) Potter's work seems unable to deconstruct the unconscious male desires which inevitably determine its structure and content. Ironically, the male perspective of *The Singing Detective* is *more* successful in acknowledging and problematising the male unconscious than *Blackeyes*, which attempts to deconstruct the very framework of the narrative itself. Marlow's *film noir* creation explicitly identifies the sadistic workings of the male psyche (showing, as it does, the female subject as the one-dimensional product of the male unconscious, yet independent in her own right), while Jessica's failed and miserable attempt at re-writing her own objectification, only re-establishes the woman as an essentially passive and powerless victim of sexual and cultural domination.

Potter's work, however, must be praised for at least addressing the very issues surrounding the cultural representation of the female subject. In both *Blackeyes* and *The Singing Detective* he directly confronted some of the harshest criticisms levelled at his work, offering a dramatic critique of the binary structures upon which his drama was driven and constructed. While clearly not always successful in its high (some might say naive) aspirations, his later television drama is nonetheless crucially important for the way it so clearly demonstrates the increasing influence of feminism upon literary, cinematic and televisual practice. Where his work seems unable to free itself from patriarchal constraints is, however, in its representation of the male gaze. Potter's female characters, clearly Blackeyes herself, are so explicitly sexualised that it is impossible often to locate the feminist agenda which he assured us was driving the narrative. It would seem that as a writer he was unable to acknowledge fully the extent to which his own psychological make-up may have penetrated the dynamics of his work and in particular, its portrayal of women. To set out on an explicitly feminist narrative like *Blackeyes* was foolish and arrogant for a writer who by his own admission had only encountered the impact of feminism late in his career. To acknowledge the misogyny in his own work was clearly a creative leap for Potter, but to be expected to tackle the issues and concerns of feminism was simply a task for which he was almost completely unsuited.

'If we have any dignity', Potter once explained, 'we don't take the labels that people put upon us. Wherever we are from, whatever class, whatever race, whatever sex. Whatever we are, we have a sovereign obligation to deal with ourselves as sovereign beings.'[74] It is this central attitude, however, which raises Potter's later drama above the straightforward accusations of misogyny which critics have given to his work as a whole. Although *Blackeyes* is, as we have seen, essentially flawed, it stands as a testament to a writer who was willing to take on uncomfortable and frequently unacceptable subjects. As he told Graham Fuller, '*Blackeyes* released a tide of polemical abuse of such huge proportions in the English tabloids that it was almost proof that I was stepping on the right nerves, if not in totally the right way.' (Fuller, 1993, p.133) When seen in context with his earlier work, one can sense the bravery of Potter to tackle issues which other male writers of his generation have not even attempted to address. For that, at least, he must be commended.

NOTES

1. Teresa Brennan, *History After Lacan*, Routledge, 1993, p.9.
2. John Wyver, 'Arrows of desire', an interview with Dennis Potter, *The New Statesman*, 24 November 1989, p.17.
3. Although Jack makes this comment in his description of the people he works with in television, the language and the sentiment is unmistakably his.
4. John Wyver, 1989, p.18.
5. Mark Steyn, 'The Great Pretender', *The Modern Review*, June–July 1994, p.8. My own reply to Steyn's article can be found in *The Modern Review* August–September, 1994, p.5.
6. Nancy Banks-Smith, *Sun*, 9 November 1965.
7. Anthony Thwaite, *New Statesman*, 13 November 1970, p.653.
8. John Carey, *The Listener*, 22 February 1973, p.254.
9. 'Explicit sex scene vetted by Grade', *The Times* 1 December 1986.
10. Ibid.
11. See Patrick Hill, 'Tebbit investigates the Detective's sex scenes', the *Daily Mail*, 1 December 1986, p.3.
12. Patrick Stoddart, 'Potter's First Black Eye?', *The Sunday Times*, 3 December 1989.

13. Maria Lexton, 'Sex, lies & misogyny', *Time Out*, 1005, Vol. 22, 29 November 1989, p.29.
14. Cited by Peter Ansorge, 'Don't be cruel to art that's true', *The Guardian* (*Media Section*), 15 March 1993, p.17.
15. Ibid.
16. Germaine Greer, interviewed for *Dennis Potter: A Life in Television*, *The Late Show's* Tribute to Potter, BBC 2, 6 June 1994.
17. Alan Plater, 'Sex, television drama and the writer', included in Andrea Millwood Hargrave (ed.) *British Broadcasting Standards Council, Annual Review 1992: Sex and Sexuality in Broadcasting*, John Libbey, 1992, p.78.
18. Juliet Mitchell, *Psychoanalysis and Feminism*, Penguin Books, 1974, pp.306–7.
19. Transcribed from a video recording, BBC TV, 1973.
20. Strangely enough the joke is never told in the play, Potter no doubt assuming the audience was aware of it.
21. Otto Fenichel, *The Psychoanalytical Theory of Neurosis*, Routledge & Kegan Paul, 1966, p.57.
22. Juliet Mitchell (ed.), *The Selected Melanie Klein*, Peregrine Books, 1986, p.123.
23. Barbara A. Schapiro, *The Romantic Mother: Narcissistic Patterns in Romantic Poetry*, The Johns Hopkins Press, 1983, p.ix.
24. John Wyver, 1992, p.20.
25. Sigmund Freud, 'Contributions to the Psychology of Love: The Most Prevalent Form of Degradation in Erotic Life.' This essay is published in various sources. See, for example, Sigmund Freud, *Collected Papers*, Vol. IV, translated by Joan Riviere, The Hogarth Press, 1957, p.207.
26. Otto Rank, *The Don Juan Legend*, translated and edited by David G. Winter, Princeton University Press, 1975, p.41.
27. See Barry Norman's review of *Casanova*, *The Times*, 17 November 1971.
28. 'TV play in "lewd" complaint', *The Times* 2 December 1971.
29. Ibid.
30. Clive James, *The Listener*, 25 November 1971, p.741.
31. Stuart Hood, *The Listener*, 30 December 1971, p.916.
32. Barry Norman, *The Times*, 17 November 1971.
33. Hilary Kingsley and Geoff Tibballs, *Box of Delights: The Golden Years of Television*, Macmillan, 1989, p.125.
34. See Graham Fuller, 1993, p.68.
35. All page references refer to Dennis Potter, *Casanova*, unpublished script.
36. The Proustian element of Potter's drama could be developed in some detail if space allowed. Certainly in *Casanova* the revelatory power of memory constructs a hidden world of superior reality.
37. See Sigmund Freud, *On Sexuality*, Vol. 7, Penguin Books, 1977, p.376.
38. According to Freud, '[w]omen whom he respects, like his mother, retain a penis for a long time', ibid.
39. Otto Rank, 1975. p.96.

40. Alain Silver and Elizabeth Ward (eds), *Film Noir*, Secker & Warburg, 1980, p.36.
41. See 'New Pennies', *The Times*, 22 March 1986, p.18.
42. See the *Radio Times*, 15–21 November 1986, pp.98–101.
43. Nicolas Shakespeare, 'Music to my eyes', *The Times*, 1 December 1986, p.9.
44. Nicolas Shakespeare, 'Series of massive promise', *The Times*, 22 December 1986, p.9.
45. Hugo Williams, 'With knobs on', *New Statesman*, 28 November 1986.
46. Vincent Canby, 'Is this Years Best Film on TV?', *New York Times* (Arts & Leisure section), 10 July 1988.
47. For a full account of Potter's time at LWT see 'Coffee Without Cream', Chapter V of Mihir Bose, 1992, pp.103–121.
48. Cited by Joost Hunningher, 'The Singing Detective', Chapter 13 of George W. Brandt (ed.), *British Television Drama in the 1980s*, Cambridge University Press, 1993, p.242.
49. Janey Place, 'Women in Film Noir', in E. Ann Kaplan (ed.), *Women in Film Noir*, BFI publishing, 1986, p.35.
50. Therese Lichtenstein, 'Syncopated Thriller: Dennis Potter's Singing Detective', *Artforum*, Vol. 28, no. 9, May 1990, p.171.
51. To make the self-reflective connections with Potter's previous work all the more explicit the schoolmistress is played by Janet Henfrey, the same actress who had so famously portrayed Nigel Barton's domineering primary school teacher in 1965.
52. Sigmund Freud, 1993, p.335.
53. Paul Delany, 'Potterland', *Dalehousie Review*, Vol. 68, part 4, 1988, p.517.
54. Otto Fenichel, 1966, p.255.
55. Paul Delany, 1988, argues that the play's 'happy ending' threatens to turn it into a 'commercial for psychoanalysis', p.518.
56. Laura Mulvey, 'Visual Pleasure and Narrative Cinema', originally published in *Screen*, Autumn 1975, Vol. 16, no. 3.
57. Gary Bushell, *The Sun*, 30 November 1989, p.13.
58. John Wyver, 1989, p.17.
59. Estimates have put the cost of the serial at around £2.4 million.
60. *Daily Mirror*, 29 November 1989, p.9.
61. Patrick Stoddart, 'Potter's First Black Eye?', *The Sunday Times*, 3 December 1989.
62. James Saynor, 'What Every Woman Knows', *The Listener*, 1 December 1989, p.46.
63. Hugh Herbert, 'Potter's Peepshow', *The Guardian*, date unknown.
64. See Tristram Kenton, 'Black and Blue', *The Listener*, 1 June 1989, p. 4.
65. Cited by James Saynor, 1989.
66. All extracts are taken from a video recording, BBC TV, 1989.
67. Raman Selden, *A Reader's Guide to Contemporary Literary Theory*, Wheatsheaf, 1989, p.79.
68. John Wyver, 1989, p.17.
69. Laura Mulvey, 1975. If Potter had never come across Mulvey's article,

he would have undoubtedly been aware of John Berger's influential BBC TV series *Ways of Seeing*, Penguin, BBC Publications, 1974. In one episode Berger addressed these issues in reference to the female nude. 'Men dream of women', he narrates, 'women dream of themselves being dreamt of. Men look at women. Women watch themselves being looked at.' (BBC TV, 1974)

70. Ibid.
71. Ibid.
72. See BBC TV, June 1994.
73. David Rodowick, *The Difficulty of Difference,: Psychoanalysis, Sexual Difference and Film Theory*, Routledge, 1991, pp.16–7.
74. See, interview with Dennis Potter, The Museum of Television and Radio, New York, 1992.

Conclusion: 'A Fitting Memorial?'

> I have to say that if I were starting out today as a writer who is able to persuade himself on at least two days of the week that drama or fiction is one of the last few remaining acres of possible truth-telling left to us in our over-manipulated and news-stuffed world, then I doubt very much that I would deliberately chose, as I did, to begin in television as it is now controlled, owned and organised.
>
> Dennis Potter, James MacTaggart Memorial Lecture, 1993 (Potter, 1994, p.41)

Although this book has constantly striven to distinguish itself from a straightforward 'chronological' approach to Potter's oeuvre, the work written in the last years of his life is perhaps best understood when considered separately from his earlier drama. After the disastrous reception of *Blackeyes* (1989) he found himself at an unusually low point in his dramatic career. Some four years later *Secret Friends* (1992), made in co-operation with Channel Four Films, did little to restore his reputation. Like its predecessor, it was also directed by Potter and similarly starred Gina Bellman, now alongside Alan Bates. Based on Potter's own novel *Ticket to Ride* (1986), it once again centred around a complex, multi-layered narrative about sexual guilt, fantasy and obsession, but went virtually unnoticed at its time of release. In contrast, a year later *Lipstick on Your Collar* (1993), with its mixture of 1950's rock 'n' roll, teenage rebellion and the re-employment of the 'lip-synch' technique, was billed as a spectacular return to form. Potter was even persuaded to give up his directorial aspirations for good, handing over to director Renny Rye and settling instead for the role of producer. This six part serial for Channel 4 did not, however, live up to expectations and only received mixed reviews in the press. 'Enjoyable though much of it was', wrote Craig Brown in *The Sunday Times*, 'it seemed strangely like a gifted troupe of actors playing at being typical Dennis Potter characters. . . .'[1] *Midnight Movie* (1994) made for the BBC and also directed by Rye, faired even worse. Financed partly by Potter himself the majority of critics simply chose to ignore it.

However, shortly after finishing *Midnight Movie* Potter's name hit the headlines. Asked to give the 1993 MacTaggart Memorial Lecture he took the opportunity to attack the directors of the BBC and their new breed of management culture which he so clearly despised. The lecture also weaved stories about his childhood in the Forest of Dean and his undying belief in public service broadcasting with his fear and concern for the future of an increasingly privatised and demoralised United Kingdom plc (Potter, 1994, p.34). It was a powerful, triumphant, humorous and moving performance, but perhaps only a rehearsal for the most memorable personal appearance of his television career. Early in 1994 he was diagnosed as suffering from terminal and incurable cancer. With only a few months to live he was invited by Michael Grade to appear on Channel 4's *Without Walls* interviewed by Melvyn Bragg.[2] It was this interview which was to capture the public imagination in a way his later drama had simply failed to do. Equipped with a flask of liquid morphine to ease the pain of the cancer, his apparent courage in the face of death and his stubborn ability to keep working right up until the very end, earned him praise and applause from critics and viewers alike. 'One of the most extraordinary events I have ever seen on TV occurred last night', wrote Peter Paterson in the *Daily Mail*, 'something that was sensational in the true meaning of the word, and a deeply moving display of courage. . . .'[3]

Channel 4 and the BBC had, however, already commissioned a six part serial *each* before Potter's diagnosis. Having already spent the advances (a total of £160,000) on financing *Midnight Movie*, he was now faced with fulfilling his contractual obligations within a limited amount of time.[4] But towards the end of his interview with Bragg, Potter described how he intended to satisfy these two separate obligations. By connecting the two serials with a central protagonist and having Channel 4 and the BBC collaborate on their production, he hoped to still fulfil the two contracts (each drama would also be cut down to four instead of six episodes). Finally he asked that they should be shown on both channels, bringing two rival corporations together in an unique collaboration of both production and scheduling. Potter was only too aware that both Michael Grade (Chief Executive for Channel 4) and Alan Yentob (Head of BBC 1) were long-time Potter fans, and the idea was instantly agreed upon. Comparing both serials to his finest work, he left no one in any doubt that they would prove to be the television event of the decade. 'I can now be arrogant and boastful and "F" it to everything', he told Bragg, 'I could go out with a fitting memorial.' (Potter, 1994, p.28)

Perhaps the name of Emma Porlock (the leading scientist in *Cold Lazarus*) gives us a possible clue to Potter's overall intentions. In Coleridge's account of the writing of *Kubla Khan* the poet describes how he awoke from an opium dream to find he had composed two or three hundred lines of poetry. Trying to write them down, however, he is interrupted 'by a person on business from Porlock.'[5] This then, was to be Potter's attempt to write through the haze of his own morphine treatment, and to recount a dream within a dream. Unlike Coleridge, Potter *did* complete his final work and after his death both Channel 4 and the BBC went onto fulfil practically every one of his last requests.[6] Although Trodd initially insisted on a more experienced director, Renny Rye did go onto to direct as Potter had intended.[7] *Karaoke* was shot in central London despite being a notoriously expensive and troublesome location, and crucial pieces of casting were carried out in the strict respect of Potter's wishes. Costing a total of £10 million both productions were certainly given sufficient financial backing, the BBC and Channel 4 bidding each other for the international rights.

Karaoke (1996), the first of the two serials, was, however, to be a disappointing swan song. Despite the inevitable hype, the story was sadly self-indulgent and repetitive. The first episode was shown on BBC 1 (Sunday 29 April 1996), repeated on Monday by Channel 4 and so on for the following three weeks. Not surprisingly it lost its audience at an incredible rate, plummeting as low as 800,000 viewers for Channel 4's repeat of Episode 2. The basic concept that the Karaoke machine would provide a dramatic metaphor for the way we are all, to some extent, controlled by other people's words, was promising. But the motif was not satisfactorily maintained or developed, except in Daniel Feeld's (Albert Finney) rather confused impression that he is seeing his script come alive in front of him – an idea originally utilised in *Double Dare* (1976). Ben Baglin's (Roy Hudd) spoonerisms are embarrassingly unfunny and Daniel's dubious relationship with the working-class Sandra (Saffron Burrows) seems nothing more than a patronising exercise in the flaunting of power and money. References to *Blackeyes* abound with one scene even including a Dennis Potter look-a-like (Ian McDiarmid) having a glass of red wine thrown into his face by a young woman he has been staring at. While it did receive some warm reviews, the majority of the critics were scathing in their scorn. 'One of the worst plays ever screened', wrote A. N. Wilson in *The Evening Standard*.[8] Perhaps *Private Eye* summed up the prevailing mood in its comment that, 'Potter's words have been treated as holy writ, a last will and testament, when they could have done with some serious editing.'[9]

In comparison, *Cold Lazarus* (1996) seemed like a return to form. In many ways it even explained *Karaoke*'s purpose as a rather unnecessary prologue, perhaps simply designed to fulfil Potter's contractual obligations with the BBC. The first episode was shown on Channel 4 (Sunday 27 May 1996) and repeated on Monday by BBC 1, and so on for the following three weeks. It not only proved that Potter could still turn out an entertaining and thought provoking piece of drama, but that Renny Rye, given the material, could direct with skill and panache. Set in the year 2368, a group of British scientists lead by Emma Porlock (Frances de la Tour) try to tap into the memories of the cryogenically frozen head of Daniel Feeld (the protagonist of *Karaoke*) who died 400 years earlier. Despite its comically kitsch costumes, futuristic furniture and seductive sci-fi score it nonetheless addressed many of the same issues and concerns as his 1993 MacTaggart Memorial Lecture had done. Potter's brave new world is a totally privatised dystopia where global corporations are in possession of peoples' bodies and minds – a logical and nightmarish conclusion of 1990s' Thatcherism. It is a society, however, which is contrasted with Daniel's *authentic* memories of the Forest of Nead (Dean spelt backwards). Such a narrative structure gave Potter one last chance to remind Britain of what it has lost and what it has in store for the future if the decline he predicted is not prevented.

Like all of Potter's major protagonists, Daniel is caught between two worlds, not only the past and present, but now even *life* and *death*. We see evocations of *Stand Up, Nigel Barton* (1965) and *Blue Remembered Hills* (1979) as we watch Albert Finney play Daniel as a 10 year old boy in his own distorted memory.

Meanwhile, David Siltz (Henry Goodman), a clear successor of Rupert Murdoch, monopolises the media industry through his broadcasting company UTE (Universal Total Entertainment). His rival and fellow marketer is Martina Matilda Masdon (Diane Ladd), a mixture of Margaret Thatcher and the Wicked Witch of the West; she devours young men and ruthlessly keeps an eye on the budget limits of her employees. However, a member of a terrorist organisation called 'Ron' (Reality or Nothing) allows Daniel to die before Siltz turns his memories into prime-time viewing for the masses. Welcomed by a host of radiant angels Potter's protagonist finally lets out a triumphant, orgasmic and Joycean 'Ye-e-e-e-e-es. . . .' (p.392).[10]

Overshadowed by the disastrous *Karaoke*, however, *Cold Lazarus* never received the critical attention or public applause it deserved. Shown on two separate evenings a week, both failed to be a televisual *event* in the same way *The Singing Detective* (1986) or *Pennies from Heaven* (1976) had previously been. In Potter's attempt to re-create the viewing conditions of 'The Wednesday Play' (by monopolising two separate channels) Potter had actually allowed his audience to become fragmented and disjointed for the first time in his television career. In some ways, these final two productions gives us an insight into many of the strengths and the weakness of Potter's later work. So over-indulged had he become by the medium that, by the end of his career, he could virtually dictate every facet of a production – even from beyond the grave.

The fact that both the BBC and Channel 4 had already commissioned two six part serials each, despite Potter's disappointing later work, gives us some idea of just how thinly he was being asked to spread his talent. What once would have made interesting and entertaining single plays were now forced to become lavish six-part serials which simply could not sustain their momentum, regardless of how impressive the original idea may have seemed. Although Potter was a solitary writer, his work needed to be produced and directed by individuals who could offer an objective and *critical* point of view. It is no coincidence that his greatest triumph, *The Singing Detective*, was made in intense collaboration with Jon Amiel, a director who not only had the courage to force Potter to undertake numerous re-writes of his original script, but the vision to bring his own ideas and that of his production team into the creative process itself. The very medium which made Potter, and which he faithfully championed, was finally responsible for producing an overweight and over-indulged *auteur* whose very name frequently become more important than the quality of the scripts he was attempting to sell.

Above all, Potter was a man of his time. He first began writing television drama during an tremendously exciting period in its early history. His desperate desire to reach the widest possible audience meant that he threw his talent into a television indus-try which could then produce an enormous impact through its relatively small number of national channels. The historical nature of television in Britain meant that he was first nurtured through a prolific career with the single play and was slowly and gradu-ally introduced to television adaptations and original serials, before finally moving into feature-length films made both for televi-sion and the cinema. Such an apprenticeship is unthinkable today with the demise of the single play, the growth of major serials and with the increasing amount of television drama made with both the small screen and big screen in mind. But if Potter entered television at the right time, it is fair to say he also left it at a surprisingly appropriate moment too. As a writer, it is clear he found the growing demands of the industry an increasing burden, unable to deal with its new management culture, with its increasing demand for larger and larger serials and with the ever expand-ing growth of competition, the very ideals with which he had entered the medium now seemed to have been abandoned. In many ways, it could even be argued that Potter had also come to a creative cul-de-sac in his career, completing his life's work with *The Singing Detective*, a climatic combination of themes and techniques stretching back some thirty years. As innovative and as exceptional as Potter's talent was, it could never sustain the prolific intensity which both he and the medium had continu-ally demanded of it.

But if Potter was a man uniquely of his time in terms of tele-vision, his work should also be seen within the context of a wider historical moment. Like cultural studies itself, Potter's work emerged in Britain out of the mid and late 1950s. The two books which helped establish this new discipline were also very close to his own heart – Richard Hoggart's *The Uses of Literacy* (1957) and Raymond William's *Culture and Society: 1780–1950* (1963). Both attempted to reflect on British life, to make sense of the enormous social, economic and political changes which had characterised British society since the industrial revolution. Like Hoggart (and Leavis), Potter's work longs to remember England before its 'Cultural Fall', a time before it had been soiled and corrupted by an American mass society which had destroyed Britain's own organic and vibrant folk communities. Appropriating William's notion of a common culture, his career began on the premise that by bringing the classes in dialogue with each other England's national sense of itself could still be reconstructed, maintaining and developing the long revolution which had established the principles of the welfare state and provided the country with its own individual and unique sense of identity. From *Between Two Rivers* (1960) to the posthumous *Cold Lazarus* his work attempted to dramatise and articulate this paradigm, never straying far from the agenda of the early New Left from which he, Hoggart and Williams had all emerged.

Above all, Potter's work needs to be located and understood within this historical context. This book has striven to show that British cultural studies is therefore the most singularly important 'context' a critic has for assessing and understanding his work. While film, literary and television studies all provide their unique and important insight into the drama as a whole, only the historical trajectory of British cultural studies enables the Potter critic to evaluate the work within the whole spectrum of post-war social, cultural and political history. Within this critical framework I have endeavoured to bring out some of the less consistent elements in Potter's drama, attempting to account for the breaks and indeterminacies which other critics, in their pursuit of thematic consistency, have failed even to acknowledge. As Stuart Hall has put it in reference to the history of British cultural studies itself:

> In serious, critical intellectual work, there are no 'absolute beginnings' and few unbroken continuities. . . . What we find, instead is an untidy but characteristic unevenness of development. What is important are the significant *breaks* – where old lines of thought are disrupted, older constellations displaced, and elements, old and new, are regrouped around a different set of premises and themes. . . .[11]

However Potter's drama is treated in the future there are surely few writers who have so completely and vividly produced such an intense and personal portrayal of British life at the end of the twentieth century. Consistently attracting audiences in the millions his oeuvre is testament to the remarkable possibility of a medium all too often undervalued by its audiences, its critics *and* its practitioners. Continually taking risks, he deliberately and consciously constructed his own distinctive grammar for the small screen, never afraid to tackle difficult and uncomfortable subjects with an individual and singular vision which for over 30 years kept his name far above any other writer the medium has ever known. His treatment of the past and present, his exploration of the conscious and unconscious, memory and desire desperately sought to dramatise the *interior* and *multiple* layers of the human mind, rather than merely attempting to portray an external and authentic reality. But Potter's work offers more than just psychological realism. In attempting to make sense of their own personal histories his characters' individual struggles reflect the social and cultural upheavals which have characterised post-war British society. The changing and complex world of sexual politics, social class, popular culture and even Britain's 'religious' sense of itself was at the centre of a body of work which was consumed by contradictions and ambiguities which go straight to the heart of contemporary Western culture. 'All clues. No solutions', Philip Marlow concludes in *The Singing Detective*, '[t]hat's the way things are' (Potter, 1986, p.140). Potter's work offers few solutions, but its contradictions, ambiguities and paradoxes may yet prove to be its most important legacy.

NOTES

1. Craig Brown, 'Song and dance routine', *The Sunday Times*, 28 February 1993.
2. Dennis Potter, an interview with Melvyn Bragg, *Without Walls*, Channel 4 March 1994.
3. Peter Paterson, 'Potter's brand of courage', *Daily Mail*, 6 April 1994, p.47.
4. See Introduction of Dennis Potter, *Karaoke and Cold Lazarus*, Faber & Faber, 1996, p.ix.
5. Samuel Taylor Coleridge, *Poetical Works*, Oxford University Press, 1973, p.296.
6. Potter died on the 7 June 1994. His wife Margaret died nine days earlier, also of cancer.

7. See 'Potter's death-bed legacy leaves £10m drama in jeopardy', *The Sunday Times*, 10 July 1994.
8. A. N. Wilson, 'The last word in drivel', *The Evening Standard*, 29 April 1996, p.9.
9. 'Couch Potato', 'TV EYE', *Private Eye*, 3 May 1996, p.10.
10. The ending is reminiscent of James Joyce's *Ulysses* which ends on a similarly affirmative note. See James Joyce, *Ulysses*, The Bodley Head, 1960, p.933.
11. Stuart Hall, 'Cultural studies: two paradigms', in Tony Bennett *et al.* (eds), *Culture, Ideology and Social Process: A Reader*, Open University, 1981, p.19.

Filmography

Dennis Potter is the writer on all titles. Dates refer to original broadcast in Britain. Unless otherwise stated all television productions can be viewed at The Museum of Television and Radio, New York.

Between Two Rivers (1960)
3 June, BBC TV. A personal report, narrated and presented by Dennis Potter. Producer: Anthony de Lotiniére. BBC archives only.

The Confidence Course (1965)
24 February, BBC 1. A BBC drama production for *The Wednesday Play*. Director: Gilchrist Calder. Producer: James MacTaggart. Only a script survives of this production.

Alice (1965)
13 October, BBC 1. A BBC drama production for *The Wednesday Play*. Director: Gareth Davies. Producer: James MacTaggart.

Stand Up, Nigel Barton (1965)
18 December, BBC 1. A BBC drama production for *The Wednesday Play*. Director: Gareth Davies. Producer: James MacTaggart.

Vote, Vote, Vote for Nigel Barton (1965)
15 December, BBC 1. A BBC drama production for *The Wednesday Play*. Director: Gareth Davies. Producer: James MacTaggart.

Emergency Ward – 9 (1966)
11 April, BBC 2. A BBC drama production for *Thirty-Minute Theatre*. Director: Gareth Davies. Producer, Harry Moore. Survives only in script form.

Where the Buffalo Roam (1966)
2 November, BBC 1. A BBC drama production for *The Wednesday Play*. Director: Gareth Davies. Producer: Lionel Harris.

Message for Posterity (1967)
3 May, BBC 1. A BBC drama production for *The Wednesday Play*. Director: Gareth Davies. Producer: Lionel Harris. Survives only in script form, but later re-made by the BBC and broadcast on 29 October, 1994, BBC 2.

The Bonegrinder (1968)
13 May, ITV. A Rediffusion London production for *The Playhouse*. Director/Producer: Joan Kemp-Welch.

Shaggy Dog (1968)
10 November, ITV. A LWT production for *The Company of Five*. Director: Gareth Davies. Producer: Stella Richman. Survives only in script form.

A Beast with Two Backs (1968)
20 November, BBC 1. A BBC drama production for *The Wednesday Play*. Director: Lionel Harris. Producer: Graeme McDonald.

Moonlight on the Highway (1969)
12 April, ITV. A Kestrel production for LWT's *Saturday Night Theatre*. Director: James MacTaggart. Producer: Kenith Trodd.

Son of Man (1969)
16 April, BBC 1. A BBC drama production for *The Wednesday Play*. Director: Gareth Davies. Producer: Graeme McDonald.

Lay Down Your Arms (1970)
23 May, ITV. A Kestrel production for LWT's *Saturday Night*. Director: Christopher Morahan. Producer: Kenith Trodd.

Angels are so Few (1970)
5 November, BBC 1. A BBC drama production for *The Wednesday Play*. Director: Gareth Davies. Producer: Graeme McDonald.

Paper Roses (1971)
13 June, ITV. A Granada Television production. Director: Darry Davis. Producer: Kenith Trodd.

Traitor (1971)
14 October, BBC 1. A BBC drama production for *Play for Today*. Director: Alan Bridges. Producer: Graeme McDonald.

Casanova (1971)
16 November–21 December, BBC 2. A BBC drama production in six parts. Directors: John Glenister (episodes 1,2,4), Mark Cunningham (3,5,6). Producer: Mark Shivas.

Follow the Yellow Brick Road (1972)
4 July, BBC 2. A BBC drama production for *Sextet*. Director: Alan Bridges. Producer: Roderick Graham.

Only Make Believe (1973)
12 February, BBC 1. A BBC drama production for *Play for Today*. Director: Robert Knights. Producer: Graeme McDonald.

A Tragedy of Two Ambitions (1973)
21 November, BBC 2. A BBC drama production for *Wessex Tales*, based on the story by Thomas Hardy. Director: Michael Tuchner. Producer: Irene Shubik.

Joe's Ark (1974)
14 February, BBC 1. A BBC drama production for *Play for Today*. Director: Alan Bridges. Producer: Graeme McDonald.

Schmoedipus (1974)
20 June, BBC 1. A BBC drama production for *Play for Today*. Director:
Barry Davis. Producer: Kenith Trodd.

Late Call (1975)
1–22 March, BBC 2. A BBC drama production in four parts. Based on
the novel by Angus Wilson. Director: Philip Dudley. Producer: Ken
Riddington.

Double Dare (1976)
6 April, BBC 1. A BBC drama production for *Play for Today*. Director:
John Mackenzie. Producer: Kenith Trodd.

Brimstone and Treacle (1976/78)
Made in 1976 but not transmitted until 25 August 1987, BBC 1. A BBC
drama production. Director: Barry Davis. Producer: Kenith Trodd.

Where Adam Stood (1976)
21 April, BBC 2. A BBC drama production, based on *Father and Son* by
Edmund Goose. Director: Brian Gibson. Producer: Kenith Trodd.

The Mayor of Casterbridge (1976)
22 January–5 March, BBC 2. A BBC drama production in seven parts.
Based on the novel by Thomas Hardy. Director: David Giles. Producer:
Jonathan Powell.

Pennies from Heaven (1978)
7 March–11 April, BBC 1. Subtitled: 'Six Plays With Music'. A BBC drama
production. Director: Piers Haggard. Producer: Kenith Trodd.

Blue Remembered Hills (1979)
30 January, BBC 1. A BBC drama production for *Play for Today*. Director:
Brian Gibson. Producer: Kenith Trodd.

Blade on the Feather (1980)
19 October, ITV. A LWT production in association with PFH Ltd. Director:
Richard Loncraine. Producer: Kenith Trodd.

Rain on the Roof (1980)
26 October, ITV. A LWT production in association with PFH Ltd. Director:
Alan Bridges. Producer: Kenith Trodd.

Cream in my Coffee (1980)
2 November, ITV. A LWT production in association with PFH Ltd.
Director: Gavin Miller. Producer: Kenith Trodd.

Tender is the Night (1985)
23 September–28 October, BBC 2. A BBC drama production in six parts.
Made in association with Showtime Entertainment and The Seven Network, Australia, based on the novel by F. Scott Fitzgerald. Director:
Robert Knights. Producer: Betty Willingale.

The Singing Detective (1986)
16 November–21 December, BBC 1. A BBC drama production in six
parts. Made in association with Australian Broadcasting Corporation.

Director: Jon Amiel. Producers: Kenith Trodd/ John Harris.

Visitors (1987)
22 February, BBC 2. A BBC production in association with Polymuse and W. W. Entertainment for *Screen Two*. Director: Piers Haggard. Producer: Kenith Trodd.

Christabel (1988)
16 November–7 December, BBC 2. Subtitled 'A film in Four Parts by Dennis Potter'. A BBC production in association with Arts & Entertainment, based on *The Past is Myself* by Christabel Bielenberg. Director: Adrian Shergold. Producer: Kenith Trodd.

Blackeyes (1989)
19 November–20 December, BBC 2. A BBC production in four parts. Made in association with the Australian Broadcasting Corporation and Television New Zealand, based on the novel by Dennis Potter. Director: Dennis Potter. Producer: Rick McCallum.

Lipstick on your Collar (1993)
21 February–28 March, Channel 4. A Whistling Gypsy Production in six parts. Director: Renny Rye. Producer: Dennis Potter. Co-Producers: Rosemarie Whitman/Alison Barnett.

Karaoke (1996)
28 April–20 May, BBC 1 and Channel 4. A Whistling Gypsy Production in four parts. Director: Renny Rye. Producers: Kenith Trodd/Rosemarie Whitman.

Cold Lazarus (1996)
26 May–17 April, Channel 4 and BBC 1. A Whistling Gypsy Production in four parts. Director: Renny Rye. Producers: Kenith Trodd/Rosemarie Whitman.

FOR THE CINEMA

Pennies from Heaven (1981)
USA; A Hera Production for MGM. Director: Herbert Ross. Producers: Nora Kaye, Herbert Ross.

Brimstone and Treacle (1982)
UK; Namara Films/Alan E. Salke in association with Herbert Solow. A PFH Film. Director: Richard Loncraine. Producer: Kenith Trodd.

Gorky Park (1983)
USA; Eagle Associates for Orion, based in the novel by Martin Cruz Smith. Director: Michael Apted. Producers: Gene Kirkwood/Howard W. Koch Jr.

Dreamchild (1985)
UK; A PFH Film for Thorn EMI Screen Entertainment. Director: Gavin Millar. Producers: Rick McCallum/Kenith Trodd.

Track 29 (1987)
UK, Hand Made Films. Director: Nicolas Roeg. Producer: Rick McCallum.

Secret Friends (1992)
UK; For *Film on Four*. Director: Dennis Potter. A Whistling Gypsy Production with Films Four International. Producer: Rosemarie Whitman.

Midnight Movie (1993)
U.K; Whistling Gypsy Productions for *Screen Two*. Director: Renny Rye. Producer: Dennis Potter. Co-producer: Rosemarie Whitman.

Mesmer (1994)
UK/AUS; Director: Roger Spottiswoode. Producer: Lance W. Reynolds/ Weiland Schulz-Keil. Co-Producer: Andras Hamori.

Bibliography

PUBLISHED WORKS BY DENNIS POTTER

Non-Fiction

The Glittering Coffin, Gollancz, 1960
The Changing Forest: Life in the Forest of Dean Today, Secker & Warburg, 1962; re-issued by Minerva, 1996
Seeing the Blossom: Two Interviews and a Lecture, Faber & Faber, 1994; re-issued as *Seeing the Blossom: Two Interviews, a Lecture and a Short Story*, Faber & Faber, 1994

Fiction

Hide & Seek, André Deutsch/Quartet Books; reissued by Faber & Faber, 1973
Pennies from Heaven, Quartet Books, 1981
Ticket to Ride, Faber & Faber, 1986
Blackeyes, Faber & Faber, 1987
'Last Pearls', *Daily Telegraph*, 4 June 1994

Plays

The Nigel Barton Plays: Two Television Plays, Penguin, 1967
Son of Man (adapted for the stage), André Deutsch, 1970
Follow the Yellow Brick Road in Robert Muller (ed.), *The Television Dramatist*, Elek, 1973
Brimstone and Treacle, *New Review*, No. 26, May, 1976
Brimstone and Treacle (adapted for the stage), Faber & Faber, Eyre Methuen, 1978
Sufficient Carbohydrate (for the stage), Faber & Faber, 1983
Waiting for the Boat, On Television: Blue Remembered Hills, Joe's Ark, Cream in my Coffee, Faber & Faber, 1984; re-issued as *Blue Remembered Hills and Other Plays*, Faber & Faber, 1996
The Singing Detective, Faber & Faber, 1986
Christabel (adapted from *The Past is Myself* by Christabel Bielenberg) Faber & Faber, 1988
Lipstick on Your Collar, Faber & Faber, 1993
Pennies from Heaven, Faber & Faber, 1996
Karaoke and Cold Lazarus, Faber & Faber, 1996

Selected Journalism and Articles

Potter's journalism is far too prodigious to list in its entirety. Below is a selection of articles either cited in the text or relevant to particular aspects of Potter's dramatic output and career.

'It's a Woman's World', *Isis*, 5 March 1958
'Base Ingratitude?', *New Statesman*, 3 May 1958
'The Most Exciting Ever', television review, *Daily Herald*, 27 March 1963
'TV is an electronic Yo-Yo', Dennis Potter column, *Daily Herald*, 28 December 1963
'Why Import this Trash?', television review, *Daily Herald*, 6 August 1964
'Cue Teleciné – Put on the Kettle', *New Society*, 22 September 1966, pp. 456–7
'George Orwell', *New Society*, 1 February 1968, pp.107–8
'Why I'm Glad to be British', Dennis Potter column, *Sun*, 8 April 1968
'The Night I Realised I, Too, Fear the Stranger', Dennis Potter column, *Sun*, 29 April 1968
'Writer Exposed', *Sun*, 20 May 1968
'Rally Round Patriots, Before Wireless Goes the Way of the Empire', Dennis Potter column, *Sun* 1 July 1968
'Mass language and the limits of sarcasm and semiology', review of Roland Barthes' *Mythologies*, *The Times*, 24 February 1972
'A Note from Mr. Milne', *New Statesman*, 23 April 1976
'Review of *Holocaust*', *Sunday Times*, 10 September 1978
'How I'm shaking Up the Mush Machine', *Daily Mail*, 25 May 1979
'Why British TV is Going to the Dogs', *Daily Mail*, 30 July 1980

Selected Interviews

Appleyard, Brian, 'Dennis Potter, making a drama out of a crisis', *The Times*, 9 September 1986.
Bakewell, Joan and Nicholas Garnham, interview in Bakewell and Garnham, *The New Priesthood*, Penguin Press, 1970, pp.82–4.
Bragg, Melvyn, *The South Bank Show: Man of Television*, LWT, 11 February 1987.
Bragg, Melvyn, *Without Walls*, Channel 4, 5 April 1994 (transcript included in Potter, 1994).
Brown, Robert, 'Dollars from Hollywood', BFI *Monthly Film Bulletin*, July 1982.
Craig, Mary, 'Grounds for religion: Dennis Potter on a 'protective institution', *The Listener*, 1 May 1976, p.613.
Cushman, Robert, 'Dennis Potter: the values of a television playwright', *Radio Times*, 3–9 April 1976.
Dean, Michael, *Late Night Line-Up* (on *Traitor*), 14 October 1971.
Fuller, Graham, 'Dennis Potter', *American Film*, Vol. 14, Part 5, 1989, pp.31–3.
Fuller, Graham (ed.), *Potter on Potter*, Faber & Faber, 1993.
James, Clive (Chair), *The Talk Show with Clive James*, BBC 2, 21 January 1990.

Kennedy, Ludovic (Chair), *Did You See?* (on *Brimstone and Treacle*), BBC 1, 25 August 1987.

Lawley, Sue (Chair), *Question Time*, BBC 1, 22 January 1987.

Lawson, Mark, 'Skin Flicks', *Independent Magazine*, 13 February 1993, pp. 28–32.

Levin, Bernard, *The Levin Interviews*, BBC 2, 17 May 1980.

Madden, Paul, *Complete Programme Notes for a Season of British Television Drama 1959–1973*, BFI, 1976, pp.35–7.

Mayhew, Christopher, *Does Class Matter?*, prog 2, 'Class in Private Life', BBC TV, 25 August 1958.

McDonald, Sheena (Chair), *Right to Reply Special: Dennis Potter in Edinburgh*, Channel 4, 30 August 1993.

Morris, Colin, *Anno Domini* (on religious belief), BBC 2, 13 February 1977.

Oakes, Philip, 'A suitable sleuth for treatment' (on *The Singing Detective*), *Radio Times*, November 1986.

Plomley, Roy, *Desert Island Discs*, BBC Radio 4, 17 December 1977.

Robinson, Robert (Chair), *Son of Man Reviewed*, BBC 1, 20 April 1969.

Saynor, James, 'Black and Blue' (on *Blackeyes*), *The Listener*, 1 June 1989, pp.4–7.

Twisk, Russell, 'Son of Man', *Radio Times*, 10 April 1969.

Wapshott, Nicholas, 'Dennis Potter: Knowing what goes on in people's heads', *The Times*, 21 April 1980.

Ward, Alex, 'TV's Tormented Master', *The New York Times*, 13 November 1988.

Wright, Patrick, 'The last Acre of Truth', *The Guardian*, 15 February 1993, sec 2, p.2.

Wyver, John, 'Paradise Perhaps', (on *Pennies from Heaven*), *Time Out*, 3 March 1987, pp.12–13.

Wyver, John, 'Arrows of Desire' (on *Blackeyes*), *The New Statesman*, 24 November 1989.

Wyver, John, The Long Non-Revolution of Dennis Potter', *Time Out*, October 1980, pp.18–19.

Yentob Alan, *Arena* interview, BBC 2, 30 January 1987 (transcript included in Dennis Potter, 1994).

Selected Potter-Related Criticism and Biography

Barker, Adam, 'What the Detective Saw or a Case of Mistaken Identity', BFI, *Monthly Film Bulletin*, 55:654, July 1988, pp.193–5.

Bell, Robert H, 'Implicated Without Choice: The Double Vision of *The Singing Detective*', *Literature and Film Quarterly*, Vol. 21, 1993, pp. 200–216.

Bondebjerg, Ib, 'Intertextuality and Metafiction: Genre and Narration in the Television Fiction of Dennis Potter', in M. Skormand, and K. C. Schroder (eds), *Media Cultures: Reappraising Transnational Media*, Routledge, 1992, pp.161–79.

Bosé, Mihir, 'Coffee without Cream', in *Michael Grade: Screening the Image*, Virgin Books, 1992, pp.103–121.

Colley, Ian and Davies, Gill, 'Pennies from Heaven: Music, Image, Text', *Screen Education*, 25, Summer, 1980, pp.63–78.

Cook, John, *Dennis Potter: A Life on Screen*, Manchester University Press, 1995.

Corrigan, Timothy, 'Music from Heaven, Bodies in Hell: *The Singing Detective*', in *A Cinema Without Walls: Movies and Culture after Vietnam*, Routledge, 1991, pp.179–93.

Coward, Rosalind, 'Dennis Potter and the Question of the Television Author', *Critical Quarterly*, 29:4, 1987, pp.79–87.

Creeber, Glen, 'Banality with a Beat: Dennis Potter and the paradox of popular music', *Media, Culture and Society*, Vol. 18, no. 3, July 1996, pp.501–08.

Delany, Paul, 'Potterland', *Dalehousie Review*, Vol. 68, part 4, 1988, pp.511–521.

Fuller, Graham (ed.), *Potter on Potter*, Faber & Faber, 1993.

Gilbert, W. Stephen, *Fight & Kick & Bite: The Life and Work of Dennis Potter*, Hodder and Stoughton, 1995.

Hunningher, Joost, '*The Singing Detective*: Who Done It?', in George, W. Brandt (ed.), *British Television Drama in the 1980s*, Cambrridge University Press, 1993, pp.234–57.

Poole, Mike (ed.), *Dennis Potter: A Life in Television*, a *Late Show* tribute, BBC 2, 7 June 1994.

Lennon, Peter, 'Dennis Potter: A man with a lash', *The Listener*, 20 November 1986, pp.14–15.

Lichtenstein, Therese, 'Syncopated Thriller: Dennis Potter's *The Singing Detective*', *Artforum*, May 1990, pp.168–72.

Pearson, Allison, 'Dennis in Heaven', *Independent on Sunday*, 12 June 1994, pp.4–7.

Purser, Philip, 'Dennis Potter', in George W. Brandt (ed.), *British Television Drama*, Cambridge University Press, 1981, pp.168–93.

Simon, Ron, 'The Flow of Memory and Desire', included in *The Television Plays of Dennis Potter*, the brochure which accompanied the complete retrospective of Potter's work at the Museum of Television and Radio, New York, 1992, pp.24–7.

Stead, Peter, *Dennis Potter*, Borderline Series, Seren Books, 1993.

Steyn, Mark, 'The Great Pretender', *The Modern Review*, June–July 1994, p.8.

Virchow-Voigts, Eckart, *Mannerphantasien: Introspektion und gebrochene Wirklichkeitsillusion im Drama von Dennis Potter*, Wissenschaftlicher Verlag Trier, 1995.

Wu, Duncan, 'Dennis Potter: The Angel in Us', in Duncan Wu *Six Contemporary British Dramatists: Bennett, Potter, Gray, Brenton, Hare, Ayckbourn*, Macmillan, 1995.

Wyver, John, 'A World Where the Songs Come True', in *The Television Plays of Dennis Potter*, New York, 1992, pp.7–23.

Relevant Books and Articles

Adorno, Theodor W., 'On Popular Music', included in John Storey (ed.), *Cultural Theory and Popular Culture: A Reader*, Harvester and Wheatsheaf, 1994.

Albrecht, W. P., *Hazlitt and the Creative Imagination*, University of Kansas Press, 1965.

Barthes, Roland, *Mythologies*, translated by Annette Lavers, Paladin, 1972.

Barthes, Roland, 'The Death of the Author', in Roland Barthes *Image, Music, Text*, Fontana Press, 1977.

Bennett, Tony, 'Cultural Studies: two paradigms', in Tony Bennett, Graham Martin, Colin Mercer, Janet woollacott (eds.), *Culture, Ideology and Social Process*, Open University, 1981.

Brandt, George, W., *British Television Drama*, Cambridge University Press, 1981.

Brandt, George, W., *British Television Drama in the 1980s*, Cambridge University Press, 1993.

Buscombe, Edward, 'Ideas of Authorship', *Screen*, Autumn, Vol. 14, no. 3, pp.75–99.

Buscombe, Edward, 'Creativity in Television', *Screen Education*, no. 35, Summer 1980.

Caughie, John (ed.), *Theories of Authorship: A Reader*, Routledge, 1990.

Coleridge, Samuel, Taylor, *Poetical Works*, Oxford University Press, 1979.

Cook, Jon, 'Television and Literature', in Thomas Elsaesser, *Writing for the Medium: Television in Transition*, Amsterdam University Press, 1993.

Corner, John (ed.), *Popular Television in Britain: Studies in Cultural History*, BFI Publishing, 1991.

Coveney, Peter, *Poor Monkey: The Child in Literature*, Rockcliff, 1957.

Fenichel, Otto, *The Psychoanalytical Theory of Neurosis*, Routledge & Keagan Paul, 1966.

Fiske, John, *Television Culture*, Routledge, 1992.

Foucault, Michel, 'What is an Author?', included in *Language – Memory, Practice*, Basil Blackwell, Oxford, 1977.

Freud, Sigmund, 'Contributions to the Psychology of Love: The Most Prevalent Form of Degradation in Erotic Life', in *Collected Papers*, Vol. IV, translated by Joan Riviere, The Hogarth Press, 1957.

Freud, Sigmund, *On Sexuality*, Vol. 7, Penguin Books, 1977.

Feuer, Jane, *The Hollywood Musical*, Indiana University Press, 1982.

Gardener, Carl and John Wyver, 'The Single Play: From Reithian Reverence to Cost- Accounting and Censorship', *Screen*, Vol. 24, nos. 4–5, 1983.

Hargrave, Andrea Millwood (ed.), *British Broadcasting Standards Council, Annual Review 1992: Sex and Sexuality in Broadcasting*, John Libbey, 1992.

Hazlitt, William, *Selected Writings*, Penguin Classics, 1982.

Hoggart, Richard, *The Uses of Literacy*, Penguin Books, 1990.

Hollingsworth, Mike, and Richard Norton-Taylor, *Blacklist*, Macmillan, 1988.

Housman, A. E., *A Shropshire Lad*, Harrap, 1940.

Hudson, Roger, 'Television in Britain: Description and Dissent', *Theatre Quarterly*, April–June, 1972.

Jacobs, Jason, *Early British Television Drama: Aesthetics, Style and Technology*, unpublished PhD, University of East Anglia, 1996.

Jarmen, Francis, 'Birth of a Playwrighting Man', interview with David Mercer, *Theatre Quarterly*, Vol. 3, no. 9, January–March 1973.

Laing, Stuart, *Representations of Working-Class Life: 1957–1964*, Macmillan, 1986.

Leavis, F. R., *Culture and Environment*, Chatto & Windus, 1993.

Ludwig, Emil, *The Son of Man*, Ernest Benn Ltd, 1928.

Maltby, Richard (ed.), *Dreams for Sale: Popular Culture in the 20th Century*, Harrap, 1989.

Macdonald, Dwight, 'A Theory of Mass Culture', in B. Rosenberg, and D. W. White (eds), *Mass Culture: The Popular Arts in America*, Macmillan, 1957.

Martin, Troy Kennedy, 'Nats Go Home: First Statement of a New Drama for Television', *Encore*, 11:2, March–April 1964, pp.21–33.

Martin, Troy Kennedy, 'Up The Junction And After', *Contrast*, Winter 1965, Spring 1966, pp.137–9.

Mercer, David, *Collected TV Plays: 1 – Where the Difference Begins, A Climate of Fear, The Birth of a Private Man*, John Calder, 1981.

Mitchell, Juliet, *Psychoanalysis and Feminism*, Penguin Books, 1974.

Mitchell, Juliet (ed.), *The Selected Melanie Klein*, Peregrine Books, 1986.

Murdock, Graham, 'Authorship and Organisation', *Screen Education*, no. 35, Summer 1980.

Mulvey, Laura, 'Visual Pleasure and Narrative Cinema', *Screen*, Vol. 16, no. 3, Autumn 1975.

Orwell, George, *The Decline of the English Murder and Other Essays*, Penguin, 1965.

Orwell, *Coming Up For Air*, Secker & Warburg, 1971.

Owen, Alun, *Three TV Plays*, Jonathan Cape, 1961.

Packard, Vance, *The Hidden Persuaders: An introduction to the techniques of mass- persuasion through the unconscious*, Penguin, 1960.

Park, Roy, *Hazlitt and the Spirit of the Age: Abstraction and Critical Theory*, Claredon Press, Oxford University Press, 1971.

Pilkington, Committee, *The Future of Sound Radio and Television: A Short Version of the Pilkington Committee*, Her Majesty's Stationery Office, 1962.

Place, Janey, 'Women in Film Noir', in E. Ann Kaplan (ed.), *Women in Film Noir*, BFI, 1986.

Purser, Ann, 'In at the birth of Kestrel Productions', interview with Kenith Trodd, *Stage & Television Today*, 25 June 1970.

Rank, Otto, *The Don Juan Legend*, translated by G. Winter, Princeton University Press, 1975.

Ritchie, Harry, *Success Stories: Literature and the Media in England 1950–1959*, Faber & Faber, 1988.

Redmond, James (ed.), *Drama and Society*, Cambridge University Press, 1979.

Rodowick, David, *The Difficulty of Difference: Psychoanalysis, Sexual Difference and Film Theory*, Routledge, 1991.

Salvensen, Christopher, *The Landscape of Memory: A Study of Wordsworth's Poetry*, Edward Arnold, 1965.

Selden, Raman, *A Reader's Guide to Contemporary Literary Theory*, Wheatsheaf, 1989.

Scannell, Paddy and David Cardiff, *A Social History of British Broadcasting*,

Vol. 1, 1922–1939: Serving the Nation, Basil Blackwell, 1991.

Schapiro, Barbara A., *The Romantic Mother: Narcissistic Patterns in Romantic Poetry*, The John Hopkins Press, 1983.

Self, David, *Television Drama: An Introduction*, Macmillan, 1984.

Shubik, *Play for Today: The Evolution of Television Drama*, Davis-Poynter, 1975.

Silver, Alain and Elizabeth Ward (eds), *Film Noir*, Secker & Warburg, 1980.

Sinfield, Alan, *Literature, Politics and Culture in Post-War Britain*, Basil Blackwell, 1989.

Sponheim, Paul, *Kierkegaard on Christ and Christian Coherence*, SMC Press Ltd, 1968.

Storey, John (ed.), *Cultural Theory and Popular Culture: A Reader*, Harvester & Wheatsheaf, 1994.

Taylor, Don, 'Style in Drama: The Gorboduc Stage', *Contrast*, Spring 1964, pp. 150–208.

Taylor, Don, *Days of Vision – Working with David Mercer: Television Drama then and now*, Methuen, 1990.

Thomas, Howard (ed.), *The Armchair Theatre*, Weidenfeld & Nicolson, 1959.

Trodd, Kenith, *Lew Stone: A Career in Music*, Joyce Stone, 1971.

Walter, David, *The Oxford Union: The Playground of Power*, MacDonald, 1984.

Watter, Reginald, *Coleridge: Literature in Perspective*, Evans Brothers, 1971.

Wheen, Francis, *Television: A History*, Century Publishing, 1985.

Williams, Raymond, *The Long Revolution*, Penguin, 1961.

Williams, Raymond, *Culture and Society 1780–1950*, Chatto & Windus, 1967.

Williams, Raymond, *Drama from Ibsen to Brecht*, Pelican, 1973.

Williams, Raymond, *Television, Technology and Cultural Form*, Fontana, 1974.

Williams, Raymond, 'A Lecture on Realism', *Screen*, 18:1, Spring 1977.

Wolff, Janet, *The Social Production of Art*, Macmillan, 1981.

Wordsworth, William, *Poetical Works*, Oxford University Press, 1978.

Index

Note: all Potter works are listed alphabetically. Major references are in **bold** type.

KING ALFRED'S COLLEGE
LIBRARY